The First Amendment and the Business Corporation

PREFACE

As this book went to print, the U.S. Supreme Court handed down its joint decision in *Sebelius v. Hobby Lobby* and *Conestoga Wood v. Sebelius* (renamed *Burwell v. Hobby Lobby* and *Conestoga Wood v. Burwell*). These two cases feature prominently in Chapter 7, and implicate matters that are central to this book and addressed throughout. Namely, whether a for-profit business corporation may invoke the religious liberty protections of the First Amendment to the U.S. Constitution. As such, a brief mention of this development is warranted.

In its 5-4 decision, the Supreme Court granted a religious exemption to two closely held, religiously grounded for-profit corporations from the Affordable Care Act's "contraceptive mandate," thereby recognizing and protecting their rights to religious liberty. Critically, the court predicated its decision on the Religious Freedom Restoration Act (RFRA), and explicitly declined to address whether the same result would be compelled via recourse to the First Amendment's free exercise clause. Further, the court also made clear that its holding concerned the claimants before them: two *closely held* corporations, and reserved for another day the question of whether a publicly traded corporation could also avail itself of religious liberty protections (statutory or constitutional). Finally, as with most of its other recent decisions adjudicating corporate rights and freedoms, the Court once again avoided any sustained discussion of corporate theory, in its majority opinion, concurring opinion, or its dissents.

The narrowness of the Court's decision underscores the importance and continued timeliness of this book's undertaking. The Court did not decide the cases before it on constitutional grounds, nor did the Court's holding extend to large, publicly traded corporations. The Court failed to justify its opinion via recourse to any theoretical conceptualization of the corporation, or to fit its ruling into a larger framework of corporate rights. As a result, the very questions and matters this book was written to address remain open and neglected.

The First Amendment and the Business Corporation

Ronald J. Colombo

OXFORD
UNIVERSITY PRESS

OXFORD
UNIVERSITY PRESS

Oxford University Press is a department of the University of Oxford. It furthers the University's objective of excellence in research, scholarship, and education by publishing worldwide.

Oxford New York
Auckland Cape Town Dar es Salaam Hong Kong Karachi Kuala Lumpur Madrid Melbourne Mexico City Nairobi New Delhi Shanghai Taipei Toronto

With offices in
Argentina Austria Brazil Chile Czech Republic France Greece Guatemala Hungary Italy Japan Poland Portugal Singapore South Korea Switzerland Thailand Turkey Ukraine Vietnam

Oxford is a registered trademark of Oxford University Press in the UK and certain other countries.

Published in the United States of America by
Oxford University Press
198 Madison Avenue, New York, NY 10016

Library of Congress Cataloging-in-Publication Data
Colombo, Ronald J., author.
The First Amendment and the business corporation / Ronald J. Colombo.
pages cm
Includes bibliographical references and index.
ISBN 978-0-19-933567-1 ((hardback) : alk. paper)
1. Corporation law—United States. 2. Freedom of expression—United States.
3. United States. Constitution. 1st Amendment. I. Title.
KF1416.C65 2014
342.7308'5—dc23

2014010453

1 3 5 7 9 8 6 4 2

Printed in the United States of America on acid-free paper

Note to Readers

This publication is designed to provide accurate and authoritative information in regard to the subject matter covered. It is based upon sources believed to be accurate and reliable and is intended to be current as of the time it was written. It is sold with the understanding that the publisher is not engaged in rendering legal, accounting, or other professional services. If legal advice or other expert assistance is required, the services of a competent professional person should be sought. Also, to confirm that the information has not been affected or changed by recent developments, traditional legal research techniques should be used, including checking primary sources where appropriate.

(Based on the Declaration of Principles jointly adopted by a Committee of the American Bar Association and a Committee of Publishers and Associations.)

For my wife, Kimberly, and my children, Isabella,
Christina, Ronald, Thomas, and Gabriella, with love.

CONTENTS

ACKNOWLEDGMENTS

This book would not have been possible but for the tremendous support I have received over the years from several individuals.

For a lifetime of love and encouragement, I thank my parents.

I thank my friend and colleague Julian Ku, who, in 2006, invited me to make the jump from private practice to academia. Without that leap, chances are this book would have never been written. Further, I count myself among the many who have received inspiration from Julian's example as a scholar.

I thank Crystal Glynn and Timothy Glynn for their assistance in preparing me for legal academia, and David Gregory and Mark Movsesian for their support and mentorship throughout my transition into the academy.

My colleagues at the Maurice A. Deane School of Law at Hofstra University are to be thanked for their encouragement and assistance since 2006. Special thanks in this regard goes to Dan Greenwood, Norm Silber, Robin Charlow, Vern Walker, and Akilah Folami for their help in sharpening my thoughts on the matters covered in this book.

I am especially indebted to Julian Velasco, Robert Miller, Brian McCall, and Lyman Johnson for their contributions not only to my thoughts on the matters presented herein but to my development as a scholar and also for their friendship.

Other scholars who have, over the past few years, contributed to my thinking about the matters addressed in this book include Marc DeGirolami, Rob Vischer, Richard Garnett, Susanna Riken, John McGinnis, Usha Rodrigues, Chapin Cimino, and Judd Sneirson. Thank you.

My students must be thanked for allowing me countless opportunities to discuss these issues with them, and for the benefit of their insights. This applies most especially to those students who have taken my seminar, "Controversies in Corporate Law."

Invaluable assistance was provided to me by Toni Aiello, one of the finest librarians I have ever known. No source I requested was too obscure for her to expeditiously find and procure for me. Substantial help was also provided to me by my research assistants Alyssa Galinsky and Lola Yellico, for which I am extremely thankful.

My assistant, Maria Filotti, must also be thanked for her tireless and cheerful help with a variety of administrative matters regarding this project.

I must also thank a number of institutions and organizations for affording me the opportunity to present and discuss many of the ideas that ultimately found their way into this book. These would include the Robert M. School of Business at the University of Maryland, the Annual Law & Religion Roundtable, Suffolk Law School, the Notre Dame School of Law, the Gruter Institute for Law and Behavioral Research, the Peter J. Tobin College of Business at St. John's University, the Association for the Study of Law, Culture, and the Humanities, and Villanova University School of Law. My own Hofstra Law School must be thanked for its support of my scholarship, in the form of research grants and special leave, among other things.

Some of the ideas expressed herein were previously articulated by me in other publications. I would like to thank those publications for giving me the first opportunity to work out my thoughts on these matters in print. I would like to especially thank the *Houston Law Review*, Sage Publications, the *Temple Law Review*, and the *Washington & Lee Law Review* for also permitting me to reuse certain portions of these prior publications in this book (specifically set forth in *The Naked Private Square*, 51 HOUS. L. REV. 1 (2013); *Rights and Responsibilities of the American Business Corporation, in* BUSINESS AND HUMAN RIGHTS (Manoj Kumar Sinha, ed., SAGE 2013; *The Corporation as a Tocquevillian Association*, 85 TEMP. L. REV. 1 (2012); and *Toward a Nexus of Virtue*, 69 WASH. & LEE L. REV. 3 (2012)).

Finally, and most of all, I need to thank my family, to whom this book is dedicated. The time I spent working on this project was time I could have spent with them. My sacrifices to see this book through to completion were their sacrifices as well. I have been blessed by their love, patience, support, encouragement, and prayers throughout this undertaking. For this and the countless other ways in which they enrich my life and everything I do, I am eternally grateful.

INTRODUCTION

Few institutions receive as much scrutiny as the modern business corporation. Whether it be from adulators (sometimes), or critics (more frequently), corporations and corporate conduct are consistently the subject of attention and discussion. This plays out on both a micro level (in which particular, individual corporations are the targets, such as, "How could *Apple* do such a thing?") and a macro level (in which corporations in general are the targets, such as, "How come so many companies get lucrative tax breaks?"). This is completely understandable, if not to be expected. For particular individual corporations, and corporations as a group, play a tremendously significant role in our society today.

Indeed, it would not be hyperbole to suggest that in these opening decades to the twenty-first century, the business corporation is well poised to becoming (if it has not already become) the dominant institution in most societies around the globe.[1]

By "dominant institution" I mean the force that has, to a varying degree, asserted its influence over the peoples and lesser institutions of its times. Institutions that, whether directly or indirectly, help shape law, culture, and practices. Institutions that might even set the pace and rhythm of daily life.

Nearly every age has such institutions. The ancient world was marked by kings and kingdoms, emperors and empires. In the West, as these figures and structures faded into history, the church and its bishops rose to supplant them—which, in turn, helped to define the Middle Ages. The ruptures and decline of the church birthed yet another era, one that led to the ascendency of the nation state—a situation that has generally persisted to our present time.

It can be argued, however, that the nation state is ceding (or perhaps has ceded) the high ground to the business corporation. To assert this is not to disregard the continued presence and role of national governments. States and governments certainly remain important societal pillars (and for that matter, so does the church in many regions of the world). But in an era of globalization, where technology and mobility have made national boundaries look increasingly irrelevant, corporations have found ways to spread their influence and generate wealth across borders which many modern governments would envy. Indeed, in terms of sheer size, some corporations today enjoy revenues that dwarf the gross domestic product of all but the largest and most prosperous of countries. According to one recent study, "of the 100 largest world economies in 2010, forty-two were private corporations."[2]

That is, however, only half the story. For the influence of the modern business corporation is as deep as it is far-reaching. In modern, free-market countries such as the United States, business corporations essentially set industry wages and working conditions. They determine, in very large part, what products will be sold, and what services will be offered. They decide what movies and televisions shows will be produced, and what music and programming is played on the radio. They select the foods that will be made available for us to eat, and the clothes and fashions that will be made available for us to wear. In short, it is difficult to imagine any facet of modern living that is entirely devoid of corporate influence.

In recent years, corporate influence over society has expanded further still. Via lobbying, corporations have long played a behind-the-scenes role in politics, exerting influence over the legislative and regulatory process. But today, corporations are more openly involved in this than perhaps ever before. Corporations increasingly bankroll political advertising campaigns to support or oppose causes of concern to them. This extends to the sponsorship of advertisements in favor of or in opposition to particular candidates for office as well.

In recognition of the corporation's ascendency, concerned individuals have reacted differently. Some have pushed for greater regulation of corporate enterprises, in order to rein in their influence. They seek the reassertion of state authority over the course of society, an option they consider fairer and more democratic. Further, and critically, they seek to free the state itself from the tentacles of corporate influence. For what faith can we have in additional regulation if the regulators are themselves controlled by the regulated?

Others, however, have chosen a different route. To them, the ascendency of the corporation is as much an opportunity as a potential threat. For despite the long-term power shift toward the corporation, the state shows no signs of withering away. Indeed, in the wake of the global financial crisis of 2008–2009 (the effects of which have persisted well into the subsequent decade), many governments have flexed their muscles and asserted powers to a greater degree than generations can recall. If the late twentieth century was the era of deregulation and privatization, the early twenty-first century can be considered an era of re-regulation and, in some instances, nationalization. Further, not wishing to let "a serious crisis go to waste,"[3] many governments that rode into power during the financial crisis have turned their energies and regulatory zeal to matters well beyond a reform of financial markets. Within such a context, some have seen the power of the corporation as a counterweight (perhaps the only effective modern counterweight) to the state.

Additionally, some have worked to harness the power of the corporation for what they consider to be more positive ends. They have attempted to supplement the corporation's focus on private goods (such as shareholder returns) with greater consideration of the common good. They have attempted to dislodge the corporation's typical, single-minded focus on profits and introduce elements of prosociality.

The fruits of these efforts are visible everywhere. Corporations are increasingly committing themselves to philanthropic undertakings, via charitable giving or by establishing nonprofit organizations of their own. Corporations are today leading initiatives that have helped alleviate humanitarian suffering and crises when governments were unwilling or unable to get involved.

Some corporate boards and executives have taken these efforts to an even higher level. Not satisfied with limiting their concern over the common good as merely an add-on component to corporate decision making, they have endeavored to build corporations that are intrinsically prosocial: corporations that are organized around a set of moral and ethical principles that guide their conduct as concretely as the desire to turn a profit.

An example of this is the large number of corporations today that have embraced a commitment to environmental stewardship, and as such have pledged to conduct their operations in environmentally friendly ways that minimize their carbon footprint. Many corporations have also adopted principles regarding the treatment of employees and customers that go well beyond that which is required by either regulation or market forces. Some also make it a priority to patronize only those suppliers who themselves ascribe to certain standards of ethical conduct.

Some corporations have been pushed further still. Recognizing the power and ubiquity of the corporate form, certain individuals have combined to build and sustain corporations that adhere to their most deeply held convictions of all: their religious values. Motivating these individuals has not been a desire to proselytize per se, but rather a desire to serve their own needs—and the needs of other people of faith. This should not be surprising, as many people of faith, from a variety of religious backgrounds, feel alienated from if not downright excluded from a marketplace and corporate world driven primarily by the pursuit of profit, in which the accumulation of wealth and other and secular concerns predominate. Predictably, they have created niche enterprises where individuals of shared religious convictions can pool resources, coming together as directors and employees, investors and customers. These corporations are commonly committed not simply to honorable business practices broadly speaking, but rather to the principles of certain, particular religious traditions.

Taken together, these undertakings to broaden the perspective of corporate purpose (whether driven by a concern for environmental stewardship, social responsibility, or religious values) arguably transform the corporation in profound ways. Indeed, it can be plausibly maintained that we have witnessed the genesis of an entirely new organizational form. For modern corporate theory is predicated upon conceptualizing the business corporation as a profit-maximizing commercial actor, created for the purpose of private enrichment. In recalibrating the focus of the corporation away from these traditional objectives, and more toward the common good and holistic personal fulfillment, we have brought corporate practice into conflict with this prevailing conceptualization.

It is within this dynamic context that our society is currently reassessing the corporation. Thus, in considering the corporation's proper role in our society, we find ourselves addressing a quickly moving target. Moreover, we address a target that manifests itself in dramatically divergent ways. Indeed, given the widely disparate reactions to the corporation, ranging from adulation to antipathy, it may very well be the case that when individuals discuss "the corporation," they have vastly different entities in mind. This observation alone, I suggest, goes a long way in explaining the apparent interminability of our society's debate over corporations.

This makes any serious discussion of the corporation and its role in our society a considerably more difficult one. It is, nevertheless, one we must persevere in having. For the choices we make today regarding the corporation may have profound consequences for us tomorrow.

If our fears of corporate ascendancy are misplaced, actions we take to rein in the corporation could very well forestall one of the most powerful forces for good that the world has ever seen. Having already proven itself a tremendously powerful entity for the creation of wealth, the corporation might also prove itself a tremendously powerful entity in service of the common good as well. The corporation might also serve as a powerful bulwark against an ever-expanding state, preserving an important sphere of private activity and perhaps even the expression of countercultural values no longer shared by public majorities.

On the other hand, if our hopes are misplaced, allowing corporate power to amass unchecked could undermine our central democratic institutions, including fair elections and majoritarian rule itself.

In the United States, the flashpoint of this debate has been the First Amendment to the U.S. Constitution. Although not necessarily the most predictable battleground for this contest, the First Amendment is nevertheless an appropriate one.

Few constitutional provisions are as hallowed as the First Amendment. Recognized worldwide, this 1791 addition to the U.S. Constitution explicitly guarantees freedom of religion and freedom of speech (in addition to freedom of the press, the right to assembly, and the right to petition government for redress of grievances). It has famously been interpreted to guarantee other implicit freedoms as well, including the freedom of association. As such, the First Amendment protects elements essential to nations considered to be free and democratic; elements essential to individuals as a matter of personal autonomy and to society as a whole as constitutive of democratic processes.

With the rise and spread of corporations across America, coupled with changing views regarding the corporation's purpose and role in society, the applicability of the First Amendment's protections to corporate activity is a question that has squarely and forcefully been raised. As business corporations increasingly engage in conduct that had previously been limited to political groups, civic associations, charities, and other such organizations, they have increasingly sought the same rights and constitutional protections that these other entities have enjoyed. Further, as individuals create corporations for these very purposes, to pursue aims that are not solely profit-driven but also imbued with concerns that are ethical, moral, political, and/or religious in nature, they too have clamored for application of the Constitution's protections to their (corporate) undertakings.

These attempts have been fiercely resisted. As with many constitutional disputes, a fair number of the adversaries appear to be simply attempting to advance political causes under the guise of constitutional argument. To the extent that corporate First Amendment rights are viewed as favoring one set of political interests or another, proponents and opponents of such rights predictably line up along the expected lines. For such combatants, arguments are pretextual—party rather than principle governs their advocacy (unless the principle subscribed to happens to be that the ends justify the means).

Far more interesting (and the subject of this book) are those arguments that tap into deeper, more sophisticated principles and concerns. What are the natures of freedom of speech, religion, and association? Are these liberties that can effectively be exercised in isolation, by individuals alone, or do they require a communitarian component in order to be fully realized? If they do require a communitarian component, what makes a business corporation qualified, or unqualified, to serve as that component? Do the vast resources of many modern business corporations counsel in favor or against recognition of corporate constitutional rights? Would such recognition serve to crowd out individual voices and rights, or would such recognition serve as a greater safeguard to individual liberty and a more effective check on government? These questions, and others like them, have driven the writing of this book.

This book is organized into ten chapters (not including this introduction and a conclusion). Chapter 1 will explain how freedom can rarely be exercised in a vacuum. Rather, to truly flourish, freedom requires the support and opportunities that only "associations" can provide. Indeed, associations and a vibrant associational life are critical components to any society that wishes to remain free, democratic, and healthy. Chapter 1 will then introduce a claim central to this book's thesis: that a business corporation can serve as an association. Not all corporations and perhaps not even most corporations can serve this role. But, as shall be explained in later chapters, certainly some corporations can. This is important for constitutional purposes because associations have long been recognized (as they should and must) as bearers of First Amendment rights.

Chapter 2 will set forth the modern business corporation and its history. In its current, typical manifestation, coupled with our prevailing understanding of its nature, the corporation does not come across as a particularly strong candidate for the "association" appellation. This is largely because the modern corporation is characterized as a *sui generis* organization where ownership is separated from control, and where management is duty-bound to prioritize profits over all else. A review of the corporation's history, however, demonstrates how the corporation has continually changed and adapted to meet the needs and wants of its time. Further, past understandings of what the corporation was, or how it ought to be viewed, have similarly evolved. This suggests, I posit, a certain openness to other ways of envisioning the corporation even within our own times. It suggests that the prevailing conceptualization of "the corporation" need not be a static one, nor be considered particularly correct, but rather can and should continue to evolve.

Building upon chapter 2, chapter 3 will assert that the evolution of the corporation has continued, and introduce what I have labeled the "postmodern corporation." Unlike the modern corporation, the postmodern corporation is not fixated solely upon the maximization of profits, but rather balances profitability with a regard for other values and principles. This is a critically important distinction, as it enables the postmodern corporation to plausibly lay claim to associational status. Harkening back to chapter 1, with this status comes a presumption of the First Amendment's applicability.

Chapter 4 explores the theory of "corporate personhood"—the vehicle through which corporate constitutional rights have traditionally been recognized. It will show how the list of corporate rights has generally grown over time and will set forth the current reach of such rights. It will show how recognition of corporate rights has proceeded without much theoretical consideration of the corporation itself, or of the appropriateness of treating the corporation as a right-bearing entity. Chapter 4 will then suggest a different approach to First Amendment jurisprudence regarding the corporation, an approach that does indeed take the nature of a corporate claimant into account when weighing questions of constitutional rights. Not only does the proposed approach lead to more just results, it also follows the traditional wisdom of linking rights with responsibilities, as it would afford greater constitutional rights to those corporate entities that embrace social responsibilities, and lesser protections to those entities that shun such responsibilities.

Chapters 5 through 8 will turn to the First Amendment. Chapter 5 will provide a background to the amendment, and chapters 6, 7, and 8 will delve into the freedoms of speech, religion, and association (respectively). This examination will reveal how the courts, when applying the First Amendment to corporate claimants, have increasingly prescinded from any detailed exploration of the corporation per se and its nature. To the extent that courts and judges have entertained corporate theory in their constitutional decision making, they have largely predicated their decisions on rough, outdated, corporate stereotypes. When one considers the values that animate these First Amendment freedoms, one quickly realizes how some corporations today (namely, postmodern corporations) can justly lay claim to First Amendment rights—a realization that has been lost upon the courts due to their undertheorized (if not incorrectly theorized) approach to the corporation. Given the timeliness and novelty of corporate claims to religious liberty, this particular question will be examined especially closely.

Chapter 9 will tie the preceding together and set forth a taxonomy of the corporation. Fundamental to doing so is the recognition that our conceptualization of the corporation need not be locked in time and wedded to a one-size-fits all paradigm. To the extent that the corporate landscape is marked by a significant amount of diversity, we ought not to adhere to a singular conceptualization of the corporation, but rather should embrace a multiplicity of conceptualizations. These conceptualizations need not be created from whole cloth, but can borrow from theoretical conceptualizations of yesteryear. Although certain understandings of the corporation are no longer popular today, they appear quite applicable to particular corporate entities of our own time given their makeup and operation.

Having suggested that we should view different corporations differently, chapter 9 will then suggest that, for First Amendment purposes, we should treat different corporations differently. A means of doing this shall be set forth in the form of a taxonomy, which will divide the universe of corporations into different categories based upon constitutionally salient characteristics. The chapter will explain why corporations falling within a particular category should (or should not) be entitled to assert the freedom of speech, religion, or association.

A number of concerns have been voiced in opposition to affording business corporations greater First Amendment protections. The most common of these concerns is that such protections would undermine the political process by giving business corporations disproportionate influence in elections and over government officials. This particular concern is raised most often in connection with corporate free speech rights and will be addressed in chapter 6 along with our discussion of freedom of speech.

Another cause of concern, however, is the specter of discrimination that corporate First Amendment rights might herald. Granting corporations freedom of religion and freedom of association threatens to undo decades of civil rights progress, some have argued, by inviting businesses to deny service or employment to certain groups of people. Chapter 10 will directly address this important concern.

The book's conclusion will make some parting observations regarding the consequences of its assessment and underscore the need to get the question of corporate constitutional rights correct.

NOTES

1. *See* Roberta Romano, *Metapolitics and Corporate Law Reform*, 36 STAN. L. REV. 923, 936 (1984).
2. Roy Peled, *Occupy Information: The Case for Freedom of Corporate Information*, 9 HASTINGS BUS. L.J. 261, 265 (2013); *see also* Anne Tucker, *The Citizen Shareholder: Modernizing the Agency Paradigm to Reflect How and Why a Majority of Americans Invest in the Market*, 35 SEATTLE U. L. REV. 1299, 1331 (2012).
3. *NPR Morning Edition* (National Public Radio broadcast, Dec. 23, 2008), *available at* 2008 WLNR 24606394 (recounting the (in)famous remarks of Rahm Emanuel, the Obama administration's incoming chief of staff in 2008).

CHAPTER 1

Associations and Freedom

One of the leading casebooks on corporate law, adopted in over one hundred law schools, is entitled: *Business Associations: Agency, Partnerships, and Corporations*.[1] There is nothing particularly original or imaginative about the title—indeed, other books on the same subject employ similar titles. I highlight the book (and its title) to underscore a simple but important point: the business corporation is an "association."

One of the hallmarks of an association is the recognition it receives as an entity independent and distinct from its constituent members. For example, would-be parents have traditionally come together for the purpose of raising children, giving rise to the family. The family, in turn, is viewed as a distinct unit in society, and not simply the aggregation of parent(s) and child(ren). It takes on a character of its own, dependent largely upon the roles played by its various members. Taken individually, no one member constitutes "the family." The family and its members are distinct.[2] As one commentator put it: "when a body of twenty, or two thousand, or two hundred thousand men bind themselves to act in a particular way for some common purpose, they create a body, which by no fiction of law, but by the very nature of things, differs from the individuals of whom it is constituted."[3]

Individuals come together to worship, giving rise to a congregation. Again, no individual congregant constitutes the congregation—the congregation is recognized as an entity separate and distinct from its members taken individually. Of particular relevance, the congregation remains identifiable as such despite the addition or subtraction of members. Thus, the congregation truly takes on a life of its own.

Individuals have come together for camaraderie, to socialize, or to take action in their particular societies. Certainly much of this is informal, giving rise to no entities that would be recognized as such. Much of it, however, is formal, or semiformal. When bowling clubs are formed, or political action committees are organized, we have the birth of new associations. These entities usually adopt names of their own by which they are recognized, along with rules and procedures that govern their criteria for membership, operations, and the like.

People have also come together for the purpose of conducting business. Be it the recognition that two heads are better than one, the want of skills beyond one's own, the need for additional resources and capital, or simply the desire for some helping hands, individuals have often reached out to others for assistance in plying their trade, making their livelihood, or embarking upon some commercial enterprise. Thus business associations are formed.

It must be admitted, of course, that associations differ from one another in some important ways. The associations mentioned above furnish a good illustration of this. The business corporation, for example, is typically understood to possess five features which, when taken together, distinguish it from other associations and indeed other business ventures as well: (1) the limited liability of owners, (2) the relative ease with which owners can transfer their ownership interests (their shares), (3) the corporation's separate legal personality, (4) the separation of the corporation's ownership (its shareholders) from the corporation's controllers (its board of directors), and (5) the possibility of perpetual corporate life. These features, and other aspects of the modern business corporation, will be addressed in chapter 2. For the time being, it suffices to acknowledge the fact that despite these distinguishing features, the business corporation is, at bottom, simply one kind of an association. With that in mind, in this chapter let us prescind from the specific (the corporation) and consider instead the general (the association).

In like manner, let us also temporarily postpone our focus upon the rights and freedoms that make up the First Amendment and turn our attention instead to freedom as a general matter. In other words, before delving into the nature of the corporation, or the rights enshrined within the First Amendment to the U.S. Constitution, let us begin our inquiry more generally. Let us start by considering associations, in general, and freedom, in general.

A good place to start a serious consideration of almost anything is with Aristotle. Writing in the fourth century BC, Aristotle famously remarked that "man is by nature a social animal."[4] Much more recently, and perhaps as famously, Thomas Jefferson proclaimed in the U.S. Declaration of Independence that human beings are "endowed by their Creator with certain unalienable Rights, that among these are Life, Liberty, and the Pursuit of Happiness." Taken together, it can be said that the prerogative to live in freedom and the propensity to associate with others have long been considered natural, constitutive components of what it means to be a human being. Although some may wish to question these fundamental premises, the vast majority of people generally accept these propositions as received wisdom, and herein I shall as well. For both history and common sense testify to their correctness, and it is not the purpose of this book to challenge them.

It is one of the purposes of this book, however, to inquire into the connection between these two important and foundational concepts: associations and freedom. More specifically, to what extent are associations necessary to the realization of freedom and to what extent is freedom necessary to the flourishing of associations? The short answer to both questions is: very necessary. For the two are symbiotically linked, with each providing essential support to the other.

ALEXIS DE TOCQUEVILLE'S THEORY OF ASSOCIATIONS

Although Aristotle long ago recognized humankind's natural inclination toward associations and associating, it is the nineteenth century's Alexis de Tocqueville who supplies us with one of the most helpful commentaries and analysis of associations. Tocqueville's analysis has been found so insightful that the U.S. Supreme Court and countless lower courts have referred to his writings when deemed relevant to the matters before them. He has been lauded as "the political scientist par excellence, and sometimes, more grandly, as a political philosopher, where he has often been ranked just behind Aristotle and Machiavelli as a political thinker."[5] Via recourse to Tocqueville, we will be well equipped to determine whether the business corporation is that kind of association to which the First Amendment's freedoms ought to apply.

Born in Paris in 1805, Tocqueville long followed with fascination the American experiment in democracy from his native France. He wondered how Americans were able to create such an apparently successful and thriving democratic republic whereas the nations of Europe seemed unable to do so. In 1831, Tocqueville procured an opportunity to travel to America and spent nearly two years observing and interviewing Americans from all walks of life. He published his findings in 1835, in a masterful two-volume treatise entitled *Democracy in America*. *Democracy in America* was received with great acclaim and continues to be cited approvingly today.

Tocqueville's treatise examines many aspects of early nineteenth-century American life, from the practicality of the American mind to the role that honor and ambition play in American society. He comments upon American manners, habits, and mores—including details such as the "American taste for physical well-being" and "the inflated style of American writers and orators." He addresses the American love of individualism and equality, along with the situation of women and slaves.

Although certainly some of Tocqueville's observations are dated, many remain strikingly accurate nearly two centuries later. Moreover, much if not most of Tocqueville's extrapolations and insights remain as trenchant as ever. That is, they accurately diagnose causes and effects and discern critical timeless principles.

Tocqueville devotes four full chapters to the subject of associations in *Democracy in America*: chapter 12 of volume I, and chapters 5, 6, and 7 of the second book of volume II. In the course of these chapters, Tocqueville remarks upon the richness of associational life in the United States and sets forth his thesis that this phenomenon helps account for the successful maintenance of a democratic republic in America. As John McGinnis summarized it, Tocqueville believed that associations were a "central and constitutive" element of American democracy.[6]

As mentioned at the onset of this chapter, there are many different kinds of associations. It is unlikely that Tocqueville's commentaries and insights apply to each and every associational form imaginable. It is certainly fair to question whether the business corporation, which was a rarity in the early nineteenth century, would have been included in Tocqueville's understanding of the term "association." For this reason, we shall have a twofold task as we proceed: we shall not only examine Tocqueville's theory of the association but must also identify the characteristics of a "Tocquevillian Association" in order to determine whether a business corporation could qualify as such.

"Political Associations"

Entitled "Political Associations in the United States," chapter 12 of volume I marks the beginning of Tocqueville's discussion of associations in *Democracy in America*. As a prefatory matter, it should be noted that chapter 12's focus, in keeping with its title, is on associations of a political nature and on the effect of associations (generally speaking) upon America's political institutions. Tocqueville expressly alerts the reader to this, declaring in one of the opening paragraphs to chapter 12: "I shall hereafter have occasion to show the effects of association upon the course of society, and I must confine myself for the present to the political world."[7] Moreover, the definition that Tocqueville supplies for "association" in chapter 12 is apparently tailored to an organization containing some ideological component: "An association consists simply in the public assent which a number of individuals give to certain doctrines, and in the engagement which they contract to promote the spread of those doctrines by their assertion."

Viewed in isolation, the preceding would suggest that Tocqueville's theory of associations is of little relevance to the business corporation. For most corporations could not be characterized as entities existing "to promote the spread of... doctrines." Two points must be offered in response, however.

First, a major premise of this book is that not all corporations are the same. There is a tremendous amount of diversity among corporate entities. As will be explained in chapter 3, corporations can conceivably embrace a particular ideological or religious philosophy, and some (which I shall label "postmodern corporations") have. Although this is certainly not the case for many corporate enterprises, it is clearly the case for some. Thus, corporations ought not to be categorically excluded from consideration as Tocquevillian Associations.

Second, Tocqueville's language must not be read in isolation. As Tocqueville's later writings in *Democracy in America* make clear, Tocqueville recognizes the existence of nonideological associations as well, associations which he refers to as "civil" or "public." Indeed, even some of the illustrations that Tocqueville employs in chapter 12 reveal his recognition that apolitical/nonideological organizations can constitute associations. He adverts, for example, to an organization created to contend with "a stoppage . . . in a thoroughfare," and "to provide for the splendor and regularity of . . . entertainment." Further, Tocqueville specifically notes in chapter 12 that associations are formed by Americans "to promote public order, commerce, industry, morality, and religion." Tellingly, this short list is not populated by organizations of an exclusively political or ideological in nature. Thus, an organization of persons need not be primarily political, or ideologically driven, in order to qualify as a Tocquevillian Association. Chapter 12's title and Tocqueville's qualification about confinement to the political world should be understood as merely the focus of his discussion in chapter 12—not as some limitation on what it means to be a Tocquevillian Association. It would be a mistake to conclude that Tocqueville's understanding of the association was limited to only those organizations that were political or doctrinal in nature. With this in mind, we can see that much of what Tocqueville has to say about associations in chapter 12, despite that chapter's title and focus, applies to associations generally, and not solely to political associations. This will be made abundantly clear when we encounter Tocqueville's reiteration of some key points initially set forth in chapter 12 in his later chapters (chapters which specifically address nonpolitical associations).

The distinction remains important, however, because our objective here is to ascertain the appropriate apportionment of rights afforded to all corporations, including those that might possess an ideological or religious component versus those that might not. We need, therefore, to consider how Tocqueville's thinking would apply to each. Thus, in our consideration of *Democracy in America*, we shall need to bear in mind which of Tocqueville's observations and arguments apply to associations generally (Tocquevillian Associations, as I shall continue to refer to them), versus those that apply only to corporations that can be said to "promote the spread of . . . doctrines" (to "political" or "ideological" Tocquevillian Associations).

The Effects of Association on Persons and Governments

Like a good Aristotelian, Tocqueville believed that the human tendency to socialize and associate with others is a natural component of what it means to be human. As such, he identifies the right of association as inalienable, and the language employed suggests that here he refers to associations in general:

> The most natural privilege of man, next to the right of acting for himself, is that of combining his exertions with those of his fellow-creatures, and of acting in common with them. I am therefore led to conclude that the right of association is almost as inalienable as the right to personal liberty. No legislator can attack it without impairing the very foundations of society.[8]

Tocqueville also observed the importance of associations due to the effects they have upon their members. He noted that when individuals bond together in association, the opinions that drew them together "assume[] a more exact and explicit form." Further, once in association together, individuals "become acquainted with each other, and their zeal is increased by their number."[9] Finally, through the act of associating, individuals provide mutual support to one another in pursuit of their common goals, thereby strengthening their resolve: "An association unites the efforts of minds which have a tendency to diverge in one single channel, and urges them vigorously toward one single end which it points out."[10]

Although Tocqueville appears to have political associations in mind with that last statement, the principles expressed can be generalized to nonpolitical associations as well. One of the reasons why the criminal law punishes conspiracy so harshly (regardless of its objective, which is rarely political in nature) is that when individuals agree to act in concert, they are much more likely to act at all. Regardless of an association's objective, the simple process of joining together with others for some common purpose serves to bolster the resolve of all involved to achieve that objective. As Tocqueville points out, the act of associating also creates relationships between and among individuals, and these relationships can also bear fruit in a variety of ways. This observation would apply across a variety of associations.

With regard to the United States specifically, Tocqueville was impressed by the broad proliferation of associations. He observed:

> In no country in the world has the principle of association been more successfully used, or more unsparingly applied to a multitude of different objects, than in America. Besides the permanent associations which are established by law under the names of townships, cities, and counties, a vast number of others are formed and maintained by the agency of private individuals.[11]

To Tocqueville, this phenomenon was not altogether surprising. For Tocqueville saw a strong connection between the role of associations and the nature of a particular society (especially vis-à-vis the size and role of its government). Tocqueville found the proliferation of associations in the United States suitable for, and supportive of, a free nation wary of a strong, encroaching, centralized government. In the course of his opening remarks on associations, Tocqueville introduces this important concept. It appears as though Tocqueville is not speaking here of associations that are necessarily political in themselves, but rather of how associations in general impact a nation's government and politics. That Tocqueville's point here applies to associations in general will become quite clear when we review volume II of *Democracy in America*.

Tocqueville posited that there is an inverse relationship between the breadth and vigor of a society's associational undertakings and that of its government. That this would be so appears sensible, perhaps even obvious.

In broad terms, individuals in every society are confronted, regularly, with a host of challenges and opportunities. How those challenges and opportunities are navigated goes a long way in defining the character of that society. At one extreme, the state would be the actor primarily responsible for handling everything. The state would attempt to solve every problem, and the state would arrogate for itself all opportunities and benefits—parceling out to its subjects a portion of those opportunities and benefits as it saw fit. As becomes quickly apparent, such an approach is not consistent with a society that most people would consider "free." Indeed, such an approach would resemble the totalitarianism depicted in George Orwell's *1984*—the very antithesis of a free society.

The other extreme is not a particularly pleasant one either: a state of affairs where each and every individual must fend for himself or herself. A survival-of-the-fittest society where everyone must face the difficulties of life alone and may only enjoy those benefits that he or she is capable of individually procuring. If such a society has ever existed, it must have been prehistoric, for no record of anything resembling it can be found.

A middle ground is made possible by the advent and proliferation of private associations—that is, associations that are not organs of the state. Private associations permit individuals to accomplish collectively that which they could not otherwise. This serves as an antidote to the problems of extreme individualism. It permits progress that would otherwise be impossible and ameliorates setbacks and challenges that would be insurmountable to an individual alone. It also serves as a preventative to Statism, as private associations form an important bulwark against the state. This is because the more that an individual can accomplish through associations and institutions of his or her own private creation, the less he or she will need the help and involvement of the state. This limits the opportunities for the state to expand, and to the extent that the state is held in check, space for individuals to live out their lives free of direct government oversight is maintained. The simple math of this equation was well understood by America's founding generation and those that came shortly thereafter. Their fondness of limited government led them to generally prefer private solutions to government ones. As Tocqueville explains:

> The citizen of the United States is taught from his earliest infancy to rely upon his own assertions in order to resist the evils and the difficulties of life; he looks upon the social authority with an eye of mistrust and anxiety, and he only claims its assistance when he is quite unable to shift without it.... If a stoppage occurs in a thoroughfare, and the circulation of the public is hindered, the neighbors immediate constitute a deliberative body; and this extemporaneous assembly gives rise to an executive power which remedies the inconvenience before anybody has thought of recurring to an authority superior to that of the persons immediately concerned. If the public pleasures are concerned, an association is formed to provide for the splendor and regularity of the entertainment. Societies are formed to resist enemies which are exclusively of a moral nature, and to diminish the vice of intemperance; in the United States associations are established to promote public order, commerce, industry, morality, and religion; for there is no end which the human will, seconded by the collective exertions of individuals, despairs in attaining.[12]

Thus, to Tocqueville, the liberty of association enjoyed in America has been essential to the preservation of freedom in the United States, as it has helped check the growth of the state by allowing citizens to do for themselves that which, in other countries, the state would do for them.

Associations as a Check on Majoritarian Tyranny

Associations have been essential to the American Republic for another reason as well according to Tocqueville: they have served as a "necessary guarantee against the tyranny of the majority."[13] In a nation predicated upon majority rule, and especially one lacking an aristocracy or nobility such as America, citizens who find themselves in the minority are exposed to oppression at the hands of the majority with few avenues of recourse. This concern was very much in the minds of America's founders and received articulate expression by James Madison in *Federalist 10*.[14] The correctives that the founders proposed were embodied in the U.S. Constitution. Tocqueville posited that the proliferation of associations served as a powerful supplement to the founders' constitutional designs.

Tocqueville observed that via associations, individuals can help guard against and combat oppression.[15] Although one ordinary citizen might not be able to take on City Hall, an association of ordinary citizens oftentimes can. This has been thoroughly demonstrated in America by the numerous organizations that have successfully protected and furthered the rights of those who found themselves to be part of an unpopular minority on account of race, color, creed, or some other characteristic.[16]

With regard to this particular role, Tocqueville appears to have political associations in mind. For here he is not discussing associations for the purpose of accomplishing some particular private commercial end, but rather associations created for the purpose of protecting minorities and minority interests. Such associations would seem, by definition, to be political in nature. Consequently, one could argue that Tocqueville's observations regarding the role of associations in protecting against majoritarian tyranny are inapplicable to the typical business corporation.

That said, we ought not discount the role that nonpolitical associations can play (and have played) in providing such protections, which serves to complicate the issue significantly. For even nonpolitical associations can "serve as refuges from the state's encompassing tendencies and unifying values."[17] In other words, although not organized to engage in politics or advocacy, a nonpolitical association can, nevertheless, serve as a vehicle within which individuals sharing a common culture or perspective can band together in mutual support, finding shelter from a society that might be neglectful to their needs, or perhaps even hostile.

Further, although not political per se, an association might mobilize and insert itself into a political debate if the interests of its constituents were somehow threatened. This may be because the interests of its constituents and its own (commercial) interests coincide, as would be the case with regard to tobacco companies lobbying on behalf of smokers' rights, or gun manufacturers lobbying on behalf of gun-owners' rights. However, it may be for other reasons as well.

Consider a corporation in which the investors, directors, officers, employees, or customers (or perhaps all five constituencies together) share a particular concern in common. Such a phenomenon would not be merely coincidental, but could very well result from interests and values that brought them into contact with the corporation in the first place. All things being equal, the director of a pet-food company probably has an affinity for animals a degree above that of an average citizen. The same may very well be true for the company's investors, officers, and employees as well; it would almost certainly be true of the company's customers. One could envision this company involving itself in politics were an issue regarding animal rights or animal cruelty to capture the public's attention, even though the company was not created and does not ordinarily operate as a political association in any way. A cynic might regard this as merely an effort on the part of the company to further ingratiate itself with its constituencies, and this might certainly play a part in the company's decision making. However, it could be the result of something else as well: a manifestation of the company's "conscience," as formed by the collective influence of its various constituencies. Thus, it would seem as though even an ostensibly nonideological company could, at times, become politically activated. This is a chastening thought, as it undermines our efforts to make principled distinctions among various corporate enterprises. For the time being, let us simply note that the role of associations in exerting political power, and of potentially checking majority impulses for the benefit of minority groups, can theoretically be played by a larger circle of corporations than might initially be imagined. We will leave to later how best to navigate these uncertain waters.

Before proceeding, let us pause to consider that the converse may be true as well: a business corporation could serve to perpetuate, rather than check, the tyranny of the majority were it to align itself with prevailing opinions. An immediate response to this supposition is that the same could be said for all associations, even those that are purely political. Is there, therefore, a justification for looking at corporate business associations differently? There may be. One may fairly suggest that, given its commercial interests, a business corporation would be more likely than other forms of association to side with the majority. As such, a business corporation is, relatively speaking, more likely to further the prospect of majoritarian tyranny. Profits are a powerful incentive, especially for an entity (such as the corporation) ordinarily designed to maximize them.

Thus, it may very well be the case that, aside from those situations where their own economic interests would suggest otherwise, business corporations generally align themselves with majoritarian winds. They perpetuate the status quo, at the expense of those for whom the status quo may be repressive.

Once again we are confronted with a complexity born of corporate diversity. Certain corporations can, and have, reinforced majoritarian trends, while others have bucked such trends. Recognition of this does not preclude our consideration of the corporation as an association. To the contrary, it helps establish the claim. For in praising associations for their potential to serve as a check upon majorities, Tocqueville is not saying that only organizations that serve such a function can qualify as an association. Rather, he is touting the importance of associations due to their ability and potentiality to serve this function. Thus, the question is not whether corporations generally reinforce versus check majoritarian impulses and trends. Instead, the question is simply whether any particular corporation can potentially act as a check upon the majority. As will be explained later (in chapter 3), this is certainly something that must be answered in the affirmative.

James Madison and the Problem of Factions

The ability of corporations to serve a salutary function in checking majoritarian excesses notwithstanding, the very real problem identified above still remains: the possibility that corporations could use their resources and influence for nefarious political ends.

Of course, whether a particular end is "nefarious" or not can very well be in the eye of the beholder. Commentators who decried Target Corporation's decision to stop donating to Planned Parenthood (over the question of abortion) cheered Intel Corporation's decision to stop donating to the Boy Scouts of America (over the question of homosexual scouts), and vice versa. For most people, the problem of corporations taking political and ideological positions matter only insofar as those positions conflict with their own. This does not provide a principled basis upon which to resolve the question of corporate constitutional rights.

Let us assume, nevertheless, that there is indeed something objectively wrongful about the manner in which certain corporations influence political and societal discourse. Assume that corporate involvement furthers "special interests" detrimental to other groups, or to society at large. (This is, of course, not much of an assumption, but rather a matter of reality. That said, I cannot resist pointing out how the pejorative "special interest" is a phrase generally devoid of any objective meaning. Rather, it is simply a label affixed to the concerns of someone other than the speaker, whose own predilections are conversely deemed enlightened articulations of the common good.)

The concern is far from new. Back in 1787, James Madison railed against the mischief caused by "factions, which could either side with or against the majority." Madison's use of the term "faction" is conventionally understood to refer to the political party.[18] That said, there is little reason not to apply it to a business corporation that has become politically active. As Madison explained:

> By a faction I understand a number of citizens, whether amounting to a majority or minority of the whole, who are united and actuated by some common impulse of passion, or of interest, adverse to the rights of other citizens, or to the permanent and aggregate interests of the community.[19]

A politically influential business corporation would seem to fit the definition of "a number of citizens . . . united and actuated by some common . . . interest."[20] Even if the interest is nothing other than the pursuit of profit, one can readily see how such an interest might lead the corporation in directions "adverse to the rights of other citizens, or to the permanent and aggregate interests of the community."

Madison proceeds to tackle the important question of how best to handle the threat posed by the faction. Of the "methods of curing the mischiefs of the faction," he counts as two in number: "by removing its causes" or "by controlling its effects."[21]

With regard to removing the causes of faction, here too Madison finds two potential solutions: "by destroying the liberty which is essential to its existence" or "by giving to every citizen the same opinions, the same passions, and the same interests."[22] Madison firmly rejects each of these possibilities. The first he calls a "remedy... worse than the disease," and the second he labels "impracticable" (an understatement to be sure).[23] We are left, therefore, only with efforts to control the effects of factions upon our society.

As mentioned previously, the solution that Madison (and the founders) devised was constitutional in nature: establish a government that was republican and national in character.[24] Via a republican government, the impulses of factions are filtered through representatives who, hopefully, are more likely to govern on behalf of the common good. Via a national government, a faction's power, although possibly quite strong in a particular region of the country, is likely to be diluted via the interposition of competitive interests.[25]

For all his adulation of associations, Tocqueville too was not blind to their potential dangers. With echoes of Madison, Tocqueville identifies anarchy as the calamity that could befall a nation of associations were its citizens inclined to "violent political passions."[26] Fortunately for the United States, Tocqueville observed that Americans were not so inclined. Whereas in Europe "numerous parties [are] so diametrically opposed to the majority," in America "differences of opinion are mere differences of hue." As a result, American associations "hope to win over to their own principles" their compatriots; in Europe, where such hopes are unrealistic, associations exist in order to simply fight. Consequently, "associations in the United States are therefore peaceable in their intentions, and strictly legal in the means which they employ."[27]

Tocqueville's observations here are certainly not universally accurate. From the KKK to the Know-Nothings, not every association in the United States has been "peacable in its intentions" and "strictly legal" in the means by which it operated. But that should not detain us. For our interest lies in comparing Tocqueville's approach to associations with Madison's approach to factions (which are, themselves, simply a form of association). In doing so we find that, despite their divergent perspectives on associations, the approaches of Madison and Tocqueville can nevertheless be harmonized in important ways.

First, each thinker saw the faction as an important check on majoritarian tyranny (even if, as in the case of Madison, it was conceded that the faction could also contribute to such tyranny). As John Inazu remarked:

> It is important to note that while Madison and Tocqueville held different views about the inherent characteristics of the group—Madison's factions

were essentially bad and Tocqueville's associations were essentially good—both theorists viewed groups as a check against majority rule.[28]

Second, neither thinker was fond of depriving associations of liberty. Madison not only propounded that such a cure would be worse than the disease, but emphatically added:

> Liberty is to faction what air is to fire, an aliment without which it instantly expires. But it could not be a less folly to abolish liberty, which is essential to political life, because it nourishes faction than it would be to wish the annihilation of air, which is essential to animal life, because it imparts to fire its destructive agency.[29]

Notwithstanding the potential risks of political associations to societal stability, Tocqueville also concluded that they were, on balance, nevertheless essential. They served as an important bulwark against the dual threats to liberty so prevalent in democratic republics such as the United States: the threat of majoritarian tyranny and of governmental encroachment into all spheres of life.

This suggests that the corporation, even if viewed as a notorious "faction," would still be entitled to liberty under both Madisonian and Tocquevillian thought. It is our purpose, in the remaining chapters of this book, to flesh out the contours of this liberty. That said, it is nonetheless significant to note that even when viewed in the harsh, negative light of Madison's discourse on factions, the politically active association is entitled to freedom of action.

Tocqueville went further still. Allowing associations to partake in America's liberties was not merely a necessary evil, but rather an indispensable good in his opinion. This was necessary, Tocqueville posited, to enable associations to effectively fulfill their important roles. One such liberty that Tocqueville identified as critical was the right of individuals to actually meet in association. As Tocqueville correctly explained, an association that is limited to conducting its business via correspondence alone is not much of an association. Conversely,

> [w]hen an association is allowed to establish centres of action at important points in the country, its activity is increased and its influence extended. Men have the opportunity of seeing each other; means of execution are more readily combined, and opinions are maintained with a degree of warmth and energy which written language cannot approach.[30]

Relevantly, Tocqueville adds that associations also need to have the freedom to promulgate their opinions—"analogous to the liberty of unlicensed writing."[31] That is, associations needed the right to engage in advocacy without receiving preauthorization of their statements from the state.[32] In other words, freedom of speech.

Civil Associations

As we move from volume I of *Democracy in America* to volume II, we see a shift away from politics per se and toward a consideration of cultural and societal factors affecting the American Republic. Here Tocqueville devotes three chapters to associations. He commences this trilogy with the following remarks—remarks which make exceedingly clear (in the event that any doubt was harbored) that Tocqueville counts as "associations" enterprises that are nonpolitical in nature as well as those that might be political in nature:

> I do not propose to speak of those political associations—by the aid of which men endeavor to defend themselves against the despotic influence of a majority—or against the aggressions of regal power. That subject I have already treated.... Those associations only which are formed in civil life, without reference to political objects, are here adverted to. The political associations which exist in the United States are only a single feature in the midst of the immense assemblage of associations in that country. Americans of all ages, all conditions, and all dispositions, constantly form associations. They have not only commercial and manufacturing companies, in which all take part, but associations of a thousand other kinds-religious, moral, serious, futile, extensive, or restrictive, enormous or diminutive. The Americans make associations to give entertainments, to found establishments for education, to build inns, to construct churches, to diffuse books, to send missionaries to the antipodes....[33]

Thus, associations in Tocqueville's mind are certainly not limited to those with a political purview—such associations are merely a subset of an "immense assemblage of associations" in the United States. Of particular relevance to us, Tocqueville explicitly includes "commercial and manufacturing" companies in his litany of associations. This would seem to situate, or at a minimum potentially qualify, the business corporation well within the Tocquevillian Association category. It now behooves us to see what Tocqueville has to say about such nonpolitical associations and to what extent the observations and conclusions drawn by Tocqueville in chapter 12 of volume I are directly applicable to them.

Early on in his volume II discussion of public or civil associations (Tocqueville's term for associations that are not "political"), Tocqueville reiterated his point that associations enable private individuals to do for themselves (in conjunction with others) that which they would otherwise turn to government for assistance: "Wherever, at the head of some new undertaking, you see the government in France, or a man of rank in England, in the United States you will be sure to find an association."[34] Thus, the observation that associations serve as a check on the expansion of the state remains salient, as one would expect, when applied to public associations as well as political associations.

Indeed, Tocqueville launched into a more sustained inquiry into the connection between associations and freedom in his volume II discussion. He observed that "the most democratic country on the face of the earth is that in which men have in our time carried to the highest perfection that art of pursuing in common the object of their common desires, and have applied this new science to the greatest number of purposes." Tocqueville then asks bluntly: "Is this the result of accident?"[35] He seemed to think not.

The equality of citizens in the United States (by which Tocqueville refers to the lack of a powerful aristocracy) generally deprives individuals of the ability to accomplish much of anything significant by themselves. "Amongst democratic nations . . . all the citizens are weak and feeble; they can do hardly anything by themselves, and none of them can oblige his fellow-men to lend him their assistance" (as might a nobleman). If they do not learn to voluntarily help each other, they would "fall into a state of incapacity," and society as a whole would slip into "barbarism." "If men are to remain civilized, or to become so," Tocqueville opined, "the art of associating together must grow and improve in the same ratio in which the equality of conditions is increased."[36]

Indeed, of the two forms of association (the public versus the political), Tocqueville considered the public association of greater importance. As he explained, in the absence of political organizations, freedom would be jeopardized, but not necessarily one's material standard of living. In the absence of public associations, civilization itself would be threatened in a democratic republic:

> If men living in democratic countries had no right and no inclination to associate for political purposes, their independence would be in great jeopardy; but they might long preserve their wealth and their cultivation: whereas if they never acquired the habit of forming associations in ordinary life, civilization itself would be endangered. A people amongst which individuals should lose the power of achieving great things single-handed, without acquiring the means of producing them by united exertions, would soon relapse into barbarism.[37]

The prospect of barbarism seems somewhat of an exaggeration. What would most likely occur, as Tocqueville himself had adverted to twice before, is that the government would step in. As discussed, however, at a certain point this tendency would transform the nation from one that was democratic and free to one that was increasingly totalitarian and statist. In Tocqueville's own words:

> It is easy to foresee that the time is drawing near when man will be less and less able to produce, of himself alone, the commonest necessaries of life. The task of the governing power will therefore perpetually increase, and its very efforts will extend it every day. The more it stands in the place of associations, the more will individuals, losing the notion of combining together, require its assistance: these are causes and effects which unceasingly engender each other. Will the administration of the country ultimately assume the management of all the manufactures, which no single citizen is able to carry on?... The morals and the intelligence of a democratic people would be as much endangered as its business and manufactures, if the government ever wholly usurped the place of private companies.[38]

Moreover, the displacement of private associational activity with governmental activity has yet another negative repercussion. It is via associational activity, according to Tocqueville, that the conditions for a healthy community and society are established. For it is via the "reciprocal influence of men upon each other" through associations that "[f]eelings and opinions are recruited, the heart is enlarged and the human mind is developed."[39]

Unfortunately, for all their importance, associations are (according to Tocqueville) "more difficult" to form in democratic nations than in other nations. The reason for this is, again, the lack of an aristocracy. An association of a small number of aristocrats can be quite powerful and effective at pursuing its aims. In a democratic nation of equals, however, a similarly small number of citizens is unlikely to amass the same amount of resources and as such is unlikely to be as effective. Thus, in nations such as America, "associated members must always be very numerous for their association to have any power."[40] The task of association formation is, therefore, both more challenging and more important in nations such as America.

The Connection between Civil and Political Associations

Tocqueville concludes his examination of associations with an especially important inquiry into the "connection of civil and political associations."[41] Having discussed each of these forms of association separately (even if in a manner somewhat overlapping), he now looks into the extent to which the two forms of association bear upon one another.

In typical Tocquevillian fashion, his approach to the question begins with an observation—a multitude of observations actually. His first two observations concern the United States:

> There is only one country on the face of the earth where the citizens enjoy unlimited freedom of association for political purposes. This same country is the only one in the world where the continual exercise of the right of association has been introduced into civil life, and where all the advantages which civilization can confer are procured by means of it.[42]

Thereafter, Tocqueville observed that the inverse situation can be seen in a review of certain other nations:

> In all the countries where political associations are prohibited, civil associations are rare.[43]

Although it is a maxim of logical thinking that correlation does not necessarily entail causation, Tocqueville is within the bounds of reason here in speculating that "[i]t is hardly probable that this is the result of accident; but the inference should rather be, that there is a natural, and perhaps a necessary, connection between these two kinds of association." Tocqueville proceeds to justify his speculation as follows, by example:

> Certain men happen to have a common interest in some concern—either a commercial undertaking is to be managed, or some speculation in manufactures to be tried; they meet, they combine, and thus by degrees they become familiar with the principle of association. The greater is the multiplicity of small affairs, the more do men, even without knowing it, acquire facility in prosecuting great undertakings in common. Civil associations, therefore, facilitate political associations....[44]

In other words, the practice of associating to accomplish nonpolitical objectives gives rise to a greater eagerness and ability to associate for the purpose of political objectives.

At the same time, however, Tocqueville also points out that individuals may be disinclined to associate initially. For by associating (especially in nonpolitical matters, such as those of a commercial nature), individuals run the risk of financial loss. Further, a degree of skill is necessary in order to successfully pull together an association—skill that might be lacking among its potentially interested members.

It is for this reason that Tocqueville suggests that civil associations owe a debt of gratitude to political associations as well. For with regard to political associations, the hesitancy to get involved is lessened due to the fact that there is less risk of financial loss (as objectives in question are political and not commercial). Further, opportunities and incentives to form political associations "present themselves every day" in a nation such as America. This is largely because Americans realize the need to associate in order to move government in their desired direction. Thus, Tocqueville viewed the creation of a certain minimal number of political associations in America as inevitable; citizens would not simply sit back and allow themselves to be swept powerlessly away by whatever direction the nation's political rivers run. For that reason, "[p]olitical associations may therefore be considered as large free schools, where all the members of the community go to learn the general theory of association."[45] Pulling together his two strands of thought on the subject, Tocqueville can be said to believe that whereas political associations provide basic training in the art of associating, civil associations serve as finishing schools—the venue where this art is perfected.

The direct connection between the proliferation of political and civil associations is, to Tocqueville, replicated when it comes to their suppression as well. That is, an attack on the freedom of one form of association is, effectively, an attack on all forms of association:

> When some kinds of associations are prohibited and others allowed, it is difficult to distinguish the former from the latter, beforehand. In this state of doubt men abstain from them altogether, and a sort of public opinion passes current which tends to cause any association whatsoever to be regarded as a bold and almost an illicit enterprise.... It is therefore chimerical to suppose that the spirit of association, when it is repressed on some one point, will nevertheless display the same vigor on all others; and that if men be allowed to prosecute certain undertakings in common, that is quite enough for them eagerly to set about them.[46]

This point bears underscoring, as it goes to an argument that we will encounter in opposition to corporate First Amendment claims. To some, the divide between associations that are political versus those that are not political should govern the recognition of First Amendment rights. Although very few serious modern thinkers would advocate stripping politically focused organizations of constitutional freedoms, many fervently advocate doing this very thing with respect to ostensibly nonpolitical associations (such as corporations). In the paragraph quoted above, Tocqueville warns against attempting any such delineation.

That said, Tocqueville concludes his discussion of associations by conceding that, due to the instability that associations might engender, certain nations at certain times may wish to impose restrictions upon them. Further, he concedes that an absolutely unlimited freedom of association would probably be unwise for any nation. He adds, however, that the importance of associations is such that restrictions and limitations on associational freedoms ought to be weighed most carefully. As he colorfully put it: "I can understand that it may be advisable to cut off a man's arm in order to save his life; but it would be ridiculous to assert that he will be as dexterous as he was before he lost it."[47]

Characteristics of the Tocquevillian Association

Tocqueville did not leave us with a checklist of factors that make for an association. Nor did he supply us with a general definition of the association (the definition he provides, in chapter 12 of book one, has as its obvious object associations of a political nature). Nevertheless, from his extensive writings on the subject certain factors can be deduced.

In Tocqueville's discussion of political associations, he provides a definition that sets forth an element of general applicability, that an association must consist of "individuals":

> An association consists simply in the public assent which a number of individuals give to certain doctrines, and in the engagement which they contract to promote the spread of those doctrines by their exertions.[48]

As elementary as this initial characteristic may seem, it actually does serve to establish an important parameter. It would disqualify as associations those entities that are mere conglomerates of other entities, or those which exist on paper only.

Next, it is important that the individuals combine for some purpose. As the definition above makes clear, combining "to promote the spread" of "certain doctrines" certainly suffices. As Tocqueville's later writings (particularly in book two) make clear, combining for seemingly any common purpose suffices as well. Tocqueville observed, for example, that associations are created for a myriad of purposes: "[Americans] have not only commercial and manufacturing companies . . . but associations of a thousand other kinds—religious, moral, serious, futile, extensive, or restricted, enormous, or diminutive."[49]

Tocqueville's discussion of the benefits of association provides insights into additional factors. Recall that he wrote that via associations, individuals "become acquainted with each other, and their zeal in increased by their number."[50] This envisions a certain level of active involvement and suggests that a purely passive attachment to a certain common cause by many does not give rise to the existence of an association.

This segues into a related observation that Tocqueville made regarding associations: their role in acclimating individuals to democratic citizenship.

This acclimation is twofold, according to Tocqueville. First, an association's members are introduced to the craft of self-government. Second, and perhaps as important, via the "reciprocal influence of men upon each other" in associations, "[f]eelings and opinions are recruited, the heart is enlarged and the human mind is developed."[51] The broadening of heart and mind contributes to the virtues of empathy and tolerance, critically important in a nation where individuals, ultimately, determine the laws of the land. This further presumes a modicum of active involvement on the part of a purported association's members, reinforcing the point made immediately above.

Finally, Tocqueville had much to say about the ability of associations to check overreaching on the part of majorities and governments. They do this by enabling individuals to accomplish that which they could not otherwise accomplish alone without recourse to government. They also enable individuals to carve out, with others, private domains in which to live out their particular values—values that might conflict with prevailing majoritarian winds. Due to their size and resources, particular associations may serve as a powerful bulwark against the state; associations in the aggregate certainly serve this end.

In sum, the Tocquevillian Association of *Democracy in America* is a genuine community with a reasonably clear identity. Its membership consists of individuals dedicated to a particular cause (whether ideological or not). Member involvement can reasonably be expected to lead to mutually enriching acquaintanceships of substance. The association enables individuals to accomplish goals and fulfill yearnings that they would otherwise not be able to on their own.

MODERN SCHOLARLY TREATMENT OF ASSOCIATIONS

No scientist is infallible, least of all a social scientist. Thus, Tocqueville's observations and commentaries in *Democracy in America* are certainly open to critique and even rejection. His writings stand or fall on their own merit. That said, in both his own day and in our own time, his work has received tremendous acclaim. Many (perhaps most) who have considered his words and weighed his thoughts have found them persuasive if not convincing. In short, he is a recognized authority on the subject matters discussed here, and is presented as such.

Nevertheless, the reader will need to form his or her own opinion of Tocqueville. Fortunately, in the years since *Democracy in America* was penned, other, modern scholars have studied the role of associations in society, and their scholarship has generally supported and deepened Tocqueville's insights and conjectures.

With regard to the importance of associations to the individual, researchers have identified a number of important effects. Among the more obvious would be the satisfaction of "pursu[ing] [one's] interests with like-minded individuals," and the "realization of an important goal or furtherance of an important belief" (especially if such would not have been possible alone).[52]

Less obvious benefits have been found as well, which include:

> Providing emotional support, friendship, solidarity, and stability; conferring economic benefits; nourishing social identity and prestige; and providing a forum in which individuals can develop and live their values.[53]

With regard to the importance of associations to society as a whole, an abundance of significant scholarship has rather convincingly verified Tocqueville's analysis. Leading the charge would be Francis Fukuyama's *Trust: The Social Virtues and the Creation of Prosperity* (1995) and Robert D. Putnam's *Bowling Alone: The Collapse and Revival of American Community* (2000). Each of these books chronicles the indispensable role of associations to any given society.

As Fukuyama, Putnam, and other scholars have discovered, certain virtues and characteristics are necessary for any society's health. Chief among these is trust. For trust facilitates relationships, both personal and commercial. In the absence of trust, less is ventured, and less is gained. Further, in the absence of trust, that which is undertaken is marked by what economists refer to as increased "transaction costs." The hallmarks of a society sickened by lack of trust are an excessive proliferation of laws, lawyers, regulations, and overseers. Every detail must be carefully scrutinized, every action policed, every employee and spouse spied upon, every counterparty rigorously vetted. In the absence of natural trust, "artificial trust" must be purchased via these mechanisms. Not only is this expensive, diverting resources to more productive uses, but it is also not nearly as beneficial. For natural, genuine trust facilitates those leaps of faith and the taking of risks that lead to the greatest of rewards. Artificial trust, on the other hand, does not lend itself to risk taking, but rather ordinarily enables only those transactions and relationships to go forward in which risk can be sufficiently reduced.

Given the fact that in any modern society most individuals are strangers to one another, a certain amount of artificial trust is both necessary and inevitable. The challenge, however, is to find ways to inculcate and nurture natural trust as well. That is where associations come into play. It is through associations and associational activity that the bonds of trust are forged, along with the other virtues helpful to living in a diverse community of others. This is exceedingly beneficial to the individual, as it leads to more numerous and richer personal relationships, along with increased opportunities for commercial success. It also serves to keep at bay the state's intrusion into spheres of personal and commercial life. For the greater the trust among a group of people, the lesser is the clamor for law, regulation, and governmental oversight. All this serves to corroborate Tocqueville's thesis on the essentiality of associations to a nation that is free and prosperous.

Modern scholars have also attested to the importance of "mediating institutions" in society. These are institutions that fill the important space between citizen and state; institutions that permit individuals to privately order their lives, in reliance upon themselves and their fellow citizens instead of the state.[54] Mediating institutions provide an important venue for transmission of important social norms, norms which foster communitarian living.[55] They serve as a forum "for the cultivation and expression of republican virtues"—those habits of character that support democratic, republican government.[56] Families, religious communities, and neighborhoods have commonly been identified as prime examples of mediating institutions.[57] Relevant for our purposes, voluntary associations are also commonly included on this list.

Still more recent scholarship permits us to further refine our categorization of Toquevillian Associations. In his book *First Amendment Institutions*, Paul Horwitz explains that associations assist in the communication of messages, the formation of individual identities, the training of citizens, the evolution of views, and a source of meaning to their members.[58] This largely overlaps with Tocqueville's assessment of the association. To the extent that Horwitz intentionally focuses on factors that are of relevance to First Amendment inquiry, he provides a valuable gloss on Tocqueville's theory.

Horwitz's gloss is echoed in the work of Meir Dan-Cohen. Dan-Cohen has proposed a distinction between "constitutive communities" and "organizations," which mirrors the divide articulated by Tocqueville and Horwitz.[59] Separating the two entities is the degree to which members identify with the groups; the degree to which they regard their membership as "a significant aspect of [their] personhood."[60] As a commentator on Dan-Cohen explains, in constitutive communities, "[p]articipation in the life of the group takes on intrinsic meaning or value—it becomes a good in itself."[61] This is to be contrasted with the situation of an organization, in which the mode of association is "detached"; where members "regard the collective's goals and values as distant from their own personal identity."[62] Again, as Dan-Cohen's assessment was undertaken specifically to address the question of First Amendment rights, it is particularly relevant and salient to our inquiry.

Modern scholarship adds further to the picture, however, by offering an opinion regarding the appropriate size of an organization deemed to be an association. Thanks to research in the fields of anthropology and psychology, we have learned that there may be upper limits to a human being's ability to form meaningful relationships. According to this research, the human brain appears best adapted for small-group environments. What exactly constitutes a "small group" is far from established, but as one scholar puts it: "the number is dramatically smaller than megastructures such as the nation-state or the global corporation."[63] Beyond that number, the benefits to association, as identified by those who have studied mediating institutions, appear to dissipate.

This introduces an interesting wrinkle to Tocqueville's theory of association. Recall that Tocqueville opined that in nations such as America, "associated members must always be very numerous for their association to have any power."[64] "Very numerous" seems to certainly conflict with the "small group" theory advanced by modern scholars.

It should be noted,, that many vociferously disagree with this psychological assessment. Even very large institutions, like megachurches, or bureaucratic and hierarchical institutions, like the U.S. Army, can exhibit tremendous cohesiveness along with other characteristics of a Tocquevillian association/constitutive community.[65]

Even if we credit this research, however, it does not pose a theoretically fatal threat to our understanding of the association. It simply requires us to recognize the fact that the important roles filled by associations are not necessarily filled simultaneously. Put differently, associations can vary significantly along a continuum of characteristics and purposes. To the extent that an association exists to protect the rights of minorities, to advocate for political change, and to serve as a bulwark against the state's expansion by carving out and preserving space for private initiative, it would seem as though power (and size) would matter. To the extent that an association exists to serve as a training ground for civic virtue and the arts of democratic republicanism, a breeding ground for virtue, and a venue for interpersonal relationships, then it would seem as though its size would need to be constrained. Although an association might have to be very large to have any real power, it need not have power in order to be an association.

It would appear that at some level, a trade-off is simply inevitable: an association can be effective in one role (its sociopolitical role) only at the sacrifice of its other (its virtue-cultivating role). Associations do indeed exist for multiple reasons and do indeed serve multiple functions in our society. They do not, however, satisfy each reason and fulfill every function equally. Depending upon their size (and probably a host of other characteristics as well, yet to be discerned), associations will be stronger or weaker in their multiple dimensions.

For those who prefer happier endings, there is a potentially superior solution to this tension. It lies in recognizing that even very large organizations can be broken down into smaller units, which in turn can serve an associational function. Under this have-your-cake-and-eat-it-too approach, a large, powerful association would be broken into smaller units, which in turn could leverage the power of belonging to the larger association in their particular sphere(s) of influence without sacrificing those benefits that require an organization of a relatively small size.[66] Indeed, this is a structure that many large organizations, from a variety of fields, have adopted. It permits an association to accumulate the power that comes from a large size while preserving the benefits of smallness.

THE SUPREME COURT AND ASSOCIATIONS

In closing, it should be noted that the importance of associations in American life, both in practice and as described in theory by Tocqueville and others, has not been lost on America's courts. Indeed, "freedom of association" has now been firmly established in the United States as a First Amendment right. The contours of this freedom will be considered, in detail, in chapter 8. Generally speaking, this freedom entails the right of individuals to join together with others in pursuit of common cause.

Tellingly, the Supreme Court has discussed the freedom of association in Tocquevillian terms. It has observed how associations serve as "critical buffers between the individual and the power of the State."[67] It has noted how associations enable individuals to join with others in accomplishing objectives in common, which helps serve as a mechanism for those whose beliefs and desires might not coincide with that of most people:

> According protection to collective effort on behalf of shared goals is especially important in preserving political and cultural diversity and in shielding dissident expression from suppression by the majority.[68]

Indeed, the Court has identified the right to associate as being one of the "foundations of our society" and has cited in support of that proposition Tocqueville himself.[69]

It must be noted, however, that the Supreme Court has not adopted a definition of the association equivalent to that set forth here as the Tocquevillian Association. Indeed, as will be seen in chapter 8, the Court has been quite unclear in its definition of what constitutes an "association" for constitutional purposes, and its approach toward designating organizations as such has changed over time (from case to case it would seem).

Further, "freedom of association" is not synonymous with granting associations the constitutional rights of religious liberty or freedom of speech, as these three constitutional freedoms are distinct. There is certainly a tremendous degree of overlap here, and the Court has long recognized that "an association may have standing in its own right to seek judicial relief from injury to itself and to vindicate whatever rights and immunities the association itself may enjoy"[70]—including First Amendment rights. That said, as with the Court's definition of an "association," the case law regarding the interplay of these First Amendment freedoms is unclear.

The Court's difficulty in articulating a definition of "association," and the rights inuring thereto is, I posit, largely remediable. Drawing upon Madison, Tocqueville, and our understanding of the importance of associations to both individuals and society as a whole, an entity that bears the characteristics of a Tocquevillian Association ought to be deemed an association, and ought to presumptively enjoy the First Amendment's freedom of association and freedom of speech protections. To the extent that the association is religious in nature, it ought to presumptively enjoy the First Amendment's freedom of religion protections as well. The reasons why this is so will be clearly elucidated in chapters 5 through 8, which address those three First Amendment freedoms.

NOTES

1. Stephen M. Bainbridge, J. Mark Ramseyer, & William A. Klein, Business Associations Agency Partnerships and Corporations (8th ed. 2012).
2. *See* Richard L. Cupp Jr., *Moving Beyond Animal Rights: A Legal/Contractualist Critique*, 46 San. Diego L. Rev. 27, 59 (2009). Some historians posit that the family, or clan, was actually recognized as a unit of society before the individual was. *See* Samuel Williston, *History of the Law of Business Corporations Before 1800*, 2 Harv. L. Rev. 105, 106 (1888) (citing Henry Maine).
3. George F. Deiser, *The Juristic Person*, 3 Penn. L. Rev. 131, 133 (1908).
4. Aristotle, Politics 6 (Benjamin Jowett trans., 1999).
5. Alexis de Tocqueville, Democracy in America, Introduction at xxxvi (Bantam Classics 2000) (introduced by Joseph Epstein).
6. John O. McGinnis, *Reviving Tocqueville's America: The Rehnquist Court's Jurisprudence of Social Discovery*, 90 Cal. L. Rev. 485, 533 (2002).
7. *See* Tocqueville, *supra* note 5, at 219.
8. *See id.* at 224.
9. *See id.* at 219.
10. *See id.* at 219.
11. *Id.* at 218.
12. *See id.* at 219.
13. *See id.* at 222.
14. *Id.* at 218.
15. *See id.* at 223.
16. *See* Jason Mazzone, *Freedom's Associations*, 77 Wash. L. Rev. 639, 696 (2002) ("According to Tocqueville, associations...generate power because in associations collective agendas are set and refined, and organized individuals are able to exercise greater influence together than if they each labor alone.").
17. Paul Horwitz, First Amendment Institutions 222 (2013).
18. *E.g.*, Daryl J. Levinson, *Separation of Parties, Not Powers*, 119 Harv. L. Rev. 2311, 2321 (2006).
19. The Federalist No. 10 (James Madison).
20. *Id.*
21. *Id.*
22. *Id.*

23. *Id.*
24. *See id.*
25. *See id.*
26. *See* TOCQUEVILLE, *supra* note 5, at 220–23.
27. *See id.* at 225.
28. John D. Inazu, *The Strange Origins of the Constitutional Right of Association*, 77 TENN. L. REV. 485, 556 (2010).
29. THE FEDERALIST NO. 10 (James Madison).
30. TOCQUEVILLE, *supra* note 5, at 219.
31. *See id.* at 219. In an era before e-mail or the Internet, Tocqueville also devotes an entire chapter to the need for associations to publish their own newspapers, in order to keep their widely dispersed membership informed. *See id.* at 636–39.
32. Tocqueville also wrote that associations ought to have the right to select, from among their number, delegates to represent their viewpoints as may be necessary or helpful. This is probably the least controversial of Tocqueville's statements on the subject of associations, and the lease relevant for our purposes. But Tocqueville was nothing if not thorough.
33. TOCQUEVILLE, *supra* note 5, at 630.
34. *See id.* at 630–31.
35. *See id.* at 631.
36. *See id.* at 635.
37. *See id.* at 631–32.
38. *See id.* at 632–33.
39. *See id.* at 633.
40. *See id.* at 632.
41. *See id.* at 640.
42. *See id.*
43. *See id.*
44. *See id.*
45. *See id.* at 642.
46. *See id.*
47. *See id.* at 645.
48. *Id.* at 219.
49. *Id.* at 630.
50. *See id.* at 219.
51. *See id.* at 633.
52. Mazzone, *supra* note 16, at 694–95.
53. *Id.* at 695.
54. *See* Richard Brooks, *Law and Civil Society in the United States, Canada, Quebec, and the First Nations*, 15 ARIZ. J. INT'L & COMP. L. 1, 11–12 (1998).
55. *See* Timothy L. Fort, *The First Man and the Company Man: The Common Good, Transcendence, and Mediating Institutions*, 36 AM. BUS. L. J. 391, 430 (1999).
56. Cass R. Sunstein, *Beyond the Republican Revival*, 97 YALE L. J. 1539, 1572 (1988).
57. *See* Fort, *supra* note 55, at 430.
58. HORWITZ, *supra* note 17, at 222.
59. *See* Meir Dan-Cohen, *Freedoms of Collective Speech: A Theory of Protected Communications by Organizations, Communities, and the State*, 79 CAL. L. REV. 1229 (1991) (*cited in* James D. Nelson, *Conscience, Incorporated*, 2013 MICH. STATE L. REV. 1565, 1581–82 (2013)).
60. *See* Nelson, *supra* note 59 (manuscript at 15).

61. *Id.*
62. *Id.* (manuscript at 16).
63. *See* HORWITZ, *supra* note 17, at 429–30.
64. *See* TOCQUEVILLE, *supra* note 5, 632.
65. *See* Nelson, *supra* note 59 (manuscript at 20).
66. *See* Fort, *supra* note 55, at 395.
67. *See* Roberts v. United States Jaycees, 468 U.S. 609, 619 (1984).
68. *See id.* at 622.
69. *See* N.A.A.C.P. v. Claiborne Hardware Co., 458 U.S. 886, 933 & 933 n.80 (1982).
70. Warth v. Seldin, 422 U.S. 490, 511 (1975).

CHAPTER 2

The Modern Business Corporation

There is general agreement with Tocqueville that associations are critically important and entitled to certain freedoms and protections. Whether these freedoms and protections should include those set forth in the First Amendment is a separate, albeit closely related question. That said, the extent to which a corporation qualifies as a Tocquevillian Association should bear heavily on the extent to which it can assert First Amendment rights, for the reasons set forth in chapter 1. Although some observations on this question were made in chapter 1, more thorough scrutiny will be undertaken here.

It should come as no surprise that many people balk at characterizing the corporation as a Tocquevillian Association. Although Tocqueville explicitly referenced and included business enterprises in his articulation of associations, Tocqueville "was not writing about organizations controlled by unaccountable managers and self-perpetuating boards."[1] The modern for-profit corporation is considered *sui generis* and, as such, outside the realm of all other associational undertakings. The reason for this, I posit, is the purpose, operation, and understanding of the typical, modern business corporation. As this chapter will demonstrate, these characteristics paint the picture of an entity that scarcely resembles Tocqueville's association.

However, this chapter will also demonstrate that things were not always so. The corporation of yesteryear differed dramatically from its modern cousin, and in some ways more closely resembled Tocqueville's concept of an association. Even more significantly, as will be explored in chapter 3, not all corporations of today resemble the typical modern version. Some corporate enterprises harken back, in many respects, to corporate forms and practices of old, breathing new relevancy into our understanding of corporate history.

THE PREMODERN CORPORATION

The modern corporation evolved over the course of centuries, with its particular defining characteristics (set forth below) making their first appearances in different times and places. Also changing over time has been corporate law itself: the rules and regulations that govern the corporation's interactions with the state, and the rights and responsibilities of the corporation's various constituencies vis-à-vis one another and the corporation. These changes, in turn, fueled an evolution in the theoretical understanding of the corporation. Over the next few sections, we shall review this evolution, with an eye toward those developments that are particularly relevant to the question of the corporation's putative classification as a Tocquevillian Association, and, *a fortiori*, the strength of its claim to the First Amendment's protections.

Scholars have traced the precursors of the modern corporation to ancient Rome. That judgment is certainly one that must be taken under advisement, for there is no tidy way to define a "precursor" to the modern business corporation. If one defines the term broadly, to include any commercial arrangement beyond mere barter, then we can trace the corporation's lineage back to Mesopotamia, 3000 BC. If one demands the presence of an organized group of investors, then the lineage is cut short by a millennium to Assyria, 2000 BC. If one's criteria for a corporate precursor includes the formal operation of law (versus strictly private arrangements), then ancient Athens of the first millennium BC becomes a contender for the honor.[2]

Rome, however, is a particularly good choice. Indeed, no less an authority than William Blackstone, master commentator on the common law, supports this view. Blackstone gives credit for the advent of the corporation specifically to Numa Pompilius, the second King of Rome (whose reign marked the seventh century BC).[3] During Numa's rule, hostilities between two tribal factions (the Romans and the Sabines) plagued the city of Rome. To resolve the situation, Numa subdivided each of these factions into several smaller units, organized by trade or profession. These smaller units received official recognition of their own in the eyes of the law, and by dividing these tribes into factions themselves, Numa hoped to dilute their unity, thereby decreasing the severity of the overall rift between Romans and Sabines.

The concept of attributing official recognition to a group of persons was soon utilized in other contexts as well. Towns, villages, colonies, and temples received such recognition, becoming official and separate members of Roman society. So did burial societies and trade guilds. This concept of separate societal membership, for a group of persons, is reflected in the very word "corporation." Although not coined at the time, the word "corporation" has at its root *corpus*, the Latin noun for "body." The development and repercussions of this concept, more formally known as "corporate personhood," will be discussed more fully in chapter 4.

Of particular relevance to us, the use of corporate status was eventually extended to business ventures as well. Ordinarily called *societates*, these ancient Roman entities resembled partnerships more than corporations. Like modern partnerships until relatively recently, the *societates* did not, for example, survive the departure of one of their participants. Further, each participant was personally liable for the debts of the *societates*. Nevertheless, the *societates* can fairly be said to represent an important milestone in the evolution of the corporation. For here we have clearly recognized, as an independent unit of society, an entity that is commercial in nature. It had certain rights and duties of its own—rights and duties that were not simply the extension of those of its participants.

By the third century BC we find in Rome *societates publicani*. These entities were generally larger than the earlier *societates* of the seventh century BC, and introduced the concept of limited partners—forerunners to the modern corporate shareholder. Like the modern shareholder, the limited partners of the *societates publicani* lacked the ability to manage the business entity and were shielded from liability arising out of the entity's operations. Further, the death of a member of a *societates publicani* did not necessarily spell the demise of the entity—it could continue in its business. This made the *societates publicani* an attractive option for those wishing to invest or wishing to procure investment. It enabled individuals to pursue wealth within a structure that provided a significant degree of protection and certitude. As Professors Henry Hansmann, Reinier Kraakman, and Richard Squire opined in their article "Law and the Rise of the Firm," these particular precursors to the modern corporation were stunningly similar to that with which we are familiar today:

> By the first century B.C., the largest *societates publicanorum* appear to have resembled the modern public company in both size and structure, with "multitudes"—presumably hundreds—of limited partners who could trade their shares on a market similar to a modern stock exchange.[4]

Although the *societates publicani* represent an important advance, the historical development of the corporation has not been a linear affair. Thus, despite the appearance of many modern corporate features in the *societates publicani*, these features did not persist throughout the centuries to come. This is particularly the case with the advent of limited liability. Although certain *societates publicani* were afforded this protection, it was not the norm for all corporate entities. Additionally, as will be discussed, much of Roman law was lost when Rome fell in the fifth century AD—including the concept of limited corporate liability.

Further, all the significant similarities between the *societates publicani* and the corporation of today should not mask some fairly profound differences between the two as well. Today's corporations are usually of an indefinite duration; premodern corporate entities were ordinarily of a fairly short temporal duration (notwithstanding their ability to survive the death of an investor). Today's corporations are usually formed to pursue any legitimate, profitable enterprise; premodern corporate entities were ordinarily created to pursue a narrow, fixed undertaking.

One of the most important similarities—and differences—had to do with the relationship between the *societates* and the state. As with our modern corporations, the *societates* were creatures of law. Their existence required the sovereign's approval, and regulations governed important aspects of their conduct. However, unlike the situation today, the objectives of the *societates* were narrowly circumscribed by the sovereign. Whereas the modern business purpose is empowered by law to pursue any legitimate, profitable enterprise, its predecessors enjoyed no such liberty. Corporate recognition was historically limited to a narrow range of putative undertakings.

The *societates* were generally permitted to exist solely to serve some particular interest of the state. They were used, as mentioned, to organize and provide legal recognition of towns and colonies. To the extent that they engaged in enterprises that could be considered commercial, *societates* were formed to collect taxes, manage public works, supply armaments, and work the mines.

This feature of premodern corporate entities persisted throughout the Middle Ages and well into the nineteenth century. Indeed, it should be considered one of the main features that distinguishes premodern corporate entities from modern ones. Sovereigns would grant an association the privilege of operating as a corporate entity only to the extent that the entity served some interest of the sovereign or of society as a whole (which would hopefully coincide in any event). As a result, practically all premodern corporate entities engaged in activities that could be deemed public-oriented in one sense or another, such as the building of roads and bridges, the maintenance of hospitals, the caretaking of religion, the provision of education, the settling of new colonies, and engagement in foreign trade.

Another distinguishing feature was that the procurement of a corporate charter was, traditionally, not routine at all (as is the case today). Rather, those wishing to incorporate were required to convince their sovereign (be it an emperor, king, or parliament) that incorporation was warranted for the entity in question. This required a showing that the organization's corporate recognition (and the privileges attached thereto) served some good that the sovereign was interested in seeing served. The granting of a corporate charter was deemed a significant privilege and was done on a case-by-case basis in accord with the sovereign's needs and wishes. Moreover, the charters themselves were not simply the product of those seeking incorporation but were often written by an agent of the sovereign. Those charters that were the product of initial private draftsmanship often saw revisions at the hands of governing authorities.

Finally, with few exceptions, the membership of premodern corporations actively participated in corporate affairs.[5] This active participation "would impart moral rectitude to the company from which legitimacy flowed" and helped justify "an independence from the state."[6] In other words, the close connection and involvement of the corporation's membership in its governance and activities imbued the corporation with a sense of innate validity. This counterbalanced the potential to characterize the corporation as a mere creature of the state, owing all its rights and even its very existence completely to the sovereign's grace.

Thus, even prior to the modern era, certain entities received independent societal and legal recognition. Such entities were permitted to exist for narrowly circumscribed objectives linked to the common good or the interests of the state. Few were commercial in nature, and those that were commercial nevertheless served some purpose deemed sufficiently beneficial to society as a whole. Investors of certain entities enjoyed limited liability, but this protection was not generally presumed and did not endure consistently over time. Moreover, most members of the corporate enterprise were actively involved in its affairs, imbuing it with a sense of legitimacy.

THEORETICAL UNDERSTANDINGS OF THE PREMODERN CORPORATION

Although what a corporation *did* as a general matter was fairly circumscribed over the centuries (from its appearance in ancient Rome to the nineteenth century), what the corporation *was* cannot be so tidily explained. For over the course of the millennia, different theories have been advanced to explain the nature of the corporate entity. Despite Felix Cohen's attack on such ruminations as "transcendental nonsense,"[7] ideas have consequences and our conceptualization of the corporation can either support, or undermine, our law's treatment of it. Thus, in the pages that follow, we shall inquire into those conceptualizations of the corporation that have made their mark upon history.

Roman jurists did not philosophize much about the nature of the corporation, but from the types of entities that were generally permitted to incorporate we can discern a pattern. For the most part, as mentioned, only those entities that served an explicit public purpose were permitted to carry on in the corporate form—and to enjoy the rights and privileges attached thereto. Indeed, it could be fairly argued that during both ancient and early medieval times, the corporation was viewed essentially as an arm of the state, and the law largely treated it as such. Corporations were permitted to exist but were made subject to rules and regulations to ensure that they continued to exist in service to the state. This is emblematic of what has come to be known as the "concession theory" of the corporation. As its name suggests, concession theory posits that the corporation is simply a creature of the state and owes its existence to the beneficence of the state. It exists to serve the will of the state, in order to further some particular state policy or some public good.

Concession theory should be contrasted with its polar opposite, "real entity" or "natural entity" theory. "Real entity theory" posits that corporations are not pure legal fabrications, but rather naturally occurring entities. State recognition of a corporation, under real entity theory, is somewhat akin to state recognition of a live birth via the bestowal of a birth certificate.

As indicated, active involvement in the affairs of the earliest corporations by their membership clothed even these entities with somewhat of a "real entity" feel. But the seeds of the real entity conceptualization as a theoretical matter were planted by the Catholic Church in the Middle Ages. For the church long needed some way to contend with its vast network of affiliated agencies (and agencies of ordinarily perpetual duration). The corporate form (or, more precisely, the "juridic person" under the canon law[8]) helped provide for the orderly transfer of property and the orderly recognition of rights and responsibilities—all without needing to peg such things to individual human persons (who have the unfortunate habit of coming and going, both in terms of geography and mortality). Far more convenient it was to declare that the University of Paris owns a particular parcel of land, than to identify the ever-changing group of individuals who constitute the university as the land's owners. In fact, the very term *persona ficta*, which captures the fact that corporations are essentially artificial persons in the eyes of the law, was purportedly coined by Sinibaldo Fieschi, a canonist who would eventually be coronated as Pope Innocent IV, and who has come to be known as the "father of modern corporations theory."[9]

Unlike the ancient Roman approach, however, the canonists did not bestow corporate recognition merely out of convenience—or out of some purported act of legislative grace. Under canon law, church recognition of the corporation was indeed practically important, but such recognition followed, rather than preceded, the corporation's appearance. In other words, in juxtaposition to the Roman view, the church's position was that society naturally gives rise to certain aggregations of individuals—aggregations that can fairly be said to take on a life of their own. Official recognition of these aggregations as corporations (juridical persons) was simply that: an act of recognition, not of creation. Put differently, the difference between the two views can be summarized as a difference over cause and effect: the Romans believed that official recognition gave rise to a corporation's existence; the canonist believed that a corporation's existence gave rise to its recognition. One real entity theorist put it this way:

> The juristic person, or collective will of the group, is not a creation of the law; the law does not create its personality, but finding a group engaged in some common pursuit, endows it with a definite legal capacity. It is capable of exercising rights, capable of committing wrongs; the former it may vindicate; the latter it must atone for.[10]

Canon law had a particularly profound effect on corporate theory generally (carrying over into the civil sphere) due to the collapse of the Roman Empire. For when the Empire collapsed (generally pegged to the overthrow of Emperor Romulus Augustulus by the barbarian Odoacer in AD 476), it fell upon the church to preserve the light of civilization through the "dark ages" that followed. Many of the chores and responsibilities of government were assumed by the church (which, quite fortunately, was well positioned to assume them given the breadth of its various institutions across the European continent). For this reason, the church's understanding of corporate entities did not remain an internal matter, but carried over into civil society.

Corporate law and theory took a major step toward its modern form in the twelfth century, when canon lawyers sought to systematize the corpus of church law. Although by this time the dark ages were over, the church continued to exert a profound influence upon secular authorities and secular thinking. Thus, the canonists' project had a profound impact on the trajectory of European corporate law and theory.

As can be seen from the historical sources, despite their theological training, the concerns and objectives of the canonists were quite mundane in nature, and not ethereal. As Harold Berman explains, they needed "to achieve practical solutions to actual legal conflicts between church and the secular polities as well as legal conflicts within the church."[11] These conflicts multiplied as the church increasingly advocated the novel proposition of separation of church and state: that the church constituted its own "corporate legal entity . . . independent of emperors, kings, and feudal lords."[12]

A review of the "kinds of practical issues that arose in litigation in the twelfth century" demonstrates that the list of items that the canonists grappled with would probably be of interest to most corporate law scholars of our own day:

> Is the head of a corporation (say, a bishop) required to consult its members (the chapter) before making a decision to sue or to answer a charge in court? Is he required not only to consult with them but also to obtain their consent? What about a decision to alienate property, or a decision to confer privileges of various kinds?

> ...
>
> Who is to exercise the powers of the head of a corporation during a vacancy...?
>
> ...
>
> Can a corporation commit crimes? Can it commit torts? Is it liable for the crimes or torts of its officers?
>
> ...
>
> If a corporation loses all its members, does it continue to exist?
>
> ...
>
> What happens to the property of a corporation that ceases to exist?
>
> ...
>
> May a corporation to which property has been given for a particular purpose lawfully decide to use that property for another purpose?[13]

During their process of corporate-law systemization, the canonists did not merely update Roman corporate law, or even church canon law, but merged these past approaches with Germanic associational theory and Christian theology.[14] This led to a greater personalization of the corporation than under traditional Roman law, as both the German and Christian influences lent themselves to the personification of groups.[15] For example, whereas under Roman law only those entities recognized by the sovereign could constitute a corporation, under the newly systematized corporate law of the canonists, "any group of persons which had the requisite structure and purpose...constituted a corporation, without special permission of a higher authority."[16] Also in contrast to Roman corporate law, "canon law imposed civil and criminal liability on a corporation when a majority of its members consented to a wrongful act...."[17]

What resulted was a neo-Roman approach. This approach generally put a greater emphasis on the natural right of associated entities to exist, and less on the concessionary perspective of classical Roman law. An example of this neo-Roman thinking is provided by Bartolus of Sassoferrato, one of the most important commentators upon the law's reform. Bartolus proclaimed: "If some people want to settle in some place, and create a city, castle, or village, they can do so, as it is permitted by the law of nations."[18] Such a view is a direct repudiation of the position that the permission of the state is required in order to establish a corporation (as each of the resulting entities was understood to be a form of corporation).[19]

In continuity with classical Roman approach, the reformers "had a clear vision of the corporation as separate from...its members."[20] With the reformer's view of corporate separateness came a fairly robust view of corporate "personality," permitting even the extension of criminal law to corporations.[21] This was an extension of the traditional approach, for the applicability of criminal law to the corporation unheard of under classical Roman law.

Thus, the European conceptualization of the corporation became an admixture of divergent understandings: that of ancient Rome, of medieval Germany, and of the church. Elements of each can be found in how authorities over the centuries approached and treated the corporation. In some contexts and in some eras one particular strand generally prevailed, and in other contexts and in other eras another generally prevailed.

Consider, for example, the persistence of the classical Roman approach during the feudal era—centuries after the fall of Rome, and during the same time as the canonists' reformulation of corporate law. This era of kings and lords was marked by a proliferation of towns across the European continent. These towns were typically organized as municipal corporations—to which an overlord would grant a charter of powers and duties in return for "the payment of a sum of money or the rendition of some other consideration."[22] Although these municipal corporations enjoyed substantial rights to self-governance, "[i]t was recognized and well settled as a principle that no town legislature might invade the limits of the royal or parliamentary law-making power."[23] There was also "the fear that the town charter of the powers granted by it might be summarily taken away by the king" if the town's government misbehaved.[24] Thus, we see the use of the corporate form to grant limited, leased independence to an organizational subset for the good of, and under the ultimate authority of, the whole. Had this arrangement reflected the canonist, church approach instead (as expressed above by Bartolus), greater weight would have been given to the autonomy and sovereignty of towns, flowing from their natural and necessary occurrence in the development of human affairs.

THE CORPORATION IN COLONIAL AMERICA

Although influential, the neo-Roman corporate law of the canonists was not adopted everywhere. Most notably, in England the more classical Roman version of corporate law generally persisted. This was the version of corporate law inherited by the United States. In fact, the first English colony in America was established by an English corporation: the Virginia Company of London, which, in 1607, settled Jamestown, Virginia. This should not come as a surprise for, as mentioned, corporate charters were routinely granted to entities that spearheaded colonization efforts.

Of course, even in England the law of corporations evolved. However, the Roman pedigree of English corporate law remained easier to discern. Consider, for example, England's treatment of commercial interests in the late Middle Ages. More specifically, consider the "earliest organization of English merchants that came in direct contact with foreigners," known as "Merchants of the Staple."[25] From 1313 to 1353, King Edward II and his successor King Edward III granted the Merchants of the Staple charters recognizing certain rights of self-governance while imposing certain rules of trade.[26] Although these charters certainly benefited the merchants, "the principle motive" for granting them "was to give the king control over the transactions with foreigners and especially to make the payment of customs more certain and convenient."[27] In fact, according to John Davis, the corporate form "was imposed by the state as a public necessity than conceded by it in response to the demands of the private interests of merchants."[28] Other such charters were granted by subsequent sovereigns over the centuries, ordinarily granting certain trade monopolies to the corporations and rights of self-governance.[29] Among such corporations were the East India Company, the African Company, the Hudson Bay Company, and the South Sea Company, which were granted powers of colonization and colonial government, as an accompaniment to their trading powers.[30] Still other corporations were created for the purpose of colonization, such as the London Company and the Plymouth Company.[31] Again, as Davis explains, the growth of these chartered corporations is traceable to the needs of the state:

> The key to an understanding of their [the corporations'] rise and growth is in a due appreciation of the extent to which the political organization in England had been perfected. The lack of closer political relations with foreign nations as well as of those between the government of England and its subjects made it necessary to leave for the exercise of groups of subjects prompted by the motive of self-interest many powers that were later to be resumed by the state. When the state became able to extend its functions over the field of activity occupied by the companies, they became obsolete, though, like most English institutions, they were maintained in form long after their efficiency as organs of government had departed.[32]

This helps explain why English merchants trading in France "were never organized in a corporation"—"close relations... existed between England and France since the Norman conquest" and the "English government... had maintained the international machinery necessary for the performance of its functions."[33] In short, corporate charters were granted to enable associations of people to do those things that the state, because of its limited reach and abilities, was unable to do.[34]

Not surprisingly, then, concession theory remained strong in England, pursuant to which corporations were deemed mere artificial entities that owed their existence "to the positive law of the state."[35] This was buttressed by the practice of chartering corporations on a case-by-case basis, via individualized acts of the sovereign. Pursuant to both theory and practice of the time, corporations were created "to subserve 'the advantage of the public,' as in 'the advancement of religion, of learning, and of commerce.'"[36]

A consequence of artificiality was the understanding that a corporation "could not be an imbecile, commit a crime, be guilty of treason or suffer an assault or battery; nor could it be imprisoned or suffer attainder, forfeiture or corruption of blood.... Having likewise no soul, it could not be bound by oath...."[37]

The conception of the corporation as an "artificial person" under the common law provided the backdrop to modern corporate law as articulated in Blackstone's *Commentaries*, which in turn adopted its approach from Sir Edward Coke's writings on the subject.[38] This was to be expected, as Coke wrote about the corporation in the sixteenth and seventeenth centuries—at a time when corporations functioned, as explained, as essentially arms of the state, and when concession theory and the view of the corporation as an artificial person reigned supreme.[39]

Thus, in the Anglo-American world at the turn of the nineteenth century, the corporation was conceived of as "an agency of the government, endowed with public attributes, exclusive privileges, and political power, and designed to serve a social function for the state."[40]

THE ADVENT OF THE MODERN CORPORATION

As governments grew in function and reach since the time of Blackstone, "the state has wholly or partially absorbed" the powers that were once the domain of corporations.[41] This undercut, to an extent, the foundational basis of concession theory—the chartering of corporations to serve public ends that were beyond the reach of the state or sovereign. For as a result of the state's expansion, "[t]he plane of corporate life has been depressed, in a sense, to a lower level. The purpose of the modern corporation is less plainly to contribute to national development and is apparently confided, to a large extent, to the amplification of the individual."[42] In other words, as the corporation became less essential to the state, it was increasingly viewed as serving ends that were primarily private, versus ends that were primarily public. One might have expected this to mark the demise of the corporation, given its long association with the state and publicly oriented ends. Of course, that is not what happened.

To the extent that a philosophical justification for the increasingly private-oriented corporation was necessary, one could be found in Adam Smith's *Wealth of Nations*. In this 1776 treatise, Smith famously propounded the observation that by freely serving their own private interests, individuals furthered the common good. Consequently, recognition of the corporation, even for undertakings that are not explicitly publicly oriented, nevertheless could be said to serve society's best interests—the same standard to which corporate recognition had traditionally been pegged. Although I cannot locate a source tying society's acceptance of the privatization of the corporation to the theories of Adam Smith, I believe it is plausible to assume that Smith's theories, which were popular at the time of the corporation's transformation, helped facilitate this transformation.

Further facilitating this transformation was the fact that the benefits of conducting business under the corporate form were simply too great to forego by this point. These included, ordinarily, the monopolization of a particular trade route or line of commerce, the ability to raise capital via the sale of stock, and the apparent efficiency of internalization (a point upon which economists are in disagreement).

Another benefit of incorporation was the potential protection of limited liability, but this advantage must be put firmly into perspective. Although such protection had been available to some extent under ancient Roman law, it had largely disappeared after Rome's fall. It did not emerge again until approximately the sixteenth century. When it did re-emerge, it was not enshrined in the law as an automatic feature of incorporation, but rather appeared only sporadically, in particular corporate charters to the extent deemed necessary or preferable.[43] It was not the norm. Thus, this particularly attractive feature of the corporation is unlikely to have played that great a role in furthering its acceptance as an entity subservient to private ends.

Of course today, the limited liability of corporate investor is the norm. Why this has not always been the case can be pegged, in large part, to the ambivalence with which society approached the issue, coupled with a lack of its need. Ambivalence existed because parties were naturally wary of doing business with an entity whose owners disclaimed personal liability (especially in an era when such was not common). The owners themselves were less concerned with limited liability because the corporate entities of the past were generally much smaller than the corporate entities of today. Many were family affairs—owned and operated by blood relatives or close business associates. Under such circumstances, trust in one's fellow business venturers was sufficient to counterbalance the risk of loss.

During the nineteenth century this began to change rather dramatically. Entities of greater size and scale (particularly the burgeoning railroad companies) increasingly sought corporate charters. Their size, and the scope of their undertakings, required them to raise large amounts of capital—more than any one family or group of business associates could amass among themselves. The ability to raise capital by selling ownership interests (stock) made incorporation an obvious choice. Coupled with this was an increased desire for the protections of limited liability. Given a large base of disparate investors, many with no connection to one another, the cost-benefit analysis of limited liability came out differently. For under these circumstances, the benefits of limited liability outweighed the costs. Without limited liability, it would have been far more difficult to raise capital from investors who had little or no relationship with each other or with the business's managers.

The demand for and importance of incorporation in the nineteenth century kicked off a chain of events that ushered in the modern era of the corporation. First, the case-by-case, charter-by-charter system of incorporation had become increasingly unwieldy. Further, this system had shown itself prone to abuses and corruption (which became increasingly inevitable as the value of a corporate charter increased).

Next, in the United States, individual state governments began to compete for charter applications, as the fees and tax revenue generated by the business of incorporation became increasingly lucrative. (This competition was enabled to a large degree by the 1839 U.S. Supreme Court decision *Bank of Augusta v. Earle*, in which the Court declared that a company incorporated in one state could not be prohibited from doing business in other states.[44])

Taken together, these factors led to a series of important corporate law developments. States began to abandon the traditional requirement that a business must serve some explicit public purpose in order to receive a charter. They started to allow businesses to incorporate for "any lawful business or purpose whatever," and not merely a purpose that had an explicitly publicly oriented thrust.[45] This follows logically from Adam Smith's insights alluded to previously, and from the growth of the state.

Further, states began to adopt statutes of general incorporation, pursuant to which a company could incorporate simply by submitting the requisite paperwork, without relying upon any independent determination by the state legislature. In other words, any individual (or group of individuals) who complied with certain specified guidelines was entitled to a corporate charter. No longer was individualized, discretionary assessment of the corporate undertaking provided for. This helped combat corruption in the chartering process and "democratized" the corporation, putting this powerful form of business organization into the hands of the common man.

Finally, the norm of shareholder liability gradually shifted from unlimited to limited. This protection enabled an individual—almost any individual—with a good enough idea to raise the capital he or she needed (via the investment of stock purchasers) to put that idea into action. The shield of limited liability allowed putative stock purchasers to take on just the amount of risk they were comfortable to take on. This is what led Nicholas Murray Butler, president of Columbia University, to famously remark in 1917: "In my judgment the limited liability corporation is the greatest single discovery of modern times... even the steam engine and electricity are far less important than the limited liability corporation and they would be reduced to comparative impotence without it."[46]

These developments were mirrored across the Atlantic, in both England and on the European continent over roughly the same time period.

Not surprisingly, this liberalization of the incorporation process was accompanied by a dramatic rise in the number of business corporations.[47] In the United States, for example, there were 335 corporations in 1800; by 1890 there were nearly 500,000.[48]

THEORETICAL CONCEPTUALIZATIONS OF THE MODERN CORPORATION

The developments discussed above sapped concession theory of much of its descriptive power, making its continued persistence increasingly indefensible. For the ability to incorporate was increasingly viewed as an individual entitlement, not an act of state concession. Yet concession theory did linger on and remained strong as the twentieth century opened. (Indeed, concession theory remains alive and well in some quarters to this very day.) This prompted John Davis, writing at the turn of the twentieth century, to criticize corporate law as a prime example of "the failure of a system of law to adequately express new social relations."[49]

In any event, concession theory did not enter the twentieth century unscathed. Further, as will be discussed, in a series of important judicial decisions American courts chipped away at concessionary orthodoxy.[50] These decisions hailed both from the U.S. Supreme Court[51] and the influential Delaware Chancery Court.[52] This led, expectedly, to the rise in competing theories of the corporation.

One challenger was the "aggregate" or "associational" theory of the corporation. Under this line of thinking, there is no such thing as a "corporation" per se; rather, what we call a "corporation" is nothing more or less than the aggregation of particular individuals (namely, the shareholders). In other words, akin to Louis XIV's purported declaration "*L'État, c'est moi*," the shareholders of the corporation are the corporation. The corporate title and nomenclature are merely matters of convenience: the corporation's rights are simply an extension of the shareholders' rights. The aggregation theory of the corporation enjoyed fleeting prominence during the close of the nineteenth century. It represented the first successful attempt to dislodge the untenable concession theory of yesteryear.

The second challenger was real entity theory. As discussed previously, this was a long-time fixture in continental corporate theorizing, but largely alien to Anglo-American corporate law. Under real entity theory, the corporation is "separate from both [its] shareholders and the state,"[53] and is primarily the natural "creation of private initiative rather than state fiat."[54] Although the corporate person might very well still be considered "artificial," the entity as a whole is not a mere legal fiction. For "artificial" is not synonymous with "fictitious"; a plastic heart used to save a patient's life is artificial, but it is at the same time quite real.

As Reuven Avi-Yonah explains, the real entity view represented a balance between the traditional artificial entity theory and the novel aggregate theory.[55] The former view afforded the state "too much power to regulate corporations," and the latter afforded the state too little.[56]

What helped enable real entity theory to displace aggregation theory was recognition of the fact that the corporation was not simply an aggregation of shareholders; indeed, it was arguably more than the sum of all its parts.

Aggregation theory essentially treated the corporation as a partnership, but the *fin de siècle* corporation was not a partnership. Partnerships are marked by a confluence of ownership of control: partners both own and manage the enterprise. Although ancient and medieval corporations could be so characterized to a large degree, that was no longer generally the case as the twentieth century dawned. By this time, the corporation was marked by one of its prime distinguishing modern characteristics: the *separation* of ownership and control. The shareholder-owners merely elected a board of directors, which in turn oversaw the management of the corporation on their behalf. The corporation was not simply a collection a shareholders, nor the board of directors, nor the officers and employees who worked for it. The combination of these constituencies gave rise to an entity that was *sui generis*—an entity that pursued policies and practices that reflected a complicated balancing of interests, and not simply some majority desideratum. As one commentator explained:

> When a body of twenty or two thousand or two hundred thousand men bind themselves together to act in a particular way for some common purpose, they create a body which by no fiction of law but by the very nature of things, differs from the individuals of whom it is composed.[57]

Natural entity theory also helped explain the phenomenon of limited liability. Partners in a general partnership didn't enjoy this protection, yet the owners of the twentieth-century corporation did. This does not make much sense if one conceptualizes the corporation as simply the aggregate of its owners; it does make sense if one conceptualizes the corporation as an entity distinct and separate from its owners.

Enthusiasm for the real entity theory of the corporation was dealt two significant blows by the 1930s. The first was the rise of the legal realists, led by John Dewey, who, in 1926, "dismissed as irrelevant the debate among the aggregate, artificial entity, and real entity views of the corporation."[58] To Dewey, any of these theories "could be deployed to suit any purpose," thereby undermining their usefulness.[59]

More significantly, perhaps, was the stock market crash of 1929 and its aftermath, which "catalyzed populist mistrust of 'financiers,' and 'Wall Street' and, ultimately, the natural entity model."[60] Filling the burgeoning theoretical vacuum were Adolf Berle and Gardiner Means, who advanced the timely "property model" of the corporation.[61] Pursuant to the property model, the corporation is the property of the shareholders, and it "is unquestionably on their behalf that the directors are bound to act.... Managerial powers are held in trust for stockholders as sole beneficiaries of the corporate enterprise."[62]

The property model cemented (if not ushered in) a corporate law norm that has remained in effect ever since: "shareholder primacy."[63] The directors are beholden—via the imposition of fiduciary duties—to govern the corporation for the benefit of shareholders. This has been equated with a mandate to maximize shareholder wealth, and as such the two terms are commonly used interchangeably.[64]

Although the shareholder primacy norm has persisted since the property model of the corporation, the property model itself has not. By the end of the twentieth century, it had largely been supplanted by the "nexus of contracts" model of the corporation.[65] Rejecting the "reification" of the corporation as an entity of any sorts (artificial or natural), the nexus-of-contracts approach envisions "the corporation" as simply a useful term to describe a variety of interrelated express and implied contracts.[66] Pursuant to this approach, "rights, expectations, and responsibilities" concerning a corporation are the result of contracting, not of property rights and fiduciary duties.[67] Stephen Bainbridge summarized the theory well when he wrote:

> Contractarians model the firm not as an entity, but as an aggregate of various inputs acting together to produce goods or services. Employees provide labor. Creditors provide debt capital. Shareholders initially provide equity capital and subsequently bear the risk of losses and monitor the performance of management. Management monitors the performance of employees and coordinates the activities of all the firm's inputs. The firm is a legal fiction representing the complex set of contractual relationships between these inputs. In other words, the firm is not a thing, but rather a nexus or web of explicit and implicit contracts establishing rights and obligations among the various inputs making up the firm.[68]

The contractarian view of the corporation was first fully formulated in Michael Jensen and William Meckling's famous 1976 article "The Theory of the Firm: Managerial Behavior, Agency Costs, and Ownership Structure."[69] It stems from Ronald Coase's scholarship regarding the problem of transaction costs and the reactions generated by this scholarship.[70] More specifically, Coase argued that activities will be included within a firm when the costs of using "markets" (that is, employing agents outside of the firm) are greater than the costs of direction by "authority" (that is, handling the activities internally).[71]

Armen Alchian and Harold Demsetz objected to Coase's theory, primarily on the grounds that the firm has no real "authority," but rather simply replicates market and contract mechanisms internally.[72] This replication, according to Alchian and Demsetz, occurs within the context of the "team production" model and is characterized by monitoring mechanisms.[73]

Jensen and Meckling took Alchian and Demsetz's insights one step further and argued that in conceptualizing the firm the emphasis should not be on "team production" and "monitoring," but rather on contracting.[74] Within the course of their argument, Jensen and Meckling coined the "nexus of contracts" terminology.[75]

The contractarian description of the corporation fit well given the nature of the modern corporation and modern corporate law. For in almost every state today, the corporate code is a mere "enabling" statute.[76] Thus, unlike yesteryear, when the internal workings of the corporation were more heavily regulated, today "what is open to free choice is far more important to the daily operation of the firm . . . than is what the law prescribes."[77] As Frank Easterbrook and Daniel Fischel put it, "[t]he corporation is a complex set of explicit and implicit contracts, and corporate law enables the participants to select the optimal arrangement for the many different sets of risks and opportunities that are available in a large economy."[78]

CHARACTERISTICS OF THE MODERN BUSINESS CORPORATION

Some of the preceding has shed light on whether the modern business corporation can plausibly be categorized as a Tocquevillian Association. Most notably, for reasons that shall be explained, the fiduciary duty of management to maximize shareholder wealth and our theoretical (contractarian) understanding of the modern corporation weigh heavily upon this question. Before revisiting these concepts, let us first consider the peculiar characteristics of the modern business corporation and how they factor into its assessment as a Tocquevillian Association.

Not every business association is a corporation. In the terms of modern parlance, some can be sole proprietorships (in which the business has one owner) or partnerships (in which the business has more than one owner). What makes a business a corporation is a set of characteristics that have evolved, over time, to demarcate it. When taken together, these characteristics distinguish the modern corporation from sole proprietorships, partnerships, and other business enterprises. As previously identified (in chapter 1), these characteristics are commonly held to be separate legal personality, limited liability, liquidity of ownership, perpetual life, and the separation of ownership and control. When viewed in their entirety, these factors suggest that the modern corporation is ill-suited for characterization as a Tocquevillian Association.

Separate Legal Personality

"Separate legal personality" refers to the fact that the corporation is deemed to be an entity separate and distinct from its owners, not merely as a matter of social consciousness but under the law as well. A high school chess club may very well be recognized as a distinct entity by all who deal with it. It may have its own website, its own e-mail address, and a charter setting forth rules and regulations for its membership. Unless incorporated, however, the club would not have an independent identity in the eyes of the law. Since it lacks a legal existence, it could not, for example, sue or be sued in its own name. To the extent that "it" becomes embroiled in a legal controversy, the club itself does not become a litigant, but rather its members, as separate individuals, would.

A distinctive and separate personality would appear to support the categorization of a corporation as a Tocquevillian Association. For what makes an association Tocquevillian is the fact that it represents the coming together of individuals for a common purpose in a way that takes on a life of its own. Within the association, the members are, to a degree, transformed—incorporated, if you will, into a collective with a purpose of its own.

As mentioned, all genuine associations have, to a greater or lesser extent, a distinct identity of their own. The fact that, with regard to corporations, this distinct identity is recognized by law should not affect the Tocquevillian analysis. It certainly does not detract from the characteristics that make an association a Tocquevillian Association and, if anything, could best be read to contribute to such a finding.

Limited Liability

A somewhat natural consequence of the corporation's distinct legal personality is that its debts and liabilities are *its* debts and liabilities, not generally those of its associates. Whereas a general partner in a partnership is ordinarily personally liable for the partnership's debts, and may be called upon to answer for them if the partnership is unable to for some reason (such as lack of funds), no one associated with the corporation faces similar liability. It is true that under the doctrine known as "piercing the corporate veil," a corporation's shareholders can, in certain limited circumstances, be held liable for a corporation's debts. Veil piercing, however, is the proverbial exception that proves the rule: unlike the situation of a partnership, the debts of the corporation are ordinarily not viewed as attributable to anyone other than the corporation itself.

Here too I see a distinction that should have little bearing upon the corporation's assessment as a Tocquevillian Association. Nothing in Tocqueville's writings leads me to conclude that the liability of an association's members is somehow relevant to the association's character as a Tocquevillian association.

An argument could be made, perhaps, that limited liability somehow distances a corporation's shareholders from the association, but I find the argument weak. The constituents of the corporation are not entirely shielded from loss due to the imposition of limited liability. Wages may be cut for employees, prices could be raised for customers, and shareholders could lose their entire investment. In sum, I do not believe limited liability so dramatically attenuates the associational connection so as to undermine the entity's potential associational status. That said, it certainly doesn't further it either, which is why I conclude that this corporate attribute should have no bearing on the Tocquevillian analysis.

Liquidity of Ownership and Perpetual Life

Also related to the concept of the corporation's separate legal personality is the liquidity of corporate ownership and perpetual corporate life. Since the corporation is not viewed as simply the alter ego of its owners, it can persist despite a change in ownership via the sale of stock from one individual to another. Although modern partnership law generally permits this as well, traditionally such was not always the case. Traditionally, a change in partners meant the dissolution of the partnership, to be replaced by a new partnership (with the new partner). Similarly, the death or loss of a partner traditionally meant the demise of the partnership too, thereby limiting the life of a partnership to the lives of its members. A corporation, by contrast, can persist indefinitely; its existence is not hampered by the limitations of human mortality.

Tocquevillian Associations can feature similar characteristics. A political party, for example, can exist for generations. Its membership can be fluid, with members coming and going over time, an attribute that can be analogized (albeit roughly) to liquidity of ownership. Thus, liquidity of ownership and perpetual life do not seem like compelling reasons to disqualify the modern corporation from categorization as a Tocquevillian Association. In fact, it would appear as though these characteristics reinforce the view of the corporation as an entity separate from its members and, consequently, as an association.

Separation of Ownership and Control

Separation of ownership and control refers to the fact that in a corporation, those traditionally considered to be the owners of the entity, its shareholders, are not empowered to manage the corporation. The power of management rests instead with a board of directors (elected by the shareholders) and the management team appointed by the board. The shareholders may have the right to vote on certain, particular corporate decisions (such as a merger or acquisition, or an amendment to the corporate charter), but such limited say on a limited number of issues does not in any real sense equate to control. This contrasts dramatically with the situation in other forms of business enterprises, namely partnerships and sole proprietorships. In these businesses, the partners (or the sole proprietor) have the legal right to control the organization and ordinarily exercise this right to a greater or lesser degree. Even if this right is delegated to a committee of partners, or via the hiring of a consultant or office manager, the right remains, ultimately, theirs under the law.

In contrast to the attributes we have thus far considered, this particular feature of the modern corporation presents a significant challenge to the corporation's identification as a Tocquevillian Association. To Tocqueville, the association occupied a pivotal role in society because of its ability to bring people together to work toward a common goal. Through this process, not only are certain objectives obtained but, almost as important, people are educated in the arts of cooperation and leadership. In this way, associations serve as training grounds for the citizens of a democratic republic such as the United States.

Certainly, associations need not be made up of equals. Each member of an association brings with him or her a different set of strengths and weaknesses. Further, within the association members can take on different roles and responsibilities. Each member is not similarly active. That said, the passive shareholder of the modern corporation appears to fall off, rather than somewhere on, any continuum of associational involvement. It is difficult to see how his or her participation in the corporate enterprise contributes to the development of an associational community. Indeed, a large percentage of shareholders in modern corporations is made up of institutional investors, such as hedge funds and mutual funds, further attenuating the link between the corporation and human control and ownership.

THE MODERN CORPORATION AND THE TOCQUEVILLIAN ASSOCIATION

A review of the fundamental characteristics that distinguish the business corporation from other enterprises yields mixed results from a Tocquevillian perspective. Many of these characteristics appear to have no bearing on the question of association, or at best a bearing that is ambiguous. Separation of ownership and control, however, would appear to present a serious obstacle in the path of such recognition.

Recall that one of the traditional grounds giving rise to the moral legitimacy of the corporation was the participation of its membership in the corporation's affairs.[79] This convergence of ownership and management justified a degree of deference to the corporate enterprise, derived from the respect owed to the individuals concerned *qua* individuals. Such premodern corporations have been called "fellowships," evoking their associational nature.[80] Divorcing ownership from participation and control gives rise to a different entity.

As will be explained in our next chapter, the separation of ownership from control is not necessarily an insurmountable obstacle with regard to the corporation's characterization as a Tocquevillian Association. Far more problematic is the shareholder primacy norm, pursuant to which those who control the corporation (its board and management) are obligated, via fiduciary duties, to operate the corporation in the best interests of its shareholders (its traditional owners). Under the corporate law as formulated in most states, this norm is understood as requiring corporate boards and management to maximize shareholder wealth, thereby committing the corporation to serving the narrow, economic interests of a particular constituency (its shareholders). All other concerns are secondary and instrumental. Thus, to the extent that a corporation rallies its other constituencies around a particular cause or proposition, it only does so (insofar as it adheres to its legal obligations and organizational conventions) in order to improve upon the price of its stock. An entity so beholden to the economic interests of only a few of its own is not Tocqueville's idea of an association.

Of course, nothing prevents an association (Tocquevillian or otherwise) from hiring agents to assist with its business. Although one would be hesitant in equating such hirelings with the association's membership, taking agents on would not necessarily pose a challenge to the organization's associational status. This raises the question of whether the corporation's managerial apparatus could be deemed to be such agents, toiling in service to a genuine association. One would posit that the board and management are somehow the agents of the shareholders; that the corporation was the property of the shareholders and is managed on the shareholders' behalf for the shareholders' benefit.

This assumes, however, that an association exists to begin with. To ascribe associational status to a corporation's shareholders stretches the imagination beyond limit. The shareholders, ordinarily dispersed across states and countries, rarely know one another—and as rarely communicate with one another. As already mentioned, many are not even human, but rather institutional investors: other corporations such as mutual funds and hedge funds. The human beings that do hold shares in a particular corporation are ordinarily marked by what economists have called "rational apathy": they typically pour little time into following the corporation and are more concerned with maintaining a balanced investment portfolio. Few bother to voice their concerns via proxy voting, and far fewer still attend the corporation's annual shareholders meeting. Indeed, a large number of individuals are invested through discretionary brokerage accounts and may not even know the companies in which their brokers have invested them. It strains credulity to see how the shareholders, as a class, can be deemed to constitute an association.

The associational characterization is made even less plausible in light of modern corporate theory. For the modern corporation is conceptualized as a nexus of contracts. Pursuant to this conceptualization, the corporation is not a "thing" at all; it is not the property of the shareholders (or anyone else for that matter). It has no "owners." Rather, the corporation is a web of contracts, explicit and implicit, and it is through these contractual arrangements that shareholder primacy is established and maintained. In other words, shareholders are held prime not because they own the corporation, but rather because they are deemed to have negotiated for ownership-like rights. It is for this reason that the law, even while recognizing shareholder primacy, does not consider the corporation's management the agents of the shareholders, but rather the agents of the corporation itself.

Can this assemblage of agents somehow constitute an association? Again, it is difficult to see how. Those who control a corporation may very well have no attachment and dedication to the organization beyond the desire to do a sufficiently adequate job to secure their employment or compensation. This does not approximate with the involvement of members in a Tocquevillian Association.

Consider an agreement between a customer and a shoemaker. The customer, Ralph, orders a pair of shoes for $300, and the shoemaker, Norton, agrees to make them. No one would posit that this transaction has berthed an association. Replicate this transaction hundredfold: Ralph hires one hundred shoemakers to make shoes for him. Add to these transactions certain others: Ralph sells these shoes in turn to others. Ralph hires a salesperson and a secretary. Investors agree to lend Ralph money; he agrees to pay them interest in return. Other investors agree to buy ownership interests in Ralph's business, in exchange for limited, circumscribed rights. Contractarian theory would posit that, just as before, we do not have an association: we simply have a large number of contracts that are related in certain ways to one another. Thus, in light of both practice and theory, it is difficult to find a Tocquevillian Association within the context of the typical modern corporation.

As an aside, it should be noted that some contest the corporation's associational status on additional grounds as well, namely that the corporation is a mere creature of state law. This invokes the long-discarded notion of concession theory, which is no longer deemed applicable to the modern corporation.

Thus, as a threshold matter, this particular objection to associational status can be set aside as resting upon an outdated presupposition. In an era where the ability to incorporate one's business is commonly viewed as more of a right than a special state privilege, analogous perhaps to the procurement of a driver's license, it is difficult to credit an argument regarding the corporation that is predicated upon the notion that the modern corporation owes its existence to the discretionary grace of the sovereign. Nevertheless, since even concession theory still has its adherents, let us consider this argument briefly.

Unlike other forms of business organization, corporations admittedly require official state recognition in order to exist. Consider a partnership, for example. The mere coming together of two or more individuals as co-owners and co-operators of a business will ordinarily be recognized as a partnership in the eyes of the law. No registration with the government is necessary for this recognition to be realized. Even if such registration is necessary in order to avoid fines and penalties, the absence of such registration does not destroy the entity's fundamental status as a partnership. This is not, however, the case with corporations. For corporations are, by contrast, creatures of the law. A corporation's very existence is dependent upon compliance with whatever rules and regulations have been laid down by the jurisdiction it wishes to incorporate in. Failure to comply with those rules generally means that a corporation has not been formed, despite what the business's participants may think.

The fact that a corporation owes its existence to the operation of law might seem to pose a challenge to its categorization as a Tocquevillian Association. Building upon Aristotle, Tocqueville believed that associations were natural human occurrences. Genuine associations should not owe their existence to the operation of positive law. A corporation, therefore, appears to be more a creature of the state than the natural product of human hands.

Even if one credits this argument, it should be noted that the state itself is the work of human hands and as per Aristotle a natural (and arguably inevitable) human achievement. Likewise, the law itself is a product of societal evolution—including the law of corporations. It is not clear to me, therefore, that the interposition of human law somehow renders the corporation any less authentically a Tocquevillian Association. In other words, one natural human achievement (the state), gives rise to another (the law), which gives rise to yet another (the corporation). One could extrapolate similarly from the family, to the clan, to the town. An Aristotelian would not categorize the town or the clan as somehow unnatural simply because each is built upon something prior. To make such an assessment, further analysis would be needed, such as an inquiry into the inevitable need of such derivative institutions and how they serve authentic human progress and flourishing. I shall not engage in such a detailed analysis here but do refer the reader to the historical record which, I suggest, demonstrates that a rather strong argument can be made regarding the inevitability and perhaps even the need for the corporate enterprise (or something like it). For thousands of years, human societies from divergent eras and nations have found the corporate structure, in conjunction with certain rights and privileges, as a beneficial component of their particular civilizations. Although certainly not dispositive, this evidence supports the view that there is more to the corporation than concession theorists would grant it. It suggests that corporations do not owe their existence to the whims of their government, but rather that governments have long come to recognize the need to license such entities for the common good.

NOTES

1. Frances R. Hill, *Exempt Organizations in the 2008 Election: Will Wisconsin Right to Life Bring Changes?*, 19 U. Fla. J. L. &. Pub. Pol'y 271, 289 (2008).
2. *See* John Micklethwait & Adrian Wooldridge, The Company 3–4 (2003).
3. William Blackstone, Blackstone's Commentaries: With Notes of Reference, to the Constitution and Laws, of the Federal Government of the United States; and of the Commonwealth of Virginia, translated by St. George Tucker, 2nd ed 469 (Philadelphia, PA: William Young Birch and Abraham Small 1803) (*quoted in* Jeffrey Bone, *Legal Perspectives on Corporate Responsibility: Contractarian or Communitarian Thought?*, 24 Can. J.L. & Juris. 277, 279 n.11 (2011)).
4. *See* Henry Hansmann, Reinier Kraakman, & Richard Squire, *Law and the Rise of the Firm*, 119 Harv. L. Rev. 1333, 1361 (2006).
5. *See* Kim Hawtrey & Stuart Dullard, *Corporate Virtue and the Joint-Stock Company*, 12 J. Markets & Morality 19, 21 (2009).
6. *Id.*
7. *See* Felix S. Cohen, *Transcendental Nonsense and the Functional Approach*, 35 Colum. L. Rev. 809, 811 (1935).
8. This usage and terminology continues to the present day. *See* Code of Canon Law, Book I, Title VI, Chapter II ("Juridic Persons").
9. Mary Szto, *Limited Liability Company Morality: Fiduciary Duties in Historical Context*, 23 Q. L. Rev. 61, 109 (2004).
10. George F. Deiser, *The Juristic Person*, 3 Penn. L. Rev. 131, 133 (1908).
11. Harold J. Berman, Law and Revolution 217 (1983).
12. *Id.* at 218.
13. *Id.*
14. *Id.* at 217.
15. *See id.*
16. *See id.* at 219.
17. *Id.*
18. *Id.* (quoting Bartolus of Sassoferrato, Commentary on Dig. 3.4.1.1. (1653)).
19. *See id.*
20. *See* Reuven S. Avi-Yonah, *The Cyclical Transformations of the Corporate Form: A Historical Perspective on Corporate Social Responsibility*, 30 Del. J. Corp. L. 767, 781 (2005).
21. *See id.* at 781–82.
22. 1 John P. Davis, Corporations 95 (1905).
23. *Id.* at 114.

24. *Id.*
25. 2 JOHN P. DAVIS, CORPORATIONS 67 (1905).
26. *Id.* at 67–69.
27. *Id.* at 72. *See also id.* at 73 ("It is plain that the primary consideration was the protection of the royal treasury; the secondary consideration was the advancement of the private interests of the merchants.").
28. *Id.* at 72–73.
29. *See id.* at 74–75, 83–85.
30. *See id.* at 114, 123–47.
31. *See id.* at 158–59; *see generally* 157–208.
32. *Id.* at 85.
33. *Id.*
34. *See id.* at 110 ("Corporations are, in a broad view, institutions of government.... For most purposes their activity may be said to have fallen into two classes, political and commercial, though the analysis is certainly superficial.").
35. *See* David Millon, *Theories of the Corporation*, 1990 DUKE L.J. 201, 206 (1990).
36. *See* DAVIS, *supra* note 22, at 211.
37. *Id.*
38. *See id.*
39. *See id.*
40. *See* Douglas Arner, *Development of the American Law of Corporations to 1832*, 55 SMU L. REV. 23, 46 (2002).
41. DAVIS, *supra* note 22, at 251. Conversely, the "strength" of corporations—in terms of their independence and privileges—had increased during periods in which state power decreased. *See* Avi-Yonah, *supra* note 20, at 782.
42. DAVIS, *supra* note 22, at 252.
43. *See* Dante Figueroa, *Comparative Aspects of Piercing the Corporate Veil in the United States and Latin America*, 50 DUQ. L. REV. 683, 695–99 (2012).
44. Bank of Augusta v. Earle, 38 U.S. 519 (1839).
45. Charles M. Yablon, *The Historical Race Competition for Corporate Charters and the Rise and Decline of New Jersey: 1880–1910*, 32 J. CORP. L. 323, 335 (2007).
46. Daniel J. Morrissey, *Piercing All the Veils: Applying an Established Doctrine to a New Business Order*, 32 J. CORP. L. 529, 534–35 (2007).
47. *See* Margaret M. Blair, *Reforming Corporate Governance: What History Can Teach Us*, 1 BERKELEY BUS. L.J. 1, 4 (2004).
48. *See id.* I also surmise that this transition was furthered by Adam Smith's publication of *The Wealth of Nations* in 1776. Despite the fact that Smith "was not fond of the idea of large companies," Arner, *supra* note 40, at 38, his basic premise, that the pursuit of their own private interest by individuals and entities redounds to the common good, would seem to provide a theoretical justification for permitting business to incorporate generally and for "any lawful business or purpose whatever." *See also* DAVIS, *supra* note 22, at 29 ("The unprecedented growth of private corporations since 1830" appears related to "the justification for their existence in the general opinion that public welfare is materially promoted by the more facile exercise in corporate form of social functions whose exercise is prompted by the pursuit of private interest"); Steven Semeraro, *Demystifying Antitrust State Action Doctrine*, 24 HARV. J.L. & PUB. POL'Y 203, 215 (2000).
49. Davis, *supra* note 22, at 211.
50. *See* Avi-Yonah, *supra* note 20, at 781.
51. *See id.* at 787–93.

52. *See* Daniel P. Sullivan & Donald E. Conlon, *Crisis and Transition in Corporate Governance Paradigms: The Role of the Chancery Court in Delaware*, 31 LAW & SOC'Y REV. 713, 728 (1997).
53. Avi-Yonah, *supra* note 20, at 793–94.
54. Sullivan & Conlon, *supra* note 52, at 728.
55. *See* Avi-Yonah, *supra* note 20, at 798. The aggregate view defined corporate property rights as "aggregated individual property rights" and as such granted the corporation "the same constitutional rights and responsibilities that society decrees are inalienable to natural persons." Sullivan & Conlon, *supra* note 52, at 728.
56. *See* Avi-Yonah, *supra* note 20, at 798.
57. John C. Coates IV, *State Takeover Statutes and Corporate Theory: The Revival of an Old Debate*, 64 N.Y.U. L. REV. 806, 819 (1989) (quoting John Dewey, *The Historic Background of Corporate Legal Personality*, 35 YALE L.J. 655, 673 (1926)).
58. Avi-Yonah, *supra* note 20, at 803.
59. *Id.*
60. Sullivan & Conlon, *supra* note 52, at 728.
61. *See id.* at 731.
62. *Id.*
63. *See* Robert Sprague & Aaron J. Lyttle, *Shareholder Primacy and the Business Judgment Rule: Arguments for Expanded Corporate Democracy*, 16 STAN. J.L. BUS. & FIN. 3 (2010).
64. *See id.* As I have pointed out elsewhere, I believe that the conflation of "shareholder primacy" with "shareholder wealth maximization" is mistaken. *See* Ronald J. Colombo, *Ownership, Limited*, 34 J. CORP. L. 247, 269 (2008).
65. *See* Sullivan & Conlon, *supra* note 52, at 732.
66. *See* Stephen M. Bainbridge, *The Case for Limited Shareholder Voting Rights*, 53 UCLA L. REV. 601, 604 (2006).
67. Sullivan & Conlon, *supra* note 52, at 734.
68. STEPHEN M. BAINBRIDGE, CORPORATION LAW AND ECONOMICS 27 (2002) (*quoted in* Harry G. Hutchison, *Choice, Progressive Values, and Corporate Law: A Reply to Greenfield*, 35 DEL. J. CORP. L. 437, 447 (2010)).
69. Michael Jensen & William Meckling, *The Theory of the Firm: Managerial Behavior, Agency Costs, and Ownership Structure*, 3 J. FIN. ECON. 305 (1976) (*cited in* Melvin A. Eisenberg, *The Conception that the Corporation Is a Nexus of Contracts, and the Dual Nature of the Firm*, 24 J. CORP. L. 819, 819 (1999)).
70. *See* Eisenberg, *supra* note 69, at 821.
71. *See id.*
72. Armen A. Alchian & Harold Demsetz, *Production, Information Costs, and Economic Organization*, 62 AM. ECON. REV. 777, 777–78 (1972) (*cited in* Eisenberg, *supra* note 69, at 821–22).
73. Eisenberg, *supra* note 69, at 821–22.
74. *See id.*
75. *See id.* at 822.
76. *See* Frank H. Easterbrook & Daniel R. Fischel, *The Corporate Contract*, 89 COLUM. L. REV. 1416, 1417 (1989).
77. *See id.* at 1418.
78. *Id.*
79. *See supra* text accompanying note 5.
80. *See* Hawtrey & Dullard, *supra* note 5, at 20.

CHAPTER 3

The Postmodern Corporation

As explained in our last chapter, certain characteristics of the modern corporation make it difficult to categorize as a Tocquevillian Association. Chief among these characteristics are separation of ownership from control, shareholder primacy, profit maximization, and its contractarian conceptualization. Whereas an association, in Tocqueville's mind, was marked chiefly by the presence of a genuine community among its members, these particular attributes of the modern corporation largely undermine the existence of such a community.

However, among today's incorporated businesses there exist some for which these attributes bear little relation. There exist corporations that renounce shareholder primacy, balance the pursuit of profits with the observance of certain principles, and for which the nexus-of-contracts theory is ill-suited. I shall refer to these entities as "postmodern corporations." (Please note that with this reference I am not invoking the postmodernism of philosophy, the arts, or literature, but rather simply wish to indicate that this new form of the corporation is the successor of the predominant, "modern" form of the corporation.) Whereas the constituents of the modern corporation are focused on financial benefit *simpliciter* (in terms of profits for its shareholders, wages for its employees, and value for its customers), the constituents of the postmodern corporation are focused on other matters in common, either in addition to or in preference to financial gain. Unlike modern corporations, postmodern corporations can fairly claim the mantle of "association" as Tocqueville used that term. This is so because the postmodern corporation embodies a genuine community.[1]

THE POSTMODERN CORPORATION AS DISTINGUISHED FROM A MODERN CORPORATION

The community embodied by the postmodern corporation is that of investors, owners, officers, employees, customers, and others coming together around a common vision or shared set of goals, values, and/or beliefs beyond those that are simply financial in nature. For some, that vision, and those values, might center on the environment, as is the case with the company Burt's Bees.[2] For others, it might concern an aversion to animal testing and cruelty, as is the case with The Body Shop.[3] For still others, the common core might be religious in nature, as is the case with Chick-fil-A.[4] Critically, its various constituencies are held together not simply via a web of contractual arrangements, with each hoping only to satisfy its own, separate economic self-interests.

This is to be distinguished from the case of the modern corporation. Aside from a commitment to profits, the modern corporation does not genuinely espouse values. Certainly, virtually every corporation sets forth an articulation of beliefs and principles, commonly called "corporate credos."[5] But in the modern corporation these are understood to be merely instrumental, subsumed under the overarching goal of profit maximization. These beliefs are not "genuine," by which I mean they generally fail to reflect a commitment that goes beyond the mouthing of platitudes for reasons of public relations or expediency. They generally do not involve taking a stand, but rather the decision *not* to take a stand by appealing to least-common-denominator moralities at a level of generality that few could gainsay. Most significantly of all, these beliefs are not genuine because they do not "cost" anything to maintain: they are purely instrumental toward financial gain and profit in the long run and lack the backing of a willingness to sacrifice profits to avoid their breach.

Indeed, constrained by the shareholder primacy norm, the directors of the modern corporation are arguably precluded from ordinarily pursuing anything other than profit maximization. This belief was given judicial expression, in its most forceful form, by the Michigan Supreme Court in the classic case of *Dodge v. Ford Motor Co.*[6] In *Dodge*, the Court held that Henry Ford's decision to withhold shareholder dividends in order to sell automobiles more cheaply to the public at large was a breach of his fiduciary duties to the shareholders.[7] The Court famously expressed its vision of the proper role and duties of the corporation's directors toward the shareholders as follows:

> A business corporation is organized and carried on primarily for the profit of the stockholders. The powers of the directors are to be employed for that end. The discretion of directors is to be exercised in the choice of means to attain

> that end, and does not extend to a change in the end itself, to the reduction of profits, or to the nondistribution of profits among stockholders in order to devote them to other purposes.[8]

More recently, and perhaps just as famously, Milton Friedman famously explained this same vision in an article entitled "The Social Responsibility of Business Is to Increase Its Profits":

> In a free enterprise system, private-property system, a corporate executive is an employee of the owners of the business. He has direct responsibility to his employers. That responsibility is to conduct the business in accordance with their desires, which generally will be to make as much money as possible while conforming to the basic rules of society.[9]

Scholars such as Lyman Johnson have persuasively argued that, contrary to the common understanding, corporations and corporate directors are actually not beholden to any rule requiring strict profit maximization.[10] As he explains, given the discretion afforded to them under the law (via the operation of the "business judgment rule"), corporate directors and officers have tremendous latitude in managing corporations as they see fit, and as such are not shackled (certainly not in practice but not even in theory) to shareholder wealth maximization.[11] Further, it should not be forgotten that much of what constitutes corporate law is merely default and supplementary and can be negotiated away should the parties in question desire to do so. As for those matters that are truly mandatory, Bernard Black has described them as "trivial."[12] Thus, even if Johnson has not accurately described corporate law as commonly implemented, he has, at a minimum, articulated an approach that parties could choose to adopt.

Although Johnson's approach is admittedly somewhat novel in Anglo-American law, it is not as alien to certain continental European traditions. Consider, for example, this description of the role of profits and business articulated by Pope John Paul II in his 1991 encyclical *Centesimus Annus*:

> The Church acknowledges the legitimate role of profit *as an indication that a business is functioning well.* When a firm makes a profit, this means that productive factors have been properly employed and corresponding human needs have been duly satisfied. But profitability is not the only indicator of a firm's condition. It is possible for the financial accounts to be in order, and yet for the people—who make up the firm's most valuable asset—to be humiliated and their dignity offended. Besides being morally inadmissible, this will eventually have negative repercussions on the firm's economic efficiency. *In fact, the purpose of a business firm is not simply to make a profit, but is to be found in its very existence as a community of persons who in various ways are endeavouring to satisfy*

> *their basic needs, and who form a particular group at the service of the whole of society.* Profit is a regulator of the life of a business, but it is not the only one; other human and moral factors must also be considered which, in the long term, are at least equally important for the life of a business.[13]

This is not to suggest that Johnson lacks domestic support for his position, however. The American Law Institute, for example, in its Principles of Corporate Governance, declared that corporations are not entirely beholden to profit maximization:

> Even if corporate profit and shareholder gain are not thereby enhanced, the corporation, in the conduct of its business:
>
> (1) Is obliged, to the same extent as a natural person, to act within the boundaries set by law;
>
> (2) May take into account ethical considerations that are reasonably regarded as appropriate to the responsible conduct of business; and
>
> (3) May devote a reasonable amount of resources to public welfare, humanitarian, educational, and philanthropic purposes.[14]

Nevertheless, many remain unconvinced, giving rise to the fundamental distinction between the modern corporation and the postmodern corporation. The modern corporation adheres to the shareholder primacy norm and considers itself bound to maximize profits. Recognizing this, the common thread linking the various constituencies in the modern corporation is ordinarily a desire for financial gain. Indeed, as Michael Phillips has suggested, "there is some reason to believe that unlike the archetypal 'organization men' of the 1950s, many managers and employees are so little attached to their firms that their corporate affiliations shape them in only the most minor ways."[15] As already mentioned, any speech or expression of values on the part of such corporation today serves merely to fulfill this common interest for financial gain. It is not a genuine association, but, when it purports to act as such, a simulacrum of association. For these reasons many are justifiably opposed to the modern corporation's invocation of constitutional rights.

Postmodern corporations choose a different path. As per the arguments of Pope John Paul II and Lyman Johnson, they do not consider themselves beholden to profits alone. Their stakeholders bargain around the rules that arguably require them to strictly maximize shareholder profits. They embrace certain principles and values as ends in themselves, willing to sacrifice potential financial gain, and to accept decreased profitability, in pursuit of them.[16] It is on account of this embrace that the corporation's various constituents come together, giving rise to a community of shared values and purpose.

THE RISE OF THE POSTMODERN CORPORATION

Multiple factors have fueled the ascendency of the postmodern corporation. Chief among these are (1) the "corporate social responsibility" movement, (2) the proliferation of "religiously expressive corporations," and (3) peoples' increased desire to live coherent, integrated lives. Although there is significant overlap among these phenomena, for ease of analysis I shall address them separately.

Corporate Social Responsibility

Their moniker notwithstanding, postmodern corporations largely recycle theories, practices, and values of yesteryear. The phenomenon of corporate social responsibility (CSR) exemplifies this. Although shareholder primacy has dominated twentieth-century corporate thinking (to such a degree that in 1962, Bayless Manning lamented that "corporate law, as a field of intellectual effort, is dead in the United States"[17]), it has never been without its detractors. As far back as the 1930s, in the pages of the *Harvard Law Review*, Merrick Dodd challenged Adolph Berle's assertion that it was a director's duty to maximize shareholder wealth.[18] Dodd argued that corporate officers and directors "serve as trustees for the corporate enterprise rather than for individual shareholders," and thus may "legitimately use corporate resources to address the interests of other constituents and behave in a socially responsible manner."[19] Thus, even in the modern era of corporate law, the concept of corporate social responsible is nearly a century old.

Of course, the notion that corporations exist to serve a purpose greater than personal profit goes back further still. Indeed, this understanding was a cornerstone upon which the modern corporation's ancient predecessors were built, as was discussed in chapter 2. Recall that premodern corporations could not be chartered simply for the sake of generating profits, but rather had to be specifically tied to an undertaking that was considered sufficiently likely to further the common good or some public policy.

What kept CSR at bay throughout the twentieth century was a greater concern over the financial safety and welfare of corporate investors, particularly shareholders. Scarred by the stock market crash of 1929, and the rampant corporate corruption that the ensuing investigations revealed, Americans readily gravitated toward the property model of the corporation, and with it the shareholder primacy norm. By conceptualizing the corporation as the property of its shareholders, by clearly identifying the purpose of the corporation as shareholder wealth maximization, and by tethering corporate directors to that end via fiduciary duties, the property model (and its accompanying shareholder primacy norm) helped restore the shaken confidence of the American investor, and with it, the capital markets of the United States. The property model provided American investors with exactly what they needed to hear, exactly when they needed to hear it.

Under such constraints, corporations and corporate directors were somewhat hamstrung in their efforts to engage in socially responsible behavior. Certainly, to the extent that such behavior would serve to maximize shareholder profits it was permissible—but such is not the typical formulation of corporate social responsibility. To most, CSR entails behaving responsibly even at the sacrifice of profits, not only in their furtherance.

The shareholder primacy norm came under renewed attack in the 1980s. This decade featured a flurry of takeover activity in corporate America, which focused attention on the wide divergence of interests between shareholders and other corporate constituencies.[20] For within the context of most corporate takeovers, shareholders of the target company receive a substantial premium in exchange for their shares, while other constituencies of the target company (especially employees) often fare quite poorly (since economies of scale usually lead to workforce reductions and layoffs following a takeover's consummation).[21] Given the prevailing shareholder primacy norm, directors were arguably powerless to take into account the interests of nonshareholders during these takeovers if doing so would have come at the expense of shareholder wealth maximization.[22] This spurred a shift in attitudes, and the previous concerns about protecting shareholders from corporate management started to give way to concerns about protecting employees (and everyone else) from the corporation. To many, it seemed unfair that of all the various components of a successful corporation, only the shareholders were entitled to the protections of corporate law. Moreover, it seemed unfair that corporate directors were largely precluded from taking the interests of the corporation's other constituents into account.

This led to developments that started chipping away at shareholder primacy. An important one was the Delaware Supreme Court's 1989 case *Paramount Communications, Inc. v. Time Inc.*[23] The Court in *Paramount* held that corporate directors need not endeavor to maximize shareholder profits within the specific context of a threatened corporate takeover. Rather, the directors could work to stave off the threatened takeover in furtherance of other priorities, including a desire to preserve the corporation's unique "culture."[24]

Around the same time, state legislatures across the United States took bolder measures. Thirty-two passed "constituency" statutes, permitting boards to take into account the interests of corporate constituencies apart from shareholders in a wide variety of corporate decision-making contexts, and not simply those involving threatened takeovers.[25]

The importance of *Paramount* and constituency statutes notwithstanding, they need to be put into the proper perspective. As for *Paramount*, the

Delaware Supreme Court did not upend the general rule of shareholder primacy, but rather carved out an exception to be applied in a narrow set of circumstances (namely, when a corporation's directors are attempting to resist a hostile takeover). And both *Paramount* and the constituency statutes merely enable a corporation to veer from the shareholder primacy norm should it elect to do so (only one state's constituency statute, Connecticut's, actually requires that the interests of other corporate constituencies be regularly taken into account by the corporation's board of directors). Thus, these developments do not themselves transform the modern corporation (with its focus on shareholder primacy) into anything different. Rather, they enable a corporation to transform itself should that be its choice. This, in turn, has contributed to the modern/postmodern dichotomy.

Whole Foods is a good example of a corporation that has taken advantage of the flexibility afforded to it under the law. Its CEO, John Mackey, has explicitly disavowed the "profit-maximization" objective.[26] He acknowledges that this may very well be the objective of some of the company's investors, but adds that it's not the objective of its other stakeholders. Under his leadership, Whole Foods strives to provide value to all its constituencies. As for its shareholders, he bluntly puts it this way, "we 'hired' our original investors. They didn't hire us."[27] Thus, the movement away from shareholder primacy, although voluntary, is not hypothetical.

Significantly, however, the transformation away from the shareholder primacy model is not identical to a transformation to a socially responsible corporation. This is because the interests of other corporate constituencies are themselves, frequently, private interests as well. A corporation with a board of directors empowered and accustomed to weighing the interests of employees and customers alongside those of shareholders may very well be preferable to one solely focused on shareholder wealth maximization, but neither necessarily concerns itself much with society as a whole. A successful company that manufactures its products very inexpensively by failing to take any measures to abate the pollution it generates may be serving the best interests of its investors (high profits), employees (high wages), and customers (low prices), but should not be considered socially responsible. Socially responsible corporations typically reach beyond the interests of their own constituencies and take into account the societal effects of their operations as well.

That said, movement away from shareholder primacy was certainly an important stepping stone toward a more socially responsible corporation. Indeed, building upon this, corporations have increasingly moved toward socially responsible behavior. Corporations have increasingly espoused, and acted upon, statements of social responsibility. Some issue regular reports on their CSR. Starbucks' CSR report details how Starbucks Corporation's activities have impacted "society," and the "environment," "health and wellness," and how the corporation has treated its employees.[28] Scholars who study the CSR phenomenon concluded in 2005:

> [R]esearch has amply confirmed the existence, vitality, and relative coherence of the corporate social responsibility movement. Governments, corporations, and their stakeholder critics take it seriously at the rhetorical level.... Disclosure is now a widespread practice, as is "engagement" with a wide range of stakeholders. This includes everything from talk to the implementation of specific environmental and social projects to the solicitation of independent CSR audits.[29]

Developments furthering CSR have continued since that time, both in the marketplace and, again, in state legislatures.

The marketplace has seen the rise of B Corporations: corporations that have voluntarily committed themselves to business practices that are "socially responsible," with subjection to third-party oversight and certification.[30] By identifying itself as a B Corporation, a for-profit business can attract investors, customers, employees, and officers who share a common commitment to socially responsible corporate conduct at the expense of strict profit maximization. Since the movement began in 2006, nearly six hundred businesses in the United States and Canada have opted for this certification.[31]

Even more interesting has been the promulgation of "benefit corporation" statutes over the past few years.[32] These statutes explicitly take aim at the shareholder wealth maximization norm.[33] Whereas the B Corporation movement could be said to represent merely a commitment to maximize profits in a manner consistent with socially and environmentally responsible business practices, the benefit corporation movement actually serves to jettison the profit-maximization norm altogether.

Adopted in twenty states as of the close of 2013, benefit corporation statutes permit for-profit businesses to incorporate as "benefit corporations" and, as such, balance their focus on shareholder primacy with a focus on certain competing, publicly oriented interests (such as environmental preservation). Significantly, the state of incorporation for most publicly traded corporations, Delaware, joined this group on July 17, 2013.[34] When coupled with the fact that, all things being equal, a company may incorporate in any state of its choice and conduct business in any other number of states of its choice, the ability to incorporate as a benefit corporation is effectively available to every company in the United States.

The New York benefit corporation statute (which is typical), proclaims that the corporation's directors and officers "shall not be required to give priority to the interests of any particular person or group [including shareholders] ... over the interests of any other person or group,"[35] effectively displacing the shareholder primacy norm. As previously discussed, the parties that make up a corporation are, most likely, already empowered to negotiate such an arrangement. By offering such arrangements via a preestablished set of off-the-shelf rules, benefit corporation statutes, however, facilitate and thereby encourage this. Further, the statutes dispel any doubt that, at least for businesses incorporated as such, an arrangement that subjugates shareholder profits to other concerns is valid and lawful, presenting no violation of the strictures of corporate law.

Thus, the CSR movement, along with changes in the law and marketplace, has helped give rise to a new kind of corporation. This is not to say that every corporation has embraced the gospel of CSR. Indeed, for many, the profit-maximizing characterization that defines the modern corporation remains remarkably accurate. Other corporations, however, differ substantially from these in both the goals they pursue and the means by which they pursue them. I suggest that this difference is not merely one of degree, but of kind—thus my adoption of a nomenclature ("modern" versus "postmodern") to distinguish the two organizations.

Many have challenged this particular assertion, remarking that the difference between the modern and postmodern corporation is not particularly clear, and certainly not one "of kind." Rather, they suggest that CSR can be envisioned as a continuum, with corporations occupying various positions between the poles of vigorously socially responsible and not socially responsible at all.

The criticism is a fair one. There can be no doubt that in terms of appearances, such a continuum exists. Admittedly, for many corporations categorization may prove difficult. I posit that a line nevertheless exists separating the modern corporation from the postmodern corporation. A line that, once crossed, affords us a compelling reason to view and treat one corporation differently than another.

By analogy, consider the concept of boiling water. Boiling water is readily distinguished from, and treated differently than, water that is not boiling. Of course, the temperature of water rests upon a continuum, and water that is a few degrees below 212 degrees Fahrenheit may feel just as hot as water that is a few degrees above 212 degrees Fahrenheit. Yet we distinguish one from another categorically because of certain significant properties that separate water on one side of 212 degrees from water on the other side of 212 degrees.

If one wishes to insist that even with regard to boiling water the difference is one of degree (no pun intended) versus kind, so be it. My interest is not in the semantics of the issue, but rather to simply suggest that at a certain point, a critical line is crossed. At a certain point, a corporation's embrace of CSR, its view of itself, and its conceptualization in the eyes of its various stakeholders give rise to an entity that is different from other corporations—even if similarities can be found with regard to other corporations. How this point can be ascertained is an interesting practical question, which we shall take up in chapter 9. For the present moment, it should suffice to simply present the theoretical proposition that the world of corporate businesses can be fairly divided into two (at least) categories: those which operate in the traditional manner and are beholden to profit maximization, and those corporations which are not and are instead beholden to other values and principles to such an extent that profit maximization is not prioritized.

The Religiously Expressive Corporation

Religiously expressive corporations are a subset of postmodern corporations. Like all postmodern corporations, they place principles on par with profits (if not ahead of profits). As such, they are willing to sacrifice profits in order to remain true to their principles. What distinguishes them from other postmodern corporations is that their principles are religiously based.[36]

Whereas the twentieth century witnessed a trend toward separating work from faith and business from religion, the twenty-first century is clearly featuring a reversal of that trend and, with it, the rise of the religiously expressive corporation. Anecdotally, this phenomenon is driven home by contrasting the decision of the Harvard Business School, in 1997, to turn down a generous offer to fund a religion-and-business lecture because it feared the controversy that such a lecture would generate, with Yale University's decision in 2003 to establish a Center for Faith and Culture, which explicitly featured a focus on "ethics and spirituality in the workplace."[37]

There is more than anecdotal evidence, however, demonstrating the growing influence of religion upon corporate America. As David Miller writes in his 2007 book, *God at Work*:

> Today, contrary to... the late 1970s, growing numbers of businesspeople of all levels are attending conferences and management seminars on spirituality and work, participating in small prayer and study groups on faith and leadership, and reading books, magazines, and newsletters for self-help as regards integrating biblical teachings with marketplace demands.[38]

Indeed, Miller proceeds to argue that the "faith at work" phenomenon qualifies as a bona fide "social movement" as sociologists would use that term.[39] It could comfortably be fit within an even broader movement, dubbed the "deprivatization" of religion.[40]

Statistically, the religious beliefs of Americans appear quite stable over the past few decades.[41] With the exception of the "nones" (individuals who claim no particular religious affiliation), Americans' attitudes toward God, religious services, and prayer have changed extraordinarily little over recent years.[42] Similarly stable is the number of Americans who claim that religion is "very important" in their lives (approximately 55 percent).[43] Even among those identifying no religious affiliation (the ascendant "nones"), only a small minority profess to be atheists or agnostics—the vast majority profess, instead, a "spirituality" divorced from organized religion.[44]

Yet, at the same time, scholars have observed that "[a]lmost everywhere you look... you can see religion returning to public life."[45] Religion is "thriving in today's America—as an economic force, an intellectual catalyst, and a political influence."[46] Further evidence of this would be the rise of the religiously expressive corporation.

It appears as though the uptick of religiosity is qualitative, not quantitative, in nature, which is why it is masked by the general statistics. In other words, of that proportion of Americans who identify religion as "very important" in their lives, there appears to be an increase in religious intensity.[47] Some of the data appear to bear that out. In a 2008 survey, 74 percent of Americans responded that "faith is becoming more important in their lives."[48]

Religious intensity is often accompanied by "religious integralism"—that form of religion which sees "religion not as one isolated aspect of human existence but rather as a comprehensive system more or less present in all domains of the individual's life."[49] Although religious integralism is not ordinarily a feature of mainstream Protestantism in America, it is a feature of the fastest growing religious groups in America: Islam, Orthodox Judaism, Mormonism, fundamentalist and evangelical Protestantism, and the more traditional expressions of Catholicism.[50] This would seem to explain, at least in part, the proliferation of workplaces and corporations that are religiously expressive.

Further propelling the religiously expressive corporation is the fact that religious intensity appears particularly pronounced among America's business executives. As John Micklethwait and Adrian Wooldridge remarked, "America's executive class is probably its second most religious elite in the country after senior military."[51] In a recent poll of 110 high-level business leaders, 70 percent agreed "a great deal" or "somewhat" with the statement that "religious beliefs and values of a corporate executive should influence their business decisions,"[52] and a "growing number of executives take their faith seriously as a source of meaning and direction."[53]

As with CSR, the concept of merging faith with work is far from novel. Prior to the industrial revolution (and thus for most of recorded human history), work was largely agricultural. Even with all its severity, such work was less alienating than the urban, factory life which was to come. People then (and perhaps today as well) felt a shared bond with nature and the earth. This supported a perspective in which one's life was fully integrated, rather than segmented into several different spheres of existence.

Moreover, regardless of whether an individual peasant or serf worked for himself or for the profit of someone else, the work in question was ordinarily performed at or close to home. Indeed, life, family, faith, and work largely overlapped, with no clear boundaries demarcating one from the other.[54] This is captured well by Jean-Francois Millet's famous 1859 painting "The Angelus," which depicts a peasant couple taking a respite from their field-work to bow their heads in prayer.

The same generally held true for nonagricultural workers as well, such as artisans and guildsmen. Work for them was a very personal affair:

> In an era of the most primitive mechanization, the only motive force was provided by [the guildsman's] own body, the only machinery his own hands and a few simple tools which permitted him to manipulate directly the raw materials. He purchased his own supplies—leather, yarn, charring wood, or whatever. Aided customarily by no more than a single journeyman, he worked directly for his clients, transforming in a series of steps the raw material into finished goods. . . .[55]

Thus, the concept of segmenting one's "work" from one's "personal" and "religious" life would have been largely alien to the pre-Industrial laborer. Indeed, for most people of this time, St. Benedict's sixth-century motto *laborare orare est* ("to work is to pray") made particularly good sense, for "humankind linked work with prayer."[56] As one commentator has explained, the understanding was that "[t]hrough his labors, man was integrated into an order that transcended him and linked him to his fellow men and to the gods."[57] Indeed, "the traditional worker justified his enterprise to himself in terms more moral and religious than economic."[58] Thus, the intermingling of work and faith was not merely a practical fact of life, but rather an intermingling grounded upon widely shared philosophical and theological beliefs. Talk of achieving an appropriate "work/life" balance, so familiar today, would have been unintelligible.

Society was also much more homogenous in the centuries preceding the Industrial Revolution.[59] In Europe, for example, the church was ubiquitous[60] and set standards and traditions that workers shared across most of the continent.[61] Moreover, many medieval peasants essentially worked for the church, as the church was "by far the largest proprietor in Europe, holding perhaps one-fourth or more of all the land," and by virtue of the fact that church properties "attracted peasants from other estates by offering more favorable conditions of life and work."[62] This furthered and reinforced the common, shared understanding of work and how it fits into one's life as an integrated whole.

Although the preceding focus was largely on the medieval European world, much of the same could be said for the classical, ancient world and non-European civilizations as well. There too we see that "work is not a separate sphere of life."[63] Indeed, in many such cultures, to this day, there "is often no separate word for work."[64] This is because in such cultures

> [t]here is a unity between raising a family and hunting or gathering; between making pots and training children; and between building homes and practicing one's religion.[65]

This, of course, contrasts dramatically with the situation today. For the laborer of today, a more appropriate motto would be *laborare* aut *orare*—"to work *or* to pray." In the West, the link between work and faith began to crumble with the Protestant Reformation, and with it the process of religious individualism. No longer would there be broad consensus on questions of faith, including the common understanding of work and its nature. The link was weakened further by the Enlightenment era that followed, which began the relegation of religion as a matter wholly private and subjective (or, according to some, as ultimately irrelevant). The link between work and faith was finally broken with the advent of industrialization and urbanization. With the factory, and the subdivision of labor that accompanied it, "everything changed":[66]

> All the threads in the fabric of popular life were unraveled and then rewoven together: how people lived in families, how they interacted with their neighbors in communities, how they thought of the politically powerful.[67]

Industrialization and urbanization served to remove a large number of workers from their homes, both in terms of their ancestral lands and their place of abode.[68] Severed from the sources of faith and family (which had, in prior generations, surrounded them) the post–Industrial Revolution worker experienced a newfound separation between his or her "work life" and his or her "personal" and "religious" life, both physically and temporally. Work had become "seculariz[ed]" to the "complete inversion of the everyday sense of religion" that had formerly prevailed.[69] As one commentator explained: "In industrialized cultures, the world of work is separated and divorced from the home, family life, religious life, and other diverse activities of citizens."[70] Emile Durkheim explained how this phenomenon contributes to a state of "anomie"—normlessness and estrangement.[71]

Old habits die hard, however. For some time, despite the overall trend toward separation, a few business owners continued to mix work and religion. It was not unusual in nineteenth-century America for businesspeople to actively integrate religion (or at least religiously grounded morals) into the workplace.[72] Indeed, the Ford Motor Company's "Americanization" programs did the same sort of thing on a secular level well into the early years of the twentieth century.[73]

Such programs became increasingly difficult to maintain, however, as the religious diversity of the West has increased exponentially over time. This increase in diversity has perhaps been experienced to no greater degree than in the United States, due to both the multiplication of American religious sects and immigration from all corners of the globe over the past century. In such a heterogeneous, multicultural society, a consensus emerged eschewing religion in the workplace.[74] It was simply seen as unwise to introduce a subject as "divisive" as religion into the business setting, which thrives on unity, stability, and peace.[75] It could generate conflict among employees and alienate customers.[76] The conventional wisdom had become "religion and business simply don't mix."[77] This is the conventional wisdom that the modern business corporation largely accepts and which many postmodern business corporations choose to reject.

Coherent, Integrated Living

A third factor contributing to the rise of the postmodern corporation is a yearning on the part of many individuals to live what I shall refer to as a coherent, integrated life. This concept was introduced in our examination of the religiously expressive association, but is not limited to religious populations. Even among nonreligious individuals there is an upsurge of those who seek ways in which to conform all of their life's choices to their beliefs and principles. They too are increasingly uncomfortable with divorcing their most cherished personal values from their financial and economic decisions (such as their choice of employment, how they invest their money, and the vendors they choose to patronize).

Once again, this phenomenon is not a novelty so much as the reintroduction of past ways of thinking. Only a couple of centuries ago, it had been well understood that "every economic decision has a moral consequence."[78] Indeed, as originally understood, "economics" as a discipline was a branch of moral philosophy. This would seem to make sense, for "[a]t its core, economics is about human action," and "[h]uman existence is on all sides a moral existence."[79] Thus, modernity (and with it, the modern corporation) has not only severed the link between work and faith (as discussed previously), but it has also largely severed the broader connection between economics and authentic (that is, morally significant) human flourishing.[80]

It is difficult to pinpoint what exactly is fueling this phenomenon of re-integration (at least with regard to nonreligiously motivated values). One factor is probably the decline in voluntary associations, chronicled so well in Robert D. Putnam's *Bowling Alone: The Collapse and Revival of American Community* (2000). The deterioration of civic groups, clubs, and community associations has narrowed the venues in which individuals can express themselves. As such, today "the workplace is the single most important site of cooperative interaction and sociability among adult citizens outside the family."[81] Consequently, an individual's development as a human being, on a variety of levels, often occurs within the context of their employment and careers.[82] This would help explain why so many people are gravitating toward workplaces and corporations congruent with their values.[83] As John McGinnis has noted, "[a]s society becomes wealthier, the distinction between what many people do for a living and what they do to express themselves blurs."[84]

The effect of this phenomenon is most likely magnified by the fact that those individuals with the greatest control over a corporation—its officers—are also those most personally concerned with its culture and values. To the extent that the workplace may be integral to an employee's personal development, it is even more likely to be integral to a corporate officer's, given the greater weightiness of the responsibilities and decisions that mark his or her tenure.[85] Corporate officers are the individuals whose lives are most closely intertwined with the corporate entity, as I have noted elsewhere:

> [A] corporate officer's development as a human being may very well turn on how she discharges the corporate duties that dominate her daily life...
>
> Not surprisingly, therefore, the call for ethics in business "does not come primarily from an outraged public, the polemics-hungry press, or publicly-minded congressional committees." Instead, "[i]t comes from executives themselves who want the opportunity to think through and clarify the conflicts in which they find themselves on a daily basis."[86]

The values embraced by a corporation are of increasing concern to investors as well, and this too contributes to the rise of the postmodern corporation. One cannot fail to observe the phenomenon of socially responsible investing, whereby investors (individual and institutional) screen their investment decisions with recourse to factors that are moral and ethical in nature.[87] Over the past couple of decades, this movement has witnessed tremendous growth, exemplified by the presence of fifty-five socially responsible mutual funds with $12 billion in assets in 1995 to 250 such funds with over $316 billion in assets in 2010.[88] This amounts to approximately $1 out of every $7 invested in the United States.[89]

A subset of this class would be those investors who steer their investments to companies whose products and services comport (or at least don't conflict with) their religious beliefs.[90] This being twenty-first-century America, there are, unsurprisingly, dozens of such funds, catering to (among others) investors who are devout Catholics, Muslims, Jews, and Protestants.[91] Here too there has been remarkable growth: the number of such funds has more than tripled since 2000, and the assets of such funds have climbed from $10 billion in the late 1990s, to over $27 billion as of 2009.[92] Thus, business corporations may be motivated to embrace a religious dimension due to pressure from shareholders and other investors.[93]

Incentives for businesses to embrace values beyond simply profit maximization come from customers as well. Customers increasingly endeavor to patronize businesses and establishments that honor their values.[94] Even if this embrace is simply a matter of smart marketing initially, over time it can certainly take on a life of its own. As a company becomes associated with certain values, it attracts a following that it may very well become beholden to. It is pushed, over time, toward a deeper embrace of those values, externally (from customers and investors who are attracted to them) and internally (by employees and officers who are attracted to them as well).

This leads to a final point: consider the possibility of *all* the above-referenced constituencies coalescing around a particular company that espouses and embraces a well-defined set of values and principles. A company that may have been founded by an individual of particularly strong convictions and who made his or her convictions felt in the company's policies and practices. A company that, in turn, attracted investors, officers, and employees who shared in those convictions and who supported the "mission" of the company. Add to this a loyal base of customers who would patronize the business in preference to others, out of support for the company's policies and practices. Such are the ingredients of the postmodern corporation.

THE POSTMODERN CORPORATION AS A TOCQUEVILLIAN ASSOCIATION

The postmodern corporation obviously differs in many important respects from the modern corporation. These differences, I posit, entitle the postmodern corporation to classification as a Tocquevillian Association, a classification not well-suited to the modern corporation.

Recall that, at its core, the Tocquevillian Association is a genuine community of individuals, coalescing around a shared goal or shared set of values. The commitment of these individuals is mutually reinforcing and ordinarily lends itself to some degree of involvement in the association's activities. As presented above, the postmodern corporation would seem to fit this description. Its various constituencies are drawn together by a common core of principles and priorities. Their concern with the corporation is not tethered solely (or even primarily) to a particular number (such as profits or share price), but to matters far more personal and sensitive (such as those of ethics, morality, or religion).

Nevertheless, many balk at such a suggestion that even the postmodern corporation can amount to an association in the Tocquevillian sense. To them, no corporation, postmodern or otherwise, can constitute a Tocquevillian Association, and, consequently, no corporation is entitled to the constitutional rights and protections that our society regularly affords to such associations. The primary stumbling block is that even postmodern corporations are fundamentally commercial in nature.

This highlights a long established divide between commercial and noncommercial activity, between for-profit and nonprofit corporations. Although Tocqueville did not make this distinction, the Supreme Court and numerous commentators have.[95] As I shall demonstrate, this distinction is premised upon two questionable presuppositions.

The first presupposition is that commercial or for-profit associations (which are ordinarily treated together) are wealthier than noncommercial or nonprofit associations (which are also ordinarily treated together). This wealth, it is feared, can overwhelm society (and societal discourse) if protected by the First Amendment. But this presupposition simply does not hold true universally. Although, commercial and for-profit enterprises may have more resources than noncommercial and nonprofit enterprises as a general matter, there are certainly some nonprofit institutions (such as Harvard University or the National Collegiate Athletic Association, for example) which dwarf the vast majority of for-profit commercial enterprises in terms of wealth and resources.[96] Moreover, as a legal matter, little restricts the profitability or wealth of "nonprofit" institutions vis-à-vis for-profit businesses.[97] Indeed, the very nomenclature of "profit" versus "nonprofit" is misleading, as both types of organizations generally seek profitability. The critical difference is that the profits of a "for-profit" enterprise are distributed to others, whereas the profits of a "nonprofit" are put back into the enterprise.[98] As Henry Hansmann explained:

> The defining characteristic of a nonprofit organization is that it is barred from distributing profits, or net earnings, to individuals who exercise control over it, such as its directors, officers, or members. This does not mean that a nonprofit organization is prohibited from earning a profit. Rather, it is only the distribution of profits that is prohibited; net income, if any, must be retained and devoted to the purposes for which the organization was formed. Moreover, it is only net income, or pure profits, that may not be distributed; nonprofits are generally free to pay reasonable compensation to individuals, including controlling individuals, for labor services or capital provided to the organization.[99]

Moreover, to the extent that commercial and for-profit corporations do indeed enjoy greater wealth and power, that actually suggests that they would serve as superior candidates when it comes to checking government power—an important role of the association in Tocquevillian thought. As Martin Redish and Howard Wasserman note, the ability to check government requires "power, resources and incentive...corporations generally possess all three."[100] Thus, contrary to being a drawback, the wealth of for-profit corporations can be viewed as supportive of their identification as Tocquevillian Associations.

The second presupposition behind the for-profit/nonprofit distinction displays a more qualitative concern. It has to do with the nature of the for-profit/commercial enterprise versus the nature of the nonprofit/noncommercial enterprise. This concern melds with another aspect of the association that can be distilled from Tocqueville's writings: the extent to which an association serves as a "mediating institution" (to apply a modern term to the phenomenon Tocqueville describes).[101]

Tocqueville believed that associations were essential because, among other things, they provided a vehicle through which "[f]eelings and opinions are recruited, the heart is enlarged, and the human mind is developed."[102] In short, associations provide individuals with community—an essential component of human flourishing. As mediating institutions, associations serve the manifold purposes of socialization, self-realization, and the inculcation of civic republicanism.

In their examination of corporations, many commentators conclude that only nonprofits embody this communitarian dimension. Drawing upon social identity theory, Usha Rodrigues argues that "[n]onprofits can create a social identity in association which for-profit corporations cannot."[103] This is because of the inability of nonprofits to distribute profits and the distinctiveness of a nonprofit's "values and practices in relation to...comparable groups."[104] This helps nonprofits carve out a distinctive kind of identity, from which those associated with it derive a certain prestige and "psychic income."[105]

The Supreme Court exhibited similar thinking in *Federal Election Commission v. Massachusetts Citizens for Life, Inc.*,[106] where it explained that "[i]ndividuals who contribute to [a politically oriented nonprofit] are fully aware of its political purposes, and in fact contribute precisely because they support those purposes."[107] The Court expressly contrasted this with the for-profit world, where an individual's investment or employment decision was characterized only as "for economic gain."[108]

Such a view is overly simplistic. As Evelyn Brody points out, "many organizations" (be they for-profit or nonprofit) "have multiple purposes," and as such individuals belong to them for a variety of reasons.[109] As has been previously observed, "[a]s society becomes wealthier, the distinction between what many people do for a living and what they do to express themselves blurs."[110] The decision to invest in, work for, or patronize a given business corporation may be (for some individuals) as political as it is economic. In an age when technology largely obliterates the distinction between on- and off-duty, mundane employment and consumer choices have increasingly become avenues by which individuals express themselves.[111]

To her credit, Rodrigues recognizes that certain philanthropic for-profit corporations have blurred the distinction between profit and nonprofit corporations (she identifies, specifically, Starbucks, Whole Foods, and Ben & Jerry's), yet nevertheless maintains that the distinction persists.[112] It is here that I part company with her and many others, for I believe that there is a point at which we have a technical distinction but not a substantive difference. For many of Rodrigues's very own arguments in support of nonprofit identity can and do apply equally to postmodern corporations as well. Instead of following her reasoning to its logical conclusion, an arbitrary and unnecessary line is drawn in the sand.

Mark Hager, for example, argues in favor of a robust protection of associations and their rights—yet would exclude from this protection for-profit business corporations.[113] He justifies this exclusion primarily due to his assertion that "[a] business corporation is not essentially a collection of people, but rather, essentially a collection of capital."[114] Hager recognizes the debatability of this assertion, and quickly works to counter those who would attack it as "excessively simplistic."[115] In doing so, he argues that "[t]he common bond among stockholders lies almost exclusively in their mutual hope of profits" whereas the membership of other (nonprofit) associations is "typically held together by a broader and more complex range of social interests and purposes: political, educational, charitable, and fraternal, as well as economic."[116]

Hager's critique of the corporation as a profit-obsessed automaton is a common one. As Dan Greenwood puts it, the corporation is, by law, beholden to "the interests of a fictional creature called a shareholder that has no associations, economic incentives or political views other than a desire to profit from its connection with this particular corporation."[117] This ties in with Rodrigues's view that the presence of shareholders constitutes an important distinguishing feature separating for-profit corporations from nonprofit corporations.[118]

Again, as a matter of general supposition, I challenge neither Greenwood's nor Hager's description.[119] I agree with Hager's assertion that nonprofit organizations "display a rich and various associational and 'political' character rarely displayed among stockholders in a corporation."[120] That said, I seize upon Hager's use of the qualifier "rarely." "Rarely" connotes that *some* corporations do indeed share in these traits.[121] The world of commercial, for-profit corporations is a richly variegated one, and we should be open to the fact that some of these enterprises (namely, postmodern corporations) will bear all the significant hallmarks of a Tocquevillian Association.[122] Indeed, as has been discussed, in the years since both Hager's and Greenwood's articles were written, many states (including, most significantly, Delaware) have adopted "benefit corporation" statutes, explicitly authorizing corporate boards to prioritize other objectives—social objectives with a view toward the common good—over shareholder profits.[123] Even before that, several states adopted "corporate constituency" statutes, "which allow managers to take into account the interests of non-shareholder stakeholders (including employees) when making decisions."[124]

Most important of all, perhaps, is that many corporations simply do not view themselves as the profit-maximizing machines described above. As Lisa Fairfax has documented, companies increasingly distance themselves from profit maximization, and instead stress their balanced commitment to a variety of corporate stakeholders.[125] This, in turn, may have important normative and behavioral effects, leading to an authentic corporate identity.[126]

The ability of a for-profit corporation to have an authentic identity is further attested to by the scores of employees, investors, and customers who are often drawn to a particular corporation because of its unique qualities. Organizational scholars have long pointed out that different corporations have "distinct cultures,"[127] and with these cultures can come a set of particular values. This extends to large companies as well as small companies:

> It is not true that all big companies are the same—they aren't.... Companies develop their own distinctive personality and ethos which is so ingrained, so much a part of them, that the corporate identity expresses itself in their every action.[128]

As such, corporations can enable people to "self-realize by engaging and investing in business and by participating in and personally benefitting from the political-economic system through the power of collective action."[129]

Indeed, a substantial body of scholarship exists affirming the for-profit corporation's ability to serve as a genuine association. Timothy Fort, for example, laments the fact that the business corporation has been "neglected" as a mediating institution in society.[130] He lists five reasons why business corporations should act and be treated as mediating institutions:

First, if being in such an institution assists in moral formation and identity, then it simply is a good thing to do regardless of whether it is good business.
Second, since so much of a person's waking hours are in business work, the corporation provides an opportunity to develop moral behavior.

Third, some scholars have argued that business demands time from employees that once was available for traditional mediating institutions like the family, neighborhood, and voluntary organizations. One then could argue that an obligation in this "takeover" is the obligation to be a mediating institution.

Fourth, a mediating institution which is primarily concerned with the development of its internal members might have a corporate analogue that is efficacious if internal "stakeholders" have priority in corporate social responsibility.

Fifth, many businesses and business strategies depend upon a notion of a business that is acting very much like a mediating institution.[131]

He is not alone in this regard, as some business ethicists "have suggested that corporations today can, and possibly must, serve as mediating institutions in society."[132] Indeed, "[t]o the extent that so many people spend most of their day working in or interacting with corporate organizations, 'the corporation represents a value-laden institution that outranks the local community as a focus of loyalty and a medium for self-realization.'"[133] As Michael Novak explains:

> The business corporation is . . . a "mediating structure," that is, a social institution larger than the individuals who make it up, but smaller than the state. An institution both voluntary and private, it stands between the individual and the state and is, perhaps (after the family), the crucial institution of civil society.[134]

Novak has gone so far as to develop what can rightly be called a "theology of the corporation."[135] Building on Aristotle's observation that human beings are "social animals," who can only flourish in "community,"[136] Novak sees the business corporation as providing that community.[137] He calls the corporation "a magnificent social invention prior in its existence to the modern nation state,"[138] the importance of which has increased given the growth of the state[139] and the decline of other mediating institutions.[140] Indeed, the demands of work today are such that it is unrealistic to expect people to develop their character and personalities entirely outside the workplace.[141] "For many of us, the two most important institutions in our lives are our families and the organizations for which we work."[142] And for many if not most people, the workplace is a corporation.

It certainly is true that not every corporation lives up to the lofty role that Fort and Novak define for it. But, with equal certainty, some do. The dividing line is not so much between the nonprofit and for-profit world, as some would contend, but rather between the modern and postmodern corporation.

NOTES

1. I first explored the possibility of categorizing a corporation as an association in Ronald J. Colombo, *The Corporation as a Tocquevillian Association*, 85 Temp. L. Rev. 1 (2012).
2. *See, e.g., Our Commitment to the Environment*, Burt's Bees, http://www.burtsbees.com/c/commitment/environment/ (last visited Jan. 18, 2014). I do not mean to certify that Burt's Bees and the other companies listed in this paragraph are necessarily postmodern. That determination turns on a variety of factors, as we shall see. I cite these companies as examples of corporations that prioritize values other than profit-making alone.
3. *See, e.g., Against Animal Testing*, TheBodyShop, http://www.thebodyshop-usa.com/values-campaigns/against-animal-testing.aspx (last visited Jan. 18, 2014).
4. *See Company Fact Sheet*, Chick-fil-A, http://www.chick-fil-a.com/Company/Highlights-Fact-Sheets (last visited Jan. 18, 2014).
5. Kathleen M. Boozang & Simone Handler-Hutchinson, *"Monitoring" Corporate Corruption: DOJ's Use of Deferred Prosecution Agreements in Health Care*, 35 Am. J.L. & Med. 89, 103 n.77 (2009); Robert C. Bird, *Employment as a Relational Contract*, 8 U. Pa. J. Lab. & Emp. L. 149, 170 (2005).
6. 170 N.W. 668 (Mich. 1919). *But see generally* Lynn A. Stout, *Why We Should Stop Teaching* Dodge v. Ford, UCLA School of Law, Law-Econ Research Paper No. 07-11, available at http://ssrn.com/abstract=1013744 (arguing that "*Dodge v. Ford* is a mistake, a judicial 'sport,' a doctrinal oddity largely irrelevant to corporate law and corporate practice.").
7. *See Dodge*, 170 N.W. at 684.
8. Other scholars have interpreted the *Dodge* case differently, arguing that Henry Ford did not issue dividends for publicly minded reasons, but rather to "depress stock prices, and thus force the Dodge brothers to sell their stock to majority shareholder Henry Ford at favorable prices (which eventually happened)." Einer Elhauge, *Sacrificing Corporate Profits in the Public Interest*, 80 N.Y.U.L. Rev. 733, 774 (2005). If so, "this would have violated Henry Ford's fiduciary duty not to use his corporate control to benefit himself financially at the expense of other shareholders... [and] the otherwise aberrational court decision to interfere with the exercise of managerial discretion about dividend levels seems best explained on the view that the case really involved a conflict of interest raising duty of loyalty concerns." *Id.* Whether this reading of the case is correct, and therefore demotes the language in the decision quoted above to mere dicta, this mere dicta remains a very influential statement of the proper role and duties of the corporation's directors. *E.g.*, Robert Charles Clark, Corporate Law 603–604, 678–79 (1986).
9. Milton Friedman, *A Friedman Doctrine: The Social Responsibility of Business Is to Increase Its Profits*, N.Y. Times, Sept. 13, 1970, §6 (Magazine), at 32, 33. *See also* Edward W. Younkins, *Morality and Character Development: The Roles of Capitalism, Commerce, and the Corporation*, 4 J. of Markets & Morality 94, 104 (2001). Edward Younkins has explained this minimalist view of social responsibility as follows:

   > The social responsibility of the corporation through its directors, managers, and other employees, is simply to respect the natural rights of

individuals. Individuals in a corporation have the legally enforceable responsibility or duty to respect the moral agency, space, or autonomy of persons. This involves the basic principle of the non-initiation of physical force and includes the obligation to honor contracts with managers, employees, customers, suppliers, and others; duties not to engage in deception, fraud, force, threats, theft, or coercion against others; and the responsibility to honor representations made to the local community.

Id.

10. *See* Lyman Johnson, *Corporate Law Professors as Gatekeepers*, 6 U. ST. THOMAS L.J. 447, 450 (2009) ("[N]o law requires that businesses pursue only the goal of corporate profit or the goal of investor wealth maximization").
11. *See id.*
12. *See* John H. Matheson & Brent A. Olsen, *A Call for a Unified Business Organization Law*, 65 GEO. WASH. L. REV. 1, 9 (1996); *see also* Henry N. Butler & Larry E. Ribstein, *Opting Out of Fiduciary Duties: A Response to the Anti-Contractarians*, 65 WASH. L. REV. 1, 10–11 (1990). The degree to which corporate law should be considered "mandatory" versus merely "default" is a matter of no small debate. *See* Eric W. Orts, *The Complexity and Legitimacy of Corporate Law*, 50 WASH. & LEE L. REV. 1565, 1569 n.12 (1993) (citing Melvin Aron Eisenberg, *The Structure of Corporation Law*, 89 COLUM. L. REV. 1461 (1989); Jeffrey N. Gordon, *The Mandatory Structure of Corporation Law*, 89 COLUM. L. REV. 1549 (1989), Roberta Romano, *Answering the Wrong Question: The Tenuous Case for Mandatory Corporate Laws*, 89 COLUM. L. REV. 1599, 1599–602, 1616 (1989)).
13. JOHN PAUL II, CENTESIMUS ANNUS ¶35 (1991) (emphasis added).
14. AMERICAN LAW INSTITUTE, PRINCIPLES OF CORPORATE GOVERNANCE: ANALYSIS AND RECOMMENDATIONS (Proposed Final Draft, Mar. 31, 1992), § 2.01(b), at 69 (*quoted in* Orts, *supra* note 11, at 1604).
15. Michael J. Phillips, *Reappraising the Real Entity Theory of the Corporation*, 21 FLA. ST. U. L. REV. 1061, 1117 (1994).
16. *See* Jane O'Brien, *US Firms Put Social Values before Big Profits*, BBC NEWS (May 20, 2012, 12:31 PM), *at* http://www.bbc.co.uk/news/business-18089604.
17. *See* Daniel P. Sullivan & Donald E. Conlon, *Crisis and Transition in Corporate Governance Paradigms: The Role of the Chancery Court in Delaware*, 31 LAW & SOC'Y REV. 713, 732 (1997).
18. *See* Lisa M. Fairfax, *The Rhetoric of Corporate Law: The Impact of Shareholder Rhetoric on Corporate Norms*, 31 J. CORP. L. 675, 676 (2006) (citing Adolph A. Berle Jr., *For Whom Corporate Managers Are Trustees: A Note*, 45 HARV. L. REV. 1365, 1367 (1932) *and* E. Merrick Dodd Jr., *For Whom Are Corporate Managers Trustees?*, 45 HARV. L. REV. 1145, 1147–48 (1932)).
19. *Id.* (citing Dodd Jr., *supra* note 18, at 1160–61). For a fuller summary of the Berle-Dodd debate, *see* Judd F. Sneirson, *Doing Well by Doing Good: Leveraging Due Care for Better, More Socially Responsible Corporate Decisionmaking*, 3 CORP. GOV. L. REV. 438, 444–46 (2007).
20. *See* Kathleen Hale, *Corporate Law and Stakeholders: Moving Beyond Stakeholder Statutes*, 45 ARIZ. L. REV. 823, 831–32 (2003).
21. *See id.*
22. *E.g.*, Revlon v. MacAndrews & Forbes Holdings, Inc., 506 A2d 173, 181 (Del. 1985) (holding that once a corporate takeover was inevitable, the directors of

the target company had a duty to "maximize[e] . . . the company's value at a sale for the stockholders' benefit. . . . [t]he directors' role changed from defenders of the corporate bastion to auctioneers charged with getting the best price for the stockholders at a sale of the company.").

23. 571 A.2d 1140 (Del. 1989). Of all state courts, the Delaware Supreme Court is the most influential in the field of corporate law given the large number of businesses that are incorporated in Delaware and thereby subject to its rulings.
24. *See id.* at 1144 n.4.
25. *See* Fairfax, *supra* note 18, at 686. Although, by 2003, constituency statutes have been adopted in forty-one states, Delaware, by far the most influential state with regard to corporate law, has not adopted such a statute. Cheri A. Budzynski, *Can a Feminist Approach to Corporate Social Responsibility Break Down the Barriers of the Shareholder Primacy Doctrine?*, 38 U. TOL. L. REV. 435, 443 (2006).
26. *Rethinking the Social Responsibility of Business*, REASON (Oct. 2005) (*available at* http://reason.com/archives/2005/10/01/rethinking-the-social-responsi/4).
27. *Id.*
28. *See* Starbucks Corporation Social Responsibility Report 2006, *available at* http://www.starbucks.com/aboutus/csrannualreport.asp.
29. John M. Conley & Cynthia A. Williams, *Engage, Embed, and Embellish: Theory versus Practice in the Corporate Social Responsibility Movement*, 31 J. CORP. L. 1, 36 (2005).
30. *See* http://www.bcorporation.net/.
31. Amanda Stephenson, *Firms Make a 'B' Line for Environmental Symbol*, CALGARY HERALD, June 20, 2012, at D1. This is, admittedly, a small fraction of the total number of business corporations in operation—which number in the millions in the United States alone. *See The 2006 Statistical Abstract: The National Data Book*, U.S. CENSUS BUREAU, https://www.census.gov/compendia/statab/2006/business_enterprise/sole_proprietorships_partnerships_corporations/ (last visited Jan. 18, 2014). But the development nevertheless underscores the fact that for at least some businesses, the corporate form is not understood as requiring the maximization of profits to the exclusion of all other values.
32. *See* Angus Loten, *With New Law, Profits Take Back Seat*, WALL ST. J., Jan. 19, 2012, at B1.
33. *E.g.*, Daniel J. H. Greenwood, *Essential Speech: Why Corporate Speech Is Not Free*, 83 IOWA L. REV. 995, 1033 (1998).
34. *See* Liam Pleven, *When Doing Good Meets Investing*, WALL ST. J., July 13–14, 2013, at B9.
35. N.Y. BUS. CORP. LAW § 1707(a)(3) (McKinney Supp. 2013).
36. Much of what follows regarding the religiously expressive corporation was originally set forth in my article Ronald J. Colombo, *The Naked Private Square*, 51 HOUS. L. REV.1 (2013). To the extent that entire phrases or sentences are repeated herein, I thank the *Houston Law Review* for granting me permission to do this.
37. *See* Michelle Conlin, *Religion in the Workplace*, BUSINESSWEEK (Nov. 1 1999), http://www.businessweek.com/1999/99_44/b3653001.htm; *Ethics and Spirituality in the Workplace*, YALE CENTER FOR FAITH AND CULTURE, http://www.yale.edu/faith/esw/esw.htm (last visited Jan. 18, 2014).
38. DAVID W. MILLER, GOD AT WORK 3, 20–21 (2007).
39. *Id.* at 20–21, 105–123.
40. REX AHDAR & IAN LEIGH, RELIGIOUS FREEDOM IN THE LIBERAL STATE 2 (2013).

41. *See* David Masci & Gregory A. Smith, *God Is Alive and Well in America*, PEW RESEARCH CTR. (Apr. 4, 2006), http://pewresearch.org/pubs/15/god-is-alive-and-well-in-america; *Religion among the Millennials*, PEW RESEARCH CTR., (Feb. 17, 2010), http://pewforum.org/Age/Religion-Among-the-Millennials.aspx; David Paul Kuhn, *The Fall of Mass Attendance But Not US Religiosity*, REALCLEARPOLITICS.COM (Apr. 9, 2009), http://realclearpolitics.blogs.time.com/2009/04/09/the-fall-of-mass-attendance-but-not-us-religiosity/. *See also* RODNEY STARK, WHAT AMERICANS REALLY BELIEVE, 9 tbl.4 (2008).
42. Cathy Lynn Grossman, *Most Religious Groups in USA Have Lost Ground, Survey Finds*, USA TODAY (Mar. 17, 2009 6:35 PM), http://www.usatoday.com/news/religion/2009-03-09-american-religion-ARIS_N.htm.
43. *See* Frank Newport, *This Christmas, 78% of Americans Identify as Christian*, GALLUP (Dec. 24, 2009), http://www.gallup.com/poll/124793/this-christmas-78-americans-identify-christian.aspx. Which, after dropping from the 1950s to the 1970s, has hovered around 55% from 1980 to 2008.
44. *See* PEW RESEARCH CTR., "NONES" ON THE RISE: ONE IN FIVE ADULTS HAVE NO RELIGIOUS AFFILIATION 42 (2012), *available at* http://www.pewforum.org/uploadedFiles/Topics/Religious_Affiliation/Unaffiliated/NonesOnTheRise-full.pdf.
45. JOHN MICKLETHWAIT & ADRIAN WOOLDRIDGE, GOD IS BACK: HOW THE GLOBAL REVIVAL OF FAITH IS CHANGING THE WORLD 12 (2009).
46. *Id.* at 26. The phenomenon is not limited to the United States, but is occurring across large parts of the globe. *See* AHDAR & LEIGH, *supra* note 40, at 2.
47. *See* Eve Tahmincioglu, *Reconciling Religious Beliefs with Work*, NBCNEWS (Sept. 30, 2007, 6:13 PM), http://www.nbcnews.com/id/20973408/ns/business-careers/t/; *see also* ROSS DOUTHAT, BAD RELIGION 4–5 (2012).
48. *See* Sue Shellenbarger, *Praying with the Office Chaplain*, WALL ST. J., June 23, 2010, at D1.
49. Fouad A. Riad, *Religious Expression in the Workplace*, 30 COMP. LAB. L. & POL'Y J. 467, 481 (2009).
50. *Id.; see also, e.g.*, Charles P. Trumbull, *Islamic Arbitration: A New Path for Interpreting Islamic Legal Contracts*, 59 VAND. L. REV. 609, 610 (2006); Ann Carey, THE CARA STUDY AND VOCATIONS, CATHOLIC WORLD REPORT (May 7, 2011) (observing that among Catholic religious orders, the fastest growing over the past twenty years are "orders that observe a traditional religious life," such as those that "wear a religious habit, work together in common apostolates, and are explicit about their fidelity to the Church and the teachings of the Magisterium"); *see also* Traci Osuna, *Promoting Worship with the Traditional Mass*, ZENIT (June 9, 2010), http://www.zenit.org/article-29545?l=english (observing that although vocations are falling in most U.S. dioceses, vocations to traditional orders of Catholic priesthood are rising); *A Traditionalist Avant-Garde*, THE ECONOMIST (Dec. 15, 2012) (*available at* http://www.economist.com/news/international/21568357-its-trendy-be-traditionalist-catholic-church-traditionalist-avant-garde); MICKLETHWAIT & WOOLDRIDGE, *supra* note 45, at 17–18; AHDAR & LEIGH, *supra* note 40, at 2.
51. MICKLETHWAIT & WOOLDRIDGE, *supra* note 45, at 156–60 ("America's executive class is probably its second most religious elite in the country after senior military.").
52. *See Business Ethics in a Time of Economic Crisis*, MARIST COLL. INST. FOR PUB. OP. & KNIGHTS OF COLUMBUS, http://maristpoll.marist.edu/wp-content/misc/us090309/Business%20Ethics%20Survey/Business%20Ethics%202009.pdf (last visited Jan. 18, 2014).

53. *See* Shellenbarger, *supra* note 48, at D2.
54. *See* Eileen Power, Medieval People 1–24 (1924).
55. Edward Shorter, *A History of Work in the West: An Overview, in* Work and Community in the West 1, 8 (Edward Shorter ed., 1973).
56. *See* Alain Supiot, *Orare/Laborare*, 30 Comp. Lab. L. & P. 641, 641–42 (2009).
57. *Id.* at 642.
58. *See* Shorter, *supra* note 55, at 10.
59. *See* James Westfell Thompson, Economic and Social History of the Middle Ages 647–48, 671 (1928).
60. *See id.*
61. *See* Power, *supra* note 54, at 14; Marc Bloch, Feudal Society 256 (1961); Harold J. Berman, Law and Revolution 322 (1983) ("By the twelfth century, all peasants in Western Christendom, including serfs, had legally protected rights.").
62. *See* Berman, *supra* note 61, at 320.
63. Herbert Applebaum, The Concept of Work 9 (1992).
64. *Id.*
65. *Id.* at 9–10.
66. *See* Shorter, *supra* note 55, at 1, 16.
67. *See id.* at 1.
68. Gerben J. N. Bruinsma, *Urbanization and Urban Crime: Dutch Geographical and Environmental Research, in* 35 Crime and Justice: A Review of Research 453, 467 (Michael Tonry & Catrien Bijleveld eds., 2007).
69. *See* Supiot, *supra* note 56, at 644, 646.
70. *See* Applebaum, *supra* note 63, at 9.
71. *See* Michael L. Rustad, *Private Enforcement of Cybercrime on the Electronic Frontier*, 11 S. Cal. Interdisc. L.J. 63, 67–70 (2001) (citing Emile Durkheim, The Division of Labor in Society 368 (1933)).
72. *See* George S. White, *The Moral Influence of Manufacturing Establishments* (1836), *in* The New England Mill Village, 1790–1860, at 345, 345–46, 351 (Gary Kulik, Roger Parks, & Theodore Z. Penn eds., 1982); S. V. S. Wilder, *Ware Factory Village* (1826–1827), *in* The New England Mill Village, 1790–1860, *supra*, at 243, 243–51; Smith Wilkinson, *Contract and Memorandum Books* (1824), *in* The New England Mill Village, 1790–1860, *supra*, at 451, 465.
73. *See* Stephen Meyer, *Adapting the Immigrant to the Line: Americanization in the Ford Factory, 1914–1921*, 14 J. Soc. History 67, 67–82 (1980).
74. *See Toppling a Taboo: Businesses Go "Faith-Friendly,"* Knowledge@Wharton (Jan. 24, 2007), http://www.knowledge.wharton.upenn.edu/article.cfm?articleid=1644.
75. *See id.*
76. *See* Maya Dollarhide, *When God Goes to the Office*, CNN (Mar. 10, 2008, 10:35 AM), http://www.cnn.com/2008/living/worklife/03/10/religion.at.the.office/index.html. "As Richard Posner argues, everyday commerce depends on the ability of parties to displace debates about 'deep issues' that have little practical payoff and that can 'disrupt and even poison commercial relations among strangers.'" Mark L. Movsesian, *Rediscovering Williston*, 62 Wash. & Lee L. Rev. 207, 216 (quoting Richard A. Posner, Law, Pragmatism, and Democracy 41, 54 (2003)).
77. Miller, *supra* note 38, at 3; *see also* Danielle Lee, *Diversifying the Religious Experience*, Corp. Resp. Mag., http://thecro.com/node/588 (last visited Jan 18, 2014). Indeed, even churches themselves had generally become "uninterested

in, if not hostile towards, the business world." *Toppling a Taboo: Businesses Go "Faith-Friendly," supra* note 74.

78. *See* George P. Schwartz & William J. Koshelnyk, Good Returns: Making Money by Morally Responsible Investing xvi (2010) (quoting Benedict XVI, *Caritas in Veritate* § 37, at 39 (2009)).
79. *See* Gerson Moreno-Riaño, *Democracy, Humane Economics, and a Culture of Enterprise*, 13 J. Markets & Morality 7, 10 (2010).
80. *See id.* at 11–12.
81. Cynthia L. Estlund, *Working Together: The Workplace, Civil Society, and the Law*, 89 Geo. L. J. 1, 3 (2000).
82. *See* Ronald J. Colombo, *Toward a Nexus of Virtue*, 69 Wash. & Lee L. Rev. 3, 57 (2012).
83. *See* Karen L. Cash & George R. Gray, *A Framework for Accommodating Religion and Spirituality in the Workplace*, Acad. Mgmt Executive, Aug. 2000, at 124, 132 (2000).
84. *See* John O. McGinnis, *Reviving Tocqueville's America: The Rehnquist Court's Jurisprudence of Social Discovery*, 90 Cal. L. Rev. 485, 538 n.268 (2002).
85. *See* Colombo, *supra* note 82, at 57.
86. *See id.* at 42 (2012) (quoting Robert C. Solomon, Ethics and Excellence: Cooperation and Integrity in Business 5 (1992)).
87. *See generally* Benjamin J. Richardson, Socially Responsible Investment Law 1–2, 43 (2008); Schwartz & Koshelnyk, *supra* note 78, at 8–10; George Djurasovic, *The Regulation of Socially Responsible Mutual Funds*, 22 J. Corp. L. 257, 258–62 (1997).
88. *See* Adam Bold, *What You Need to Know about Socially Responsible Investing*, U.S. News (Apr. 19, 2011), http://money.usnews.com/money/blogs/the-smarter-mutual-fund-investor/2011/04/19/what-you-need-to-know-about-socially-responsible-investing.
89. *See* Barbara Wall, *Financial Goals, Spiritual Needs*, Int'l Herald Trib., June 5, 2005, at 18.
90. *See* Richardson, *supra* note 87, at 111–20; Schwartz & Koshelnyk, *supra* note 78, at 10–11 (distinguishing between "socially responsible investing" and "morally responsible [faith-based] investing").
91. *See* Wall, *supra* note 89; Erin Joyce, *Impact Investing: The Ethical Choice*, Forbes (May 26, 2010, 6:38 PM), http://www.forbes.com/2010/05/26/impact-investing-ethical-personal-finance-responsible.html (explaining how impact investing now includes faith-based investing); Lisa Smith, *A Guide to Faith-Based Investing*, Investopedia (Feb. 29, 2012), http://www.investopedia.com/articles/stocks/12/investing-and-faith.asp#axzz2J6tiKGR8 (explaining Catholic, Islamic, Jewish, and Protestant investing and mutual funds); Mark Thomsen, *Catholic Values-Based Investment Products Rise in Number*, Soc. Funds (June 7, 2001), http://www.socialfunds.com/news/print.cgi?sfArticleId=595 (commenting on increase of investment products targeting Catholic investors). Examples of such funds are plentiful. *See, e.g.*, *About Amana Mutual Funds Trust*, Amana Mut. Funds Tr., http://www.amanafunds.com/retail/about/index.shtml (last visited Jan. 18, 2014) (partnering with an investment adviser that selects companies that do not violate the requirements of the Islamic faith at the time of investment); *About Us*, U. Islamic Fin., http://www.myuif.com/about-us/ (last visited Jan. 18, 2014) (announcing a community bank targeting Muslims through Shariah conscious practices); *Ave Maria Catholic Values Fund*, Ave Maria

MUT. FUNDS, http://www.avemariafunds.com/funds/avemxSummary.php (last visited Jan. 18, 2013) ("Ave Maria Catholic Values Fund seeks long-term capital appreciation from equity investments in companies that do not violate core values and teachings of the Roman Catholic Church."); *Hall of Shame*, TIMOTHY PLAN (2013), http://www.timothyplan.com/Download/HallofShame.pdf (last visited Jan. 18, 2013) ("The Timothy Plan® is a family of mutual funds designed to help investors own morally clean portfolios. By screening out (avoiding to own) companies involved in activities contributing to the moral decline of America, the Timothy Plan® is committed to keeping its portfolios morally responsible.... The Timothy Plan® family of mutual funds, avoids investing in companies that are involved in practices contrary to Judeo-Christian principles.").

92. *See* Daren Fonda, *Faith & Finance: A Boom in Religious Funds*, SMARTMONEY MAG., Dec. 22, 2009.
93. Jonathan Burton, *Investing with Principles*, WALL ST. J., Apr. 4, 2011, at R8; *see generally* RICHARDSON, *supra* note 87, at 111–20; SCHWARTZ & KOSHELNYK, *supra* note 78, 6–7, 10–11.
94. See CONE, RESEARCH REPORT: CONE CAUSE EVOLUTION & ENVIRONMENTAL SURVEY 8 (2007), *available at* http://www.conecomm.com/stuff/contentmgr/files/0/a8880735bb2e2e894a949830055ad559/files/2007_cause_evolution_survey.pdf (explaining the contradiction whereby consumers consider a company's commitment to social issues during purchasing decisions yet make fewer purchases); SHEILA M. J. BONINI, KERRIN MCKILLOP, & LENNY T. MENDONCA, *The Trust Gap Between Consumers and Corporations*, MCKINSEY Q., No. 2, 2007, at 7, 10, *available at* http://cecp.co/summitmaterial/2007summit/pdfs/Mendonca%20_handout1.pdf; *BBMG Study: Three-Fourths of U.S. Consumers Reward, Punish Brands Based on Social and Environmental Practices*, BBMG (June 2, 2009), http://www.csrwire.com/press_ releases/27052-BBMG-Study-Three-Fourths-of-U-S-Consumers-Reward-Punish-Brands-Based-on-Social-and-Environmental-Practices ("America's consumers are rewarding brands that align with their values, punishing those that don't and spreading the word about corporate practices...."); *Benefits of Becoming a Sustainable Business*, ECO-OFFICIENCY, http://www.eco-officiency.com/benefits_becoming_sustainable_business.html (last visited Jan. 18, 2014) (explaining that consumers are more likely to patronize sustainable businesses); Lawrence Glickman, *Whole Foods Boycott: The Long View*, WASH. POST (Sept. 2, 2009, 5:30 AM), http://voices.washingtonpost.com/shortstack/2009/09/whole_foods_boycott_the_long_v.html?hpid=news-col-blog (examining the American boycott tradition).
95. *E.g.*, Roberts v. United States Jaycees, 468 U.S. 609, 619 (1984); Usha Rodrigues, *Entity and Identity*, 60 EMORY L. J. 1257, 1320 (2011).
96. *See* Jeff Trexler, *Design Jurisprudence and the Nonprofit Style*, 14 YALE J.L. & HUMAN. 321, 382–83 (2002).
97. *See* Henry B. Hansmann, *Reforming Nonprofit Corporation Law*, 129 U. PA. L. REV. 497, 501 (1981).
98. *See id.* But even this can be misleading, as the line between the distribution of profits, and the payment of exorbitant salaries, can sometimes differ little conceptually. Robyn Blumner, *Aiding the Poor Shouldn't Make You Rich*, ST. PETERSBURG TIMES, Apr. 19, 2009, *available* at 2009 WLNR 7426098; Stephanie Strom, *Lawmakers, Tightening Belts, Question Nonprofit Salaries*, N.Y. TIMES, July 27, 2010, *available* at 2010 WLNR 14905614.
99. *Id.*

100. *See* Martin H. Redish & Howard W. Wasserman, *What's Good for General Motors: Corporate Speech and the Theory of Free Expression*, 66 GEO. WASH. L. REV. 235, 263 (1998). *See also* MICHAEL NOVAK, THE SPIRIT OF DEMOCRATIC CAPITALISM 178 (1982) ("Without the large private corporation, there would be one fewer among the private forces strong enough to check the growing ambitions of the administrative state.").
101. *See* Timothy L. Fort, *The First Man and the Company Man: The Common Good, Transcendence and Mediating Institutions*, 36 AM. BUS. L. J. 391, 430 (1999).
102. *See* ALEXIS DE TOCQUEVILLE, DEMOCRACY IN AMERICA 633 (Bantam Classics 2000).
103. *See* Rodrigues, *supra* note 95, at 1320.
104. *Id.* at 1282.
105. *Id.* at 1284.
106. 479 U.S. 238 (1986).
107. *Id.* at 260.
108. *Id.* at 260.
109. *See* Evelyn Brody, *Entrance, Voice, and Exit: The Constitutional Bounds of the Right of Association*, 35 U.C. DAVIS L. REV. 821, 863–64 (2002).
110. *See* McGinnis, *supra* note 84, at 537 n.268.
111. Olivera Perkins, *Smartphones Let You Take Work Anywhere... That's a Problem Mobility Blurs Lines Between Workplace, Home*, CLEVELAND PLAIN DEALER, July 27, 2009, available at 2009 WLNR 14464958.
112. *See* Rodrigues, *supra* note 95.
113. Mark M. Hager, *Bodies Politic: The Progressive History of Organizational "Real Entity" Theory*, 50 U. PITT. L. REV. 575, 648–49 (1989).
114. *Id.* at 650.
115. *Id.* at 650–51.
116. *Id.* at 651.
117. *See* Greenwood, *supra* note 33, at 1033.
118. *See supra* note 95.
119. Although, as I and others have argued, the law does not necessarily compel a corporation to maximize shareholder profits. *E.g.*, Ronald J. Colombo, *Ownership, Limited: Reconciling Traditional and Progressive Corporate Law via an Aristotelian Understanding of Ownership*, 34 J. CORP. L. 247 (2008).
120. *Id.*
121. Hager also makes the argument that for-profit associations are less deserving of First Amendment rights due to the fact that they are not governed by the "one-person, one-vote" paradigm, but rather by the "one-stock, one-vote." *Id.* at 652. This calls to mind the "fervor for democracy" that, during the Revolutionary Era, "led some states to recognize the rights of churches only if they follow democratic internal decision making processes." *See* Brody, *supra* note 109, at 862. In short, it strikes me as Orwellian to deny people the right to organize in the manner they see fit in the name of democracy and freedom.
122. *Cf.* David Graver, *Personal Bodies: A Corporeal Theory of Corporate Personhood*, 6 U. CHI. L. SCH. ROUNDTABLE 235, 248–49 (1999) (recognizing critical differences among commercial corporations, such that some ought to possess free speech rights while others should not).
123. *See* Max Abelson, *The New Be Good Business: Albany Gives Birth to New York's Benefit Corporation*, N.Y. OBSERVER, June 22, 2010.
124. Barbara J. Fick, *The Changing Face of the American Workplace*, 12 NOTRE DAME J.L. ETHICS & PUB. POL'Y 1, 7 (1998).

125. *See* Fairfax, *supra* note 18, at 676–78.
126. *See id.*
127. Pamela H. Bucy, *Corporate Ethos: A Standard for Imposing Corporate Criminal Liability*, 75 MINN. L. REV. 1095, 1123–27 (1991).
128. *Id.* at 1123 (quoting W. OLINS, THE CORPORATE PERSONALITY 82 (1978)).
129. *See* Redish & Wasserman, *supra* note 100, at 254.
130. *See* Fort, *supra* note 101, at 433–34.
131. *See id.*
132. *See* Susana Kim Ripken, *Corporations Are People Too*, 15 FORDHAM J. CORP. & FIN. L. 97, 146 (2009).
133. *Id.*
134. *See* MICHAEL NOVAK, THREE IN ONE 233 (2001).
135. *See* MICHAEL NOVAK, TOWARD A THEOLOGY OF THE CORPORATION (1990).
136. *See* ARISTOTLE, POLITICS; Richard J. Regan, *Virtue, Religion, and Civic Culture, in* MIDWEST STUDIES IN PHILOSOPHY VOL. XIII 343 (Peter French et al. eds., 1988).
137. *See* NOVAK, *supra* note 134.
138. *See* MICHAEL NOVAK, THE FUTURE OF THE CORPORATION 5 (1996).
139. MICHAEL NOVAK, THE SPIRIT OF DEMOCRATIC CAPITALISM 178 (1982).
140. *See* Ripken, *supra* note 132, at 153.
141. *See id.*
142. *See id.* (quoting Michael Naughton, *The Corporation as a Community of Work*, 4 AVE MARIA L. REV. 33, 40–41 (2006)).

CHAPTER 4

Corporate Personhood, Rights, and Responsibilities

Over the next few chapters, we shall examine the various freedoms protected by the First Amendment and assess the degree to which they ought to be deemed applicable to the business corporation. Driving our assessment will be the divide between the modern versus the postmodern corporation, and the associational status enjoyed by the latter. Before proceeding, however, let us consider first the prevailing approach to assessing corporate constitutional rights.

At the crux of the prevailing approach has been the concept of "personhood" and what it means to be a "person." Paradoxically, the courts have used this concept in different ways to reach different results. "Corporate personhood" has served (and continues to serve) as the vehicle by which American courts have recognized corporate constitutional rights. At the same time, the courts have also invoked what has been called the "purely personal rights" test to deny recognition of corporate constitutional rights. In this chapter, I shall explain the development of corporate personhood and criticize how it has furthered the recognition of corporate rights divorced from any serious consideration of relevant corporate theory. I shall also explore the purely personal rights test and criticize its indeterminability if not its irrelevance.

Finally, on a related note, I shall criticize the overall debate about corporate constitutional rights insofar as its participants have generally failed to appreciate the important, perennial linkage between rights and responsibilities. For recognition of the relationship between rights and responsibilities promises an understanding of these issues that is both more measured and better theorized.

CORPORATE PERSONHOOD

As discussed in chapter 2, changes in corporate theory have largely matched the evolving realities of the corporation. Proceeding simultaneously has been the advance of corporate constitutional rights. Curiously, however, these two phenomena have not closely tracked one another. Recognition of corporate constitutional rights did not readily follow the path that corporate theory cut nor the evolving realities of the corporate form. Instead, these two phenomena have generally operated along their own trajectories, marching to the beat of their own drummers.[1] In fact, for the most part, the development of corporate constitutional rights has largely been untheorized and unmoored to the reality (or understanding) of the corporation itself. This presents a foundational shortcoming of the prevailing approach.

The prevailing approach used to recognize corporate constitutional rights is the concept of "corporate personhood." As the term suggests, "corporate personhood" refers to the law's practice of treating the corporation as a *persona ficta*—an artificial, fictitious person, but a person nonetheless when it comes to the assessment of legal status, rights, and obligations.[2] Via fictitious personhood, the state affirmatively bestows upon certain groups or collectives rights and privileges ordinarily enjoyed by natural persons: among other things, these groups are permitted to "own property, inherit legacies, and appear in legal proceedings."[3]

At the heart of the personhood debate is an almost classic "chicken-or-the-egg" problem: do we recognize corporate personhood merely out of convenience, because it gives us the ability to convey rights and privileges to the corporation? Or, conversely, do we grant right and privileges to the corporation because the corporation rightfully lays claim to some notion of "personhood"?[4]

The latter approach developed in the late Middle Ages in the heart of Europe and is a manifestation of the "real entity theory" of the corporation. As discussed in chapter 2, this approach grew out of Germanic associational theory and the theology of church canonists. Pursuant to this approach, corporations were considered naturally occurring entities and as such were entitled to certain rights and privileges. Corporate personhood, according to this understanding, was a means of recognizing and operationalizing this entitlement.

Those who embrace the former approach (the approach more usually associated with the terms *persona ficta* and "legal fiction") frequently refer to it in conjunction with concessionary theories of the corporation.[5] This is not necessary, but mutually supportive. For if there is nothing "real" about the corporation, if it is merely a legal construct invented for convenience's sake, it is easy to see why the corporation would owe its very existence to the state and its laws. Such an approach generally endorses a minimalist understanding of corporate rights—and, one could say, a minimalist understanding of "corporate personhood." As we have seen, the minimalist understanding of corporate personhood is, arguably, its earliest and most common understanding. This characterizes the approach to the corporation's ancient Roman predecessors—where the concept of fictitious personhood is thought to have first arisen.[6] Over the next two millennia, this concessionary vision of corporate personhood remained the dominant one, and it characterized the common law tradition that the United States inherited from England.[7] This vision served as backdrop to the first U.S. Supreme Court case to consider the question of corporate constitutional rights: *Trustees of Dartmouth College v. Woodward*.[8]

Corporations are nowhere mentioned in the U.S. Constitution. Yet in the 1819 case of *Trustees of Dartmouth College v. Woodward*, within barely a generation of the Constitution's 1789 adoption, the U.S. Supreme Court ruled that at least one of the provisions of the Constitution applied to corporations.[9]

At issue in *Trustees of Dartmouth College* was a state's (New Hampshire's) attempt to unilaterally modify the corporate charter of Dartmouth College.[10] In this case, the Supreme Court articulated its view of the corporation with well-cited words that reflect the entrenchment of concession theory during that era:

> A corporation is an artificial being, invisible, intangible, and existing only in contemplation of law. Being the mere creature of law, it possesses only those properties which the charter of its creation confers upon it, either expressly, or as incidental to its very existence.[11]

With such a view of the corporation, one might have expected the Court to uphold the actions of New Hampshire's legislature against the college's protestations. But the Court did otherwise. Implicated was Section 10 of Article I of the U.S. Constitution, which states: "No State shall . . . pass any . . . Law impairing the Obligations of Contracts."[12] The Court held that the corporation's charter was a contract, and the state's efforts to unilaterally amend the charter amounted to an impermissible impairment of contract in violation of the Constitution.[13] Thus, despite the fact that the corporation was viewed as a mere concession from the sovereign at the time, the Court nevertheless held that the protections of the Constitution (at least the "Contracts Clause" of Article I) applied to it.

The next milestone along the march of corporate constitutional rights was the Court's 1886 case *Santa Clara Co. v. S. Pac. R.R.*[14] Implicated in *Santa Clara* was the Fourteenth Amendment to the U.S. Constitution—an amendment not yet twenty years old, adopted in the wake of the U.S. Civil War. Designed to secure the rights of newly freed slaves, the Fourteenth Amendment declares, in relevant part, that no state shall "deny any person within its jurisdiction the equal protection of the laws."[15] At issue in *Santa Clara* was the propriety of certain taxes that the state of California had sought to assess against a railroad corporation. The railroad claimed, among other things, that these taxes violated the Fourteenth Amendment.

By the time of *Santa Clara*, a very different view of the corporation had taken hold, displacing the artificial entity/concession theory. This was the "aggregate" view of the corporation, pursuant to which it can be said that the "corporation" does not really exist at all.[16] Under this view, the moniker "corporation" is merely a helpful way of referring to an aggregation of individuals. In other words, what we call a "corporation" is essentially an association, or a partnership—an entity that has no identity of its own aside from that of its individual members.[17] When it comes to an assessment of corporate rights, aggregation theory suggests looking past the corporate form and seeing the individuals themselves.

With this as backdrop, it is perhaps not surprising that the *Santa Clara* decision marked another step forward in the recognition of corporate constitutional rights. But the precise interplay between corporate (aggregation) theory and applicable (constitutional) law is difficult to discern. For the Court, without explanation or any further elucidation, revealed its position on the matter in just two short sentences. During the oral argument of the case, Chief Justice Waite remarked to counsel:

> The Court does not wish to hear argument on the question whether the provision in the Fourteenth Amendment to the Constitution, which forbids a State to deny to any person within its jurisdiction the equal protection of the laws applies to these corporations. We are all of the opinion that it does.[18]

Santa Clara opened the floodgates with regard to the rights of corporations: if corporations are deemed "persons" for purposes of the Fourteenth Amendment, for what other purposes can they be considered "persons" under the U.S. Constitution? Moreover, thanks to the doctrine of "incorporation" (a most unfortunate term in this context as it has nothing to do with corporate chartering), many of the rights set forth in the Bill of Rights to the U.S. Constitution are "incorporated" into the Fourteenth Amendment and applicable not only to the federal government (as originally conceived) but to every state government as well.[19] For these reasons, the significance of *Santa Clara* is difficult to overestimate.

Thus, as would be expected, the Supreme Court has recognized other rights enshrined in the U.S. Constitution as applicable to business corporations in the years since *Santa Clara*.[20] As with the *Santa Clara* decision, this has generally occurred without reference to corporate theory and without regard to changes in thinking about the corporation as an entity. Although the predominant conceptualization of the corporation shifted from aggregation theory, to real entity theory, to the property model, and, finally, to the contractarianism of today,[21] the march toward greater recognition of corporation constitutional rights proceeded rather steadily—and increasingly without any reference to such theoretical conceptualizations.[22]

One might have expected the concept of corporate personhood, and the rights associated therewith, to manifest itself differently depending upon an era's overall understanding of the corporation. For example, the apogee of corporate personhood might logically be expected in the concession-theory era, when the corporation was seen as nothing other than a legal fiction. Or, perhaps, during the current period of contractarianism, pursuant to which there is no independent "corporation," but rather simply a nexus of contracts referred to as an entity for the sake of convenience.

Similarly, the apex of corporate personhood might logically be expected in the real entity era, when the corporation was seen as a naturally occurring feature of human society. But this has not been the case. As Michael Phillips has observed: "Historically, there seem to be few clear links between the real entity theory and the emergence of corporate legal rights."[23] Similarly, given the movement away from real entity theory, through the property rights era, to the modern contractarian conceptualization, one might have expected the idea of corporate personhood to wane. After all, the movement from a naturally occurring real entity, to private property, to the nothingness of a nexus, would suggest a move away from the personalization of the corporation—a move away from notions of corporate personhood (and, concomitantly, corporate rights). But this is not what happened. Instead, the robustness of corporate personhood (and the accretion of corporate constitutional rights and protections) has waxed largely unabated.

An explanation for this phenomenon is possible. Whereas the changes in corporate theory were pegged to changing corporate realities, changes in the Court's treatment of the corporation were pegged primarily to changing understandings of the U.S. Constitution.[24] The period of ascendency for corporate rights occurred within the same period during which the Supreme Court increasingly read the U.S. Constitution to protect economic interests generally. This development need not be, and apparently was not, related to the realities of the corporate form or the nuances of corporate theory.

This explanation would also help illuminate why the advance of corporate rights and personhood continued throughout the managerial (private property) era—a time when corporate theorizing was basically dormant. As Elizabeth Pollman explains, "the twentieth century staged a significant expansion of corporate rights" but without articulating "a coherent concept of corporate personhood."[25] Although, during the first half of the managerial era, when the corporation was deemed little more than the private property of its owners, the Supreme Court would occasionally make mention of corporate theory in its decisions regarding corporate rights, by 1960 the Supreme

Court avoided such discussions altogether.[26] By 1960, it had become quite clear that the Court's focus was on the Constitution and the particular constitutional right in question—not on corporate theory.[27] This focus is on full display in the Supreme Court decision *Citizens United v. FEC*, examined more fully in chapter 6.[28]

In *Citizens United*, the Court held that the First Amendment's prohibition on government efforts to abridge speech applied to corporate speech as well as the speech of individuals.[29] As such, the Court declared unconstitutional the McCain-Feingold Bipartisan Campaign Finance Reform Act of 2002. As with many of its predecessors, the *Citizens United* decision was promulgated with nary a reference to corporate theory.[30] Nowhere in the decision does the Court (in an opinion authored by Justice Kennedy) invoke a conceptualization of the corporation, or address the nature of the corporation. Instead, the Court's analysis focuses solely on the First Amendment to the Constitution and its limitations on congressional power.[31]

The lengthy dissent, authored by Justice Stevens, argued in favor of the act's validity on a number of grounds.[32] Stevens, however, not only failed to invoke a conceptualization of the corporation but explicitly disavowed the importance of theory altogether:

> Nothing in this analysis turns on whether the corporation is conceptualized as a grantee of a state concession, *see, e.g., Trustees of Dartmouth College v. Woodward*, 4 Wheat. 518, 636, 4 L. Ed. 629 (1819) (Marshall, C. J.), a nexus of explicit and implicit contracts, *see, e.g.*, F. Easterbrook & D. Fischel, The Economic Structure of Corporate Law 12 (1991), a mediated hierarchy of stakeholders, *see, e.g.*, Blair & Stout, *A Team Production Theory of Corporate Law*, 85 VA. L. REV. 247 (1999) (hereinafter Blair & Stout), or any other recognized model.[33]

Thus, in *Citizens United*, we are treated to a discussion of the First Amendment's applicability to corporations, entirely devoid of any serious analysis of the theoretical nature of corporations.

Admittedly, corporate law and constitutional law are two distinct fields. The focus of constitutional law is on the powers (and limitations) of the U.S. federal government, and, via the Fourteenth Amendment, certain limitations on state and local governments as well. By contrast, corporate law and theory focuses on the fundamental powers and structure of a private entity—the corporation. Further, the concerns of corporate law are not so much with relations between the corporation and the outside world, but rather with relations intrinsic to the corporation. Even with this acknowledgment, however, one would be reasonable in expecting that developments in one field would at the very least influence the other. After all, how society structures and conceptualizes the corporation would seem to bear upon the question of what a corporation is and how it ought to be treated under the U.S. Constitution. Thus, there is something incongruous with the Supreme Court granting the twenty-first-century business corporation rights and privileges beyond those possessed by any such enterprise in history during the very era in which the corporation is understood to be little more than a nexus of contracts. Developments in one field need not drive developments in the other, but they should, at a minimum, be acknowledged and addressed. In short, some cross-pollination is long overdue. By evaluating corporate constitutional rights in light of evolving corporate realities, a more justifiable approach toward corporate constitutional adjudication can be established.

PURELY PERSONAL RIGHTS

In contrast to the approach taken when the language of corporate personhood is invoked, there is the "purely personal rights" approach to constitutional adjudication. In the Supreme Court, this approach seems to have received its first serious articulation in *United States v. White*.[34]

The Court in *White* was confronted with a labor union that invoked the Fifth Amendment right against self-incrimination in an effort to withhold the production of documents in response to a subpoena. The Court ruled against the union, holding that the Fifth Amendment right against self-incrimination was inapplicable to "any organization." In so doing the Court provided as an example the corporation.

This was not coincidental: precedent had already established that the corporation could not invoke the Fifth Amendment.[35] But that precedent had been based on notions of the state's "visitatorial" powers.[36] In *White*, however, a different rationale was employed: the rationale that some rights, such as the right against self-incrimination, are "personal" in that they apply "only to natural individuals."[37] As the Court explained:

> The constitutional privilege against self-incrimination is essentially a personal one, applying only to natural individuals. It grows out of the high sentiment and regard of our jurisprudence for conducting criminal trials and investigatory proceedings upon a plane of dignity, humanity and impartiality. It is designed to prevent the use of legal process to force from the lips of the accused individual the evidence necessary to convict him or to force him to produce and authenticate any personal documents or effects that might incriminate him. Physical torture and other less violent but equally reprehensible modes of compelling the production of incriminating evidence are thereby avoided. The prosecutors are forced to search for independent evidence instead of relying upon proof extracted from individuals by force of law.[38]

Decades later, the Supreme Court picked up upon the language of purely personal rights again, this time in the case *First National Bank of Boston v. Bellotti*.[39] The Court in *Bellotti* noted that in two contexts, constitutional rights were deemed "purely personal" and hence unavailable to the corporation: the Fifth Amendment right against self-incrimination and the "right to privacy."[40] In an effort to flesh out the "purely personal" rule, the Court declared:

> Whether or not a particular guarantee is "purely personal" or is unavailable to corporations for some other reason depends on the nature, history, and purpose of the particular constitutional provision.[41]

Since *Bellotti*, however, the Court has not frequently invoked the "purely personal" rights theory, and the last time it did so was nearly a quarter of a century ago.[42] Indeed, in its most recent pronouncement on corporate constitutional rights, *Citizens United v. FEC*, no justice on the Court, in the majority, concurrence, or dissent, referred to this concept—despite addressing the weighty issue of corporate First Amendment rights.[43]

Admittedly, some lower courts have continued to invoke the "purely personal" standard, most recently the Third Circuit Court of Appeals in *Conestoga Wood Specialties Corp. v. Secretary of the Department of Health and Human Services*.[44] This case concerned corporate invocation of the Free Exercise Clause and will be discussed in more detail in chapter 7. What the Third Circuit failed to recognize, however, is that the Free Exercise Clause, along with the other First Amendment rights addressed herein, has already been extended to groups and organizations. To argue that somehow these freedoms are "purely personal," and can only be asserted by individuals, ignores several decades of established case law, in which various groups have successfully invoked these freedoms. Thus, it appears as though the "purely personal" test for assessing the applicability of corporate constitutional rights could not be used to deny the First Amendment rights of speech, religion, and association to the business corporation. Further, as has been explained, it appears as though the Supreme Court has little appetite in adverting to this test in the context of the First Amendment.

CORPORATE RIGHTS AND RESPONSIBILITIES

To the extent that courts can be criticized for disregarding corporate theory in their corporate jurisprudence, commentators can similarly be criticized for failing to acknowledge the connection between corporate rights and responsibilities. Like two ships passing in the night, scholarship extolling the virtues of corporate constitutional rights and scholarship extolling the virtues of corporate social responsibility have seldom interacted with one another. This too must change.

At their core, the concepts of corporate social responsibility (CSR) and of corporate constitutional rights both implicate the role of the business corporation in our society. Further, both involve a certain humanization of the corporation. As just discussed, the very concept of rights and privileges is so closely tethered to human beings that, when rights and privileges are extended to corporations, they are done so under the rubric of corporate "personhood." Conversely, when they are denied the corporation, until recently it has been pursuant to a theory that the rights are "purely personal" in nature. Similar thinking can be found in discussion of social responsibility. We don't treat plants, animals, and machines as morally culpable agents, because they lack the central feature of moral agency: the free will that marks human nature. Thus, we do not chide a cow for being socially irresponsible in its flatulent release of carbon dioxide gas into the atmosphere, or a tree for falling on someone's house. Given these important commonalities, any discussion of corporate rights without reference to corporate responsibilities, or of corporate responsibilities without reference to corporate rights, is incomplete.[45]

The Implications of Corporate Social Responsibility

As has been discussed in chapter 3, corporations are under increasing pressure to conduct themselves in socially responsible ways. By "socially responsible," I refer to salutary practices that go beyond the minimal requirements of law. Many have embraced these calls, some willingly, some begrudgingly.

In the latter category of companies would be those for which social responsibility is mere window dressing—little more than a ploy to curry favor with socially sensitive employees, customers, investors, and citizens. Such corporations will safely commit to the bare minimum of socially acceptable behavior necessary to create and maintain their image as a responsible corporation. They will approach social responsibility like all other business decisions—through the lens of cost-benefit analysis. Such companies will generally not be leaders in the field of CSR, but rather will follow public opinion when pressure demands that they do so. Due to market forces, practically every corporation has adopted, at a minimum, this form of CSR—including those I have referred to as modern corporations.

Although for some companies, even this minimalist embrace of CSR would be an improvement upon the status quo, it is not exactly the form of social responsibility that has inspired the CSR movement. What advocates of CSR yearn for are companies willing to do the right thing even when it might not be the most cost-effective choice; companies that abstain from misconduct not only when public opinion demands as much but also when the public is not even watching. As discussed in chapter 3, the postmodern corporation provides an example of such a company.

CSR advocates have encountered significant difficulty in philosophically justifying the position that a corporation bears social responsibilities. Many have invoked a "stakeholder model" of the corporation in support of their arguments, itself a proposition that has been difficult to justify, and one the articulation of which has varied from proponent to proponent.[46] Although the stakeholder model and CSR have often been linked, I suggest that the relationship between the two can be overstated.

Under the stakeholder model of the corporation, directors must operate the business for the benefit of all its various stakeholder groups. This varies dramatically with the prevailing approach, pursuant to which shareholder primacy (operationalized as profit maximization) is the touchstone of corporate decision making. The theory is premised upon the notion that since all of a corporation's various stakeholder groups contribute to the corporation's success (or failure), fairness and justice demands that the interests of all such groups be considered (and furthered) by the board of directors (whether equally or in varying degrees proportional to their contribution to the corporation).[47] Another justification often advanced in support of the model is that it is in the best long-term interests of the corporation as a whole (and thus in the best long-term interests of corporate shareholders) for directors to consider the interests of all corporate stakeholders.[48] As becomes readily apparent, however, this second justification essentially folds the stakeholder model into the shareholder model[49] and evades the more difficult question of what a board's obligations ought to be in the situation where there is an intractable divergence of interests between shareholders and other stakeholders.

Another common feature among proponents of the stakeholder model is a shared, practical critique of the shareholder wealth maximization norm as deleterious to the interests of other stakeholders and of society as a whole.[50] This certainly sounds like a page from the gospel of CSR, but an important gap must be acknowledged. Unless considered quite broadly, the list of corporate stakeholders is limited, usually consisting of investors, employees, customers, and the local community. Thus, as has been touched upon in our previous discussion of CSR in chapter 3, the stakeholder model essential proposes replacing the private interests of one particular group (the shareholders) with the combined private interests of a number of particular groups. A genuine commitment to society, however, would best be demonstrated via a commitment to the common good, and not merely a collection of certain private interests (even if broadened to include constituencies heretofore excluded via the shareholder primacy norm). For this reason, one ought not to conflate CSR with the stakeholder model. That said, the stakeholder model certainly represents a step in the right direction (if one considers movement toward the socially responsible corporation to be the right direction).

Although, as set forth above, there is some consensus among stakeholder theorists with regard to what a board of directors ought to be doing with regard to nonshareholder stakeholders (and why it ought to be doing it), there is apparently little consensus on the nature of the corporation itself.[51] Some stakeholder theorists continue to view the corporation as a bona fide entity (often referring to it as a "community") and not merely an artificial theoretical legal construct. To many of these theorists, what corporate law needs to do is recognize "the property rights of [all] stakeholders over corporate assets and their functioning," and not simply the property rights of shareholders.[52] Others, while still apparently maintaining a vision of the corporation as an entity, nevertheless contest the claim that the modern shareholder can be conceived of as its "owner" in any real sense given the fact that "from a practical perspective, shareholders ... do not resemble traditional owners."[53]

Many stakeholder theorists (most, perhaps) have adopted the "nexus of contracts" model of the corporation.[54] This is not surprising, as viewing the corporation in this way can seriously undermine the notion of shareholder primacy. As Jill Fisch has aptly noted, "[d]escribing the corporation as shareholder property is a powerful rhetorical device, because property rights convey a sense of absolutism."[55] Displacing this older model via acceptance of the contractarian approach would seem, therefore, to benefit the stakeholder and CSR movements.

But the contractarian characterization has its own difficulties to if one wishes to impose upon the corporation social responsibilities. For if the corporation is a mere nexus of contracts, a convenient fiction, from whence would "its" duties arise?

If one takes yet another approach, and reverts to a real entity model of the corporation, he or she runs into the common philosophical objection that only actual human beings can be said to possess moral agency.[56] Consequently, in line with this perspective, perhaps the best that can be argued is that the obligations of CSR are little more than the independent, personal obligations of the individuals who make up the firm (its shareholders, directors, officers, and employees). In other words, the moral obligations that these individuals personally possess carry over to the corporation(s) with which they interact. When we speak of CSR, therefore, we are really referencing the personal responsibility of these various human beings. Pursuant to this line of thinking, the corporation *itself* would lack moral agency.[57] A morally questionable "corporate" decision is the moral responsibility of the individuals who made that decision (along with those who supported it) and not the responsibility of the corporation per se. Indeed, it has often been observed that a corporation has "no body to kick and no soul to damn."[58]

This is, of course, not how CSR has generally proceeded. When a corporation morally errs, the corporation itself is ordinarily the target of castigation—much more so than the list of individuals who are responsible (causally, at least) for the corporation's (mis)conduct. Thus, without resolving the question of the responsibility's origin, we can confidently observe that the advocates of CSR generally ascribe this responsibility to the corporate entity itself. They maintain that the corporation, directly, bears certain responsibilities to society as a whole. As such, a corporation that acts inappropriately commonly becomes the target of a boycott, but its officers and directors largely remain unknown and unaccountable.

Regardless of the difficulties that CSR advocates have had in getting corporations to behave in a more social responsible fashion and in offering a convincing philosophical justification for their advocacy, their argument that corporations are moral creatures with moral responsibilities and therefore subject to moral praise or opprobrium has indeed resonated with the public[59] and received some philosophical support as well (including, perhaps most notably, Peter French's).[60] The repercussions of this perspective are significant. To the degree that the corporation possesses certain social responsibilities, the corporation is being endowed with moral agency. For it makes no sense to attach morally laden terms such as "responsibility" to an entity lacking moral agency.

Further, once moral agency and moral obligations are attributed to the corporation, we have an entity that is, in important respects, more human than not. Assuredly, corporations lack a variety of human characteristics. That said, in the corporation beholden to social responsibility we have an actor with both the capacity and duty to make morally significant decisions.[61] At least in this respect, it can be said that the corporation has been created in the image of man.[62]

Concomitant with such capacities and duties should flow the liberty to exercise them.[63] It has long been understood that actors must have those freedoms necessary to fulfill their moral obligations, for "ought implies can."[64] Thus, to the extent that we laden business corporations with moral obligations, we must grant them the liberty necessary to discharge these obligations. This understanding has ramifications with regard to the corporation's treatment under the U.S. Constitution (and, indeed, the constitutions of most nations).[65]

The precise contours of the "liberty necessary" for corporations are difficult to define. It is beyond the scope of this book to articulate exactly which constitutional rights a corporation ought to possess and which ones it ought not to possess. Our focus is on the First Amendment alone. That said, as a general proposition, the more we expect from corporations in terms of social responsibility, the more ought to be granted to them in terms of constitutional rights and protections. The more we welcome corporations as contributors to a society beyond the simple production of goods and supply of services, the more we should bestow upon them the freedoms that other contributors to society enjoy. This basic point was grasped by Thomas Donaldson over three decades ago, in his book *Corporations and Morality*:

> What is the moral status of a corporation? Is it, common as the legal metaphor suggests, an "invisible person"? Or does it more closely resemble an impersonal machine, geared toward generating rules, procedures, and profits? If corporations are moral agents as are persons, then we must demand that they assume the burdens of morality just as people do, and that they develop something akin to consciences. If they are like persons, then they should also have the rights that people have: to own property, to conclude contracts, and to exercise freedom of speech, even when it means using their vast financial reserves to promote personal political views.[66]

The converse is true as well: the more rights and privileges that corporations are held to possess, the more society should be able to expect from them in terms of socially responsible behavior.

Interestingly, in the opening decades of the twenty-first century, both the CSR movement and the recognition of constitutional rights appear to be cresting together. More than ever before, businesses are expected to be responsible corporate citizens. In the wake of *Citizens United*, never before have corporations enjoyed such extensive constitutional rights.

For the reasons discussed, this is sensible and mutually reinforcing. Yet, ironically, most commentators do not see it that way. Those who advocate greater CSR generally decry the *Citizens United* decision, and those who champion the *Citizens United* decision generally dismiss CSR.

This can probably best be explained by the general ideological and political predispositions of such advocates and turns on worldviews that go well beyond an assessment of the corporation per se. To be blunt, CSR is generally considered to further values and objectives cherished by those on the political Left, and corporate constitutional rights (especially the right to freedom of speech) are generally considered to further values and objectives cherished by those on the political Right. Not surprisingly, therefore, neither political camp is eager to grant or concede a proposition of value to its opposition. Although I take serious issue with this assessment of how CSR and corporate speech break down politically, it does, I suggest, accurately reflect the common perspective.

Only by casting aside such ends-oriented thinking and by focusing closely on the corporation and its nature (rather than on social justice or the role of government, for example) does this linkage between rights and responsibility become apparent.

Certainly, some commentators have recognized this perennial connection.[67] Philosopher John Ladd, for example, has openly acknowledged that the imposition of moral duties upon a corporation is suggestive of moral rights.[68] As he opposes vesting corporations with the moral rights of individuals, he has, with virtuous consistency, argued that a corporation's responsibilities "should be exhausted by their legal responsibility."[69] In short, he has abandoned the supralegal responsibilities of CSR out of recognition of what this portends with regard to the question of corporate rights.

Proceeding to the same conclusion from the opposite direction is Christopher Slobogin, who has considered the implications of corporate First Amendment rights upon corporate criminal liability.[70] The concept of corporate criminal liability has long been a contested one, with many arguing that although certain officers, directors, and employees of a corporation should fairly be held criminally liability for corporate misconduct, the corporate entity itself should not.[71] There are multiple reasons for adhering to this view, the most germane of which, for our purposes, is the belief that the corporation could not possess the free will, and therefore the moral blameworthiness, required for a criminal conviction (at least with regard to crimes in which intent is an element).[72] As Slobogin points out, "that argument makes less sense after *Citizens United*."[73] For *Citizens United* endorses a view of the corporation that (in the words of another commentator) "substantively distinguishe[s] [it] from its owner, managers and employees by its capacity to express independent moral judgments in the discourse of the public square."[74] Slobogin concludes that "an entity that has political will," such that it "must be allowed to participate in the 'marketplace of ideas,'" will also have "free will," and thus can be held subject to criminal liability.[75]

It must be noted that many have argued that corporations are already endowed with a panoply of special rights, and these alone support the imposition of special responsibilities (in the form of CSR) upon the corporation. They point primarily to the fact that corporations enjoy limited liability and assert that this particular privilege, without more, requires that society demands more from its corporate citizens. As one commentator summarized this position: "corporations, which owe their very existence, including such identifying characteristics as limited liability, to society, must therefore also owe a reciprocal duty to nonshareholders."[76]

In response, I freely admit that I have not worked out the precise calibration of rights to responsibilities. In other words, I do not presume to know what particular basket of rights should yield a particular basket of responsibilities, and vice versa. I simply suggest that these two baskets should generally be filled or emptied together; their weight should be directly proportionate to one another.

That said, this particular argument in support of CSR evinces adherence to a concessionary view of the corporation: the theory that the corporation is merely a creature of the state, and as such owes its existence to the state. Concession theory supports assertions on the part of the state to define, with broad latitude, the rights and obligations of the corporation. As discussed in chapter 2, concession theory has long been abandoned by the vast majority of corporate law scholars and commentators. And for good reason: with the advent of statues of general incorporation, the ability of individuals to incorporate their business ventures increasingly took on the feel of a right rather than a concession.[77] Consequently, limited liability itself has come to be seen as more of a right, rather than a privilege. Perhaps a century or two ago this was viewed differently, but given developments since then, along with present realities, it strikes me as unconvincing to predicate a relatively modern imposition of new corporate responsibilities (in the form of CSR) upon the long-standing possession of a fundamental corporate feature—whether it be characterized as a "privilege" or a "right" (namely, limited liability).

Social Responsibility as Expression

The linkage between rights and responsibilities reinforces the dichotomy between modern and postmodern corporations that has run throughout this book. Recall that the modern corporation is fixated on profit maximization, and as such eschews any commitment to values and beliefs that would interfere with this fixation. In service to profit maximization, the modern corporation may adopt a patina of principle and behave in an ostensibly responsible manner to the extent that the market demands that it do so. Few would equate this with genuine corporate social responsibility.

The postmodern corporation, however, is the poster child of the CSR movement. The postmodern corporation authentically embraces principles that guide corporate conduct, even to the point of impeding true profit maximization. This embrace is, essentially, a form of expression and further supports the linkage of corporate rights with corporate responsibilities. Regardless of what other constitutional rights ought to be afforded the socially responsible corporation, the "expressive" rights of the First Amendment (freedom of speech, religion, and association) should certainly seem to be among them. For in order to adhere to these principles, postmodern corporations will often desire, and at times require, the protections of the First Amendment.

For example, consider a corporation that recognizes and takes seriously an obligation to pay its workers an appropriate wage. How can such a corporation realistically do this if it must compete with companies whose products are manufactured overseas via child labor? Consider also a corporation dedicated to the environment, that internalizes the costs of pollution by utilizing more expensive production methods that diminish the environmental impact of its activities. How can such a corporation long endure if its competitors externalize these same costs by polluting up to the legal limits? In both cases, the goods and services of the responsible corporation are likely to be priced out of the market. Without some governmental action, ranging from tightened standards to better product labeling, the corporation's responsible business model may not be viable. In order to do what is right—and to survive while doing it—corporations will oftentimes need to involve the political process and lobby for industry-wide standards and/or international agreements.

Consider next the corporation that wishes to sell only those products known to be safe. Perhaps the corporation is a toy company, and it scrupulously avoids the use of materials associated with health problems in children. Over the years, through its own research and its study of independent research, the corporation has developed significant expertise regarding child safety and the health hazards of certain manufacturing components. Would a "socially responsible" corporation such as this company sit idly by if the government were about to permit the use of, or relax a restriction on, a chemical or substance known by the company to be unsafe? Should the company's opposition be limited to correspondence and lobbying, or should it be able to take its concerns to the public directly, out in the open via political speech? I think the answer is clear: part of being socially responsible would include recourse to the political process, to inform public opinion and influence the promulgation of law and regulation. As experts in their respective fields, responsible corporations should weigh in on controversies over which they are well informed and have developed strong opinions. Efforts to silence such corporations—or otherwise restrict their ability to influence public policy—inhibits these corporations from having the impact that they should want to have and that society would benefit from.

Finally, consider the practice of corporate charitable giving, a typical way of demonstrating good corporate citizenship. Although many charities and nonprofit organizations are benign and noncontroversial, one person's charity may be another person's political cause. Take, for example, the Planned Parenthood Federation of America (Planned Parenthood), or the Boy Scouts of America. Each of these organizations receives millions of dollars in corporate donations, yet many individuals react strongly to each of these groups. When the Susan G. Komen Foundation, itself a nonprofit charity focused on battling breast cancer, decided to cut its contributions to Planned Parenthood in 2012, a political firestorm erupted.[78] This decision was viewed by some as no mere reallocation of charitable giving, but rather as a dramatic political statement.[79] And although not every donation is as controversial as one made (or not made) to Planned Parenthood, a political or controversial angle can be found to many.

Moreover, the same can be said for a large number of business decisions. Consider decisions to grant or deny employee benefits to unmarried domestic partners, or to purchase parts and supplies from foreign companies known to violate domestic standards regarding child labor. Could not these choices, however they are made, be deemed to some "socially responsible," to others "political," and to still others "strictly business"?

Corporate activity is subject to various interpretations. One such interpretation is the mechanistic, amoral one: the corporation is a mere legal fiction that exists to maximize profits for the benefit of its shareholders. In the terms of Aristotelian logic, such a corporation is "good" if it succeeds in this undertaking and "bad" if it fails.[80] Other considerations are secondary—if not irrelevant. This exemplifies the modern corporation.

The postmodern corporation, with its embrace of CSR, challenges this view. This is because CSR speaks of the corporation in distinctly moral terms—using "good" and "bad" in their more traditional senses, and not merely in reference to the corporation's profitability. This humanizes the corporation, endows it with moral and ethical obligations. To the extent that a corporation accepts these obligations, it has become politicized in the classical sense of the term—for politics "is generally understood as the fight over whose views and values should prevail in the allocation of scarce societal resources, the struggle over who receives various social benefits and who bears the costs."[81] Once so politicized, and thereby invited into the public square, it becomes inconsistent and counterproductive to deny the corporation those rights that are essential to its participation in the public square and to the maintenance of its particular identity. Although not every right that a natural human being possesses should be bestowed upon the socially responsible corporation, certainly those that can be reasonably associated with the associational nature of such entities should be.

NOTES

1. *See* David Graver, *Personal Bodies: A Corporeal Theory of Corporate Personhood*, 6 U. CHI. L. SCH. ROUNDTABLE 235, 236 (1999). *But see* Stephen G. Wood & Brett G. Scharffs, *Applicability of Human Rights Standards to Private Corporations: An American Perspective*, 50 AM. J. COMP. L. 531, 540–41 (2002). Wood and Scharffs argue that "the choice of theory affects the content and scope of rights and duties assigned to the corporation." *Id.* at 540. I acknowledge that how a corporation is theorized can influence the rights that are granted to the corporation. Indeed, I believe that it should influence the question of rights. I observe, however, that the historical linkage between theory and rights is a weak one at best. Thus, I disagree with Wood and Scharffs' assertion that the "content and scope of the rights and duties of corporations have developed over the years in response to evolving theoretical understandings of the nature of the corporate persona." *Id.* at 541.
2. John Dewey, *The Historic Background of Corporate Legal Personality*, 35 YALE L. J. 655, 668–69 (1926).
3. André M. Peñalver, *Corporate Disconnect: The Blackwater Problem and the FCPA Solution*, 19 CORNELL J.L. & PUB. POL'Y 459, 475 (2010).

4. *See* Gregory A. Mark, *The Personification of the Business Corporation in American Law*, 54 U. Chi. L. Rev. 1441, 1469 (1987).
5. *See id.*
6. *See* Mary Szto, *Limited Liability Company Morality, Fiduciary Duties in Historical Context*, 23 Q.L.R. 61, 108 (2004).
7. *See* Susanna K. Ripken, *Corporations Are People Too: A Multi-Dimensional Approach to the Corporate Personhood Puzzle*, 15 Fordham J. Corp. & Fin. L. 97, 107–108 (2009).
8. 17 U.S. 518 (1819).
9. *Id.* at 638.
10. *Id.* at 558.
11. *Id.* at 636.
12. U.S. Const. art. I, §10.
13. 17 U.S. at 654.
14. 118 U.S. 394, 396 (1886).
15. U.S. Const. amend. XIV, §1.
16. *See* Ripken, *supra* note 7, at 109–111.
17. *Id.*
18. Santa Clara Co., 118 U.S. at 396.
19. Laurence H. Tribe, American Constitutional Law 772 (1988).
20. Wood & Scharffs, *supra* note 1, at 540–41 (setting forth constitutional rights recognized by the U.S. Supreme Court as applicable to business corporations).
21. *See* Michael J. Phillips, *Reappraising the Real Entity Theory of the Corporation*, 21 Fla. St. U. L. Rev. 1061, 1063–73 (1994).
22. *See* Graver, *supra* note 1, at 236; *but see* Wood & Scharffs, *supra* note 1, 540–41.
23. *See* Phillips, *supra* note 21, at 1098.
24. *See* Tribe, *supra* note 19, at 567–74 (discussing the *Lochner* era of constitutional interpretation).
25. Elizabeth Pollman, *Reconceiving Corporate Personhood*, 2011 Utah L. Rev. 1629, 1647 (2011).
26. *See* Graver, *supra* note 1, at 240.
27. *See* Elizabeth Salisbury Warren, *The Case for Applying the Eight Amendment to Corporations*, 49 Vand. L. Rev. 1313, 1320 (1996).
28. 558 U.S. 310 (2010).
29. *Id.*
30. *See* Amy J. Sepinwall, *Citizens United and the Ineluctable Question of Corporate Citizenship*, 44 Conn. L. Rev. 575, 578 (2012).
31. *See Citizens United*, 558 U.S. at 336–37.
32. *See id.* at 929 *et seq.*
33. *Id.* at 871 n.72.
34. 322 U.S. 694, 698 (1944).
35. *See id.* (citing Hale v. Henkel, 201 U.S. 43 (1906); Wilson v. United States, 221 U.S. 361 (1911); Essgee Co. v. United States, 262 U.S. 151 (1923)).
36. Wilson v. United States, 221 U.S. 361, 379 (1911).
37. *See* 322 U.S. at 698.
38. *Id.*
39. 435 U.S. 765, 778 n.14 (1978).
40. *Id.*
41. *Id.*
42. Baltimore City Dept. of Soc. Svcs. v. Bouknight, 493 U.S. 549, 566–67 (1990).

43. 558 U.S. 310 (2010).
44. Conestoga Wood Specialties Corp. v. U.S. Sec'y of Dep't of Health and Human Servs., 724 F.3d 377, 383 (3d Cir. 2013).
45. I first articulated my belief that corporate rights should be linked to corporate responsibilities in Ronald J. Colombo, *Rights and Responsibilities of the American Business Corporation, in* BUSINESS AND HUMAN RIGHTS (Manoj Kumar Sinha ed., SAGE 2013).
46. *See* Lisa Fairfax, *The Rhetoric of Corporate Law: The Impact of Stakeholder Rhetoric on Corporate Norms*, 31 J. CORP. L. 675, 679 (2006).
47. *See* Roberta S. Karmel, *Implications of the Stakeholder Model*, 61 GEO. WASH. L. REV. 1156, 1171 (1993).
48. *See* ROBERT CHARLES CLARK, CORPORATE LAW 689 (1986).
49. *See id.*
50. *See id.* at 688–89.
51. *Cf.* David Millon, *Communitarianism in Corporate Law: Foundations and Law Reform Strategies, in* PROGRESSIVE CORPORATE LAW 12–13 (Lawrence E. Mitchell ed., 1995).
52. Lynne L. Dallas, *Working Toward a New Paradigm, in* PROGRESSIVE CORPORATE LAW 37 (Lawrence E. Mitchell ed., 1995); *see also* Jeff Gates, *Reengineering Ownership for the Common Good, in* RETHINKING THE PURPOSE OF BUSINESS 281 (S. A. Cortright & Michael J. Naughton eds., 2002) ("[A]s human capital becomes the most valued asset in a business organization, it makes no sense to limit ownership to those who provide financial capital"); Stephen M. Bainbridge, *Interpreting Nonshareholder Constituency Statutes*, 19 PEPP. L. REV. 971, 972–73 (1992) ("Dodd... saw shareholders as absentee owners whose interests can be subjugated to those of other corporate constituencies and those of society at large.").
53. Jill E. Fisch, *Measuring Efficiency in Corporate Law: The Role of Shareholder Primacy*, 31 J. CORP. L. 637, 649 (2006). Consider, for example, that a large number of shareholders own shares in mutual funds, which in turn may invest in other mutual funds—in short, the connection between the shareholder and the specific corporation he or she ultimately "owns" can easily be several steps removed. *Cf.* Karmel, *supra* note 47, at 1158.
54. *See* Ronald M. Green, *Shareholders as Stakeholders: Changing Metaphors of Corporate Governance*, 50 WASH. & LEE L. REV. 1409, 1415–17 (1993); Millon, *supra* note 51, at 16–19; Lee A. Tavis, *Modern Contract Theory and the Purpose of the Firm, in* RETHINKING THE PURPOSE OF BUSINESS 216, 218 (S. A. Cortright & Michael J. Naughton eds., 2002); Bainbridge, *supra* note 52, at 1006–1007.
55. Fisch, *supra* note 53, at 649.
56. *See* Michael B. Metzger & Dan R. Dalton, *Seeing the Elephant: An Organizational Perspective on Corporate Moral Agency*, 33 AM. BUS. L. J. 489, 492 (1996); "Collective Responsibility," STANFORD ENCYCLOPEDIA OF PHILOSOPHY (June 14, 2010), *available at* http://plato.stanford.edu/entries/collective-responsibility/.
57. *See* Ripken, *supra* note 7, at 120.
58. Thermatool Corp. v. Department of Revenue Services, 651 A.2d 763 (Conn. Super. Ct. 1994).
59. *See* THOMAS DONALDSON, CORPORATIONS & MORALITY 1 (1982). It is beyond the scope of this chapter to explain the philosophical arguments for and against corporate moral agency. For an excellent discussion thereof, *see* Ripken, *supra* note 7, at 119–30. For present purposes, I simply point out that the language and logic of the CSR movement assume corporate moral agency.

60. *See* Kenneth E. Goodpaster & John B. Matthews Jr., *Can a Corporation Have a Conscience?*, 60 HARV. BUS. REV. 132 (1982); Metzger & Dalton, *supra* note 56, at 527–38.
61. *See* DONALDSON, *supra* note 59, at 21. An important component of moral agency is the existence of intentionality—that is, the ability of an actor to intend that which he/she/it does. *See id.* Because corporate decision making is a complicated phenomenon (as is all group decision making), the question of corporate intentionality is an exceedingly difficult one. *See id.* In these short pages I do not purport to "prove" that the corporation actually possesses moral agency. Rather, I simply endeavor to point out that our society (and especially the CSR movement) certainly seems to have embraced this position. *See id.*
62. *See id.* at 3.
63. *But see id.* at 30. Donaldson distinguishes "moral agency" from "moral personhood," concluding that although some corporations might be "moral agents," none are "moral persons." *Id.* I sidestep this important distinction by adverting to the modesty of my argument: I do not suggest that corporations are, philosophically speaking, "persons," nor that they should be afforded all the rights and privileges that flesh-and-blood persons enjoy. Instead, I suggest that the degree to which we hold corporations morally accountable ought to inform the level of rights and protections we afford them.
64. *See* DONALDSON, *supra* note 59, at 25 ("[N]o entity should be held responsible for behavior unless it can control its behavior"); AUSTIN FAGOTHEY, RIGHT AND REASON 166 (2d ed. 1959) (reprinted 2000).
65. It is interesting to note that John Rawls included corporations, alongside churches and individuals, as entities occupying the "original position" in his work *A Theory of Justice*. *See* DONALDSON, *supra* note 59, at 15 (citing JOHN RAWLS, A THEORY OF JUSTICE 146 (1971)).
66. DONALDSON, *supra* note 59, at 18; *see also id.* at 22. Peter French also concluded that the corporation was a moral agent. *See* Peter A. French, *Principles of Responsibility, Shame, and the Corporation* 19–55, *in* SHAME, RESPONSIBILITY, AND THE CORPORATION 60–62 (Hugh Cutler ed., 1986). Donaldson adds, however, that corporations can be "moral agents," but are not "moral *persons*," and as such do not deserve the full panoply of rights that moral *persons* enjoy. *See* DONALDSON, *supra* note 59, at 30. *Accord* Richard T. De George, *Corporations and Morality, in* SHAME, RESPONSIBILITY, AND THE CORPORATION 60–62 (Hugh Cutler ed., 1986).
67. *E.g.*, Michel J. Kelly, *The Status of Corporations in the* Travaux Preparatoires *of the Genocide Convention: The Search for Personhood*, 43 CASE W. RES. J. INT'L L. 483, 490 (2010) ("Along with rights come responsibilities.").
68. *See* Ripken, *supra* note 7, 122–24 (discussing John Ladd, *Persons and Responsibility: Ethical Concepts and Impertinent Analogies, in* SHAME, RESPONSIBILITY, AND THE CORPORATION 77, 95 (Hugh Curtler ed., 1986)).
69. *See id.* at 123.
70. *See* Christopher Slobogin, Citizens United & *Corporate & Human Crime*, 14 GREEN BAG 2D 77, 82 (2010).
71. *See* V. S. Khanna, *Corporate Criminal Liability: What Purpose Does It Serve?*, 109 HARV. L. REV. 1477 (1996).
72. *See id.* at 1479–80.
73. Slobogin, *supra* note 70, at 82.
74. Lawrence Friedman, *In Defense of Corporate Criminal Liability*, 23 HARV. J.L. & PUB. POL'Y 833, 848 (2000).

75. Slobogin, *supra* note 70, at 83.
76. Colin Marks & Nancy B. Rapoport, *The Corporate Lawyer's Role in a Contemporary Democracy*, 77 FORDHAM L. REV. 1269, 1273 (2009).
77. *See* P. M. Vasudev, *Corporate Law and Its Efficiency: A Review of History*, 50 AM. J. LEGAL HIST. 237, 253 (2010).
78. *See* David Morgan & Anna Yukhananov, *Kamen Reverses Move to Cut Planned Parenthood Funding*, REUTERS (Feb. 3, 2012, 5:02 p.m.), http://www.reuters.com/article/2012/02/03/us-usa-healthcare-komen-idUSTRE8111WA20120203.
79. *See id.*
80. *Cf.* Brian McCall, *The Corporation as an Imperfect Society*, 36 DEL. J. CORP. L. 509 (2011).
81. Bradley W. Joondeph, *The Many Meanings of "Politics" in Judicial Decision Making*, 77 UMKC L. REV. 347, 348 (2008).

CHAPTER 5

The First Amendment

Background

Our efforts to evaluate the strength of corporate claims to the protections of the First Amendment involve a two-step process. The first step, which we have completed, is to familiarize ourselves with the business corporation. The second step, upon which we shall now embark, is to review the purposes of the First Amendment's protections and the values that undergird them. In so doing, we shall simultaneously consider the degree to which these purposes and values are served by extending the First Amendment's protections to the corporation.

Of course, when I write of "the corporation," we understand by now that this encompasses at least two very distinct manifestations: the modern and the postmodern. To our understanding of the postmodern corporation is conjoined our appreciation of the Tocquevillian Association, which further informs our consideration of the First Amendment's applicability to the corporate enterprise.

Indeed, the significance of the postmodern corporation's associational status is difficult to overestimate. As has already been mentioned, the importance of associations to society has been recognized by the courts, and with this recognition has come favorable treatment, at least with regard to the applicability of the First Amendment. Although the jurisprudence is not particularly clear (as we shall see), one can comfortably claim that Tocquevillian Associations ordinarily enjoy the First Amendment freedoms and protections that many corporations today seek for themselves.

This lack of jurisprudential clarity, however, is what in large part requires us to proceed. Classification as a Tocquevillian Association (or not) simply serves as an essential backdrop to the ultimate question that is the focus of this book. To fully assess the applicability of the First Amendment to the business corporation we must examine the First Amendment itself.

That said, we shall find that the values served by the association overlap to a great degree with the values served by the First Amendment. Not surprisingly, therefore, we shall find that our review of the First Amendment vis-à-vis the corporation mirrors, to a large degree, our review of the Tocquevillian Association vis-à-vis the corporation. More specifically, just as the modern corporation presents a weak claim to classification as an association, we shall find that it also presents a weak claim to classification as a First Amendment rights-bearing entity. Conversely, the postmodern corporation presents a rather strong claim to both classifications.

Our examination of the First Amendment will begin with some pertinent background, set forth in this chapter. The chapters to follow will focus on the freedom of speech, freedom of religion, and freedom of association (in turn), and the applicability of these freedoms to the corporation.

THE TEXT

> Congress shall make no law respecting an establishment of religion, or prohibiting the free exercise thereof; or abridging the freedom of speech, or of the press, or the right of the people peaceably to assemble, and to petition the Government for a redress of grievances.[1]

Thus reads the First Amendment to the U.S. Constitution, in its entirety.

Since the amendment's ratification, courts have grappled with how to interpret and apply its text in a wide variety of contexts. This includes the amendment's invocation by business corporations. To properly assess and critique the courts' efforts, let us begin with an examination of the amendment itself.

What becomes immediately clear is that the First Amendment makes no reference to corporations. This certainly hinders our effort to ascertain whether or how the amendment's provisions should apply to the business corporation.

Further, when the amendment was drafted in 1789, the business corporation was not as omnipresent as it is today. Although most of the amendment's framers were probably aware of the business corporation, "[p]rior to 1789[,] corporations were few."[2] By some accounts, the number may have been barely more than thirty.[3] Thus, we cannot be assured that the amendment's framers (let alone those who ratified the amendment) foresaw its potential applicability to the corporation, making it particularly difficult to glean the original intent behind the First Amendment in this regard.

Nevertheless, the origins and history of the First Amendment have been well-researched. A review of this scholarship can help shed light on the amendment's applicability to the corporation. Additionally, even if America's founding generation was not awash in corporations, it was, as previously discussed, awash in associations.[4] Thus, even though the amendment's adopters might not have considered the prospect of a corporation invoking the First Amendment, they likely considered the amendment's applicability to groups and associations in general. To the extent that we can discern their expectations in this regard, we should be able to extrapolate and gain helpful insight into the amendment's appropriate application to corporations—both those properly characterized as associations and those not so characterized.

THE BILL OF RIGHTS

Let us begin our constitutional inquiry by contextualizing the First Amendment.

The First Amendment, as its name suggests, was not part of the U.S. Constitution as adopted at the Constitutional Convention in Philadelphia, 1789.[5] The cherished rights of this and all the amendments comprising the Bill of Rights (which has been referred to as "the high temple of our constitutional order—America's Parthenon"[6]) were not enshrined in the Constitution as originally drafted. There were multiple reasons for this, with the primary one being that the Constitution's framers believed such guarantees were unnecessary.[7] The Constitution would be establishing a government of limited, enumerated powers, and for that reason it seemed redundant to include a set of provisos explicitly denying the government powers that it had not been granted. As Alexander Hamilton explained in *Federalist 84*, "why declare things shall not be done, which there is no power to do? Why, for instance, should it be said that the liberty of the press shall not be restrained, when no power is given by which restrictions may be imposed?"[8]

Nevertheless, the absence of such safeguards proved to be a significant deficiency and hampered the constitutional ratification effort. Several prominent and influential men, including Edmund Randolph, Samuel Adams, George Mason, James Monroe, and Patrick Henry, seized upon this absence in rallying their compatriots against ratification.[9] In an effort to quell the uproar that had ensued, the Constitution's supporters capitulated and acceded to the demands for an articulation of rights within the Constitution.[10]

At the urging of James Madison, the First Congress under the new Constitution took up the question of a Bill of Rights. In doing so, Congress culled through nearly two hundred proposed amendments that had been submitted by the states.[11] The proposals that coalesced to form our First

Amendment explicitly address freedom of speech, press, assembly, and petition.[12] Although not mentioned in the amendment's text, courts have read the First Amendment to protect freedom of association as well.[13]

When one speaks of a corporation invoking the First Amendment, freedom of speech is what usually comes to mind and, to an increasing degree, freedom of religion as well. Not far behind is the closely related freedom of association. All three of these freedoms implicate personal expression, autonomy, and self-actualization. These are the freedoms which, when invoked by business corporations, have generated the most intense controversy (or, with respect to the freedom of association, will generate intense controversy if and when invoked). These, therefore, are the freedoms upon which we shall focus the bulk of our attention.

There are, of course, other important First Amendment freedoms as well: the freedom of assembly, petition, and press. These freedoms do not implicate the concerns of expression, autonomy, and self-actualization so much as (put quite broadly) the right of a people to hold its government accountable. These particular freedoms have not been at the forefront in the debate over corporate constitutional rights. Nevertheless, before moving on, let us briefly consider these freedoms and take from them that which might be of value to our chief inquiry.

THE FREEDOMS OF ASSEMBLY AND PETITION

With regard to the freedom of assembly and of petition, one might suppose that they are inapplicable to corporations given their very language. The First Amendment speaks of the "right of *the people* peaceably to assemble, and to petition the Government for a redress of grievances." This formulation is distinctly different from that employed earlier in the First Amendment, which read that "Congress shall make no law respecting an establishment of religion, or prohibiting the free exercise thereof; or abridging the freedom of speech, or of the press."[14] Whereas the language regarding freedom of religion, speech, and the press is framed as a restriction on the powers of Congress, the language regarding assembly and petition is framed, as an affirmative right "of the people." This would furnish a rather solid basis upon which to distinguish those rights that can be claimed by a corporation and those that cannot. For if the question is one of Congress's powers, the identity of the right's bearer would appear to be of secondary importance. If, on the other hand, we are speaking of a right belonging to "the people," it would seem to be critically important that the right's bearer be one of "the people." Taken together, this would suggest that corporations have far stronger claims with regard to the rights of freedom of religion, speech, and press, and weaker claims with regard to the rights of assembly and petition. (As the right to freedom of association is not located in the language of the First Amendment, this textual analysis does not shed much light on how best to treat it.)

Unfortunately, things are not so simple. The language of the Constitution has been interpreted in a number of ways that, to put it mildly, could be considered counterintuitive. For example, the bold prohibitory language declaring that "Congress shall make no law..." has been interpreted flexibly to permit exceptions.[15] The term "the people" has been interpreted to mean different things in different contexts. At times "the people" has been read to encompass corporations and at times it has been read to exclude corporations.[16] Thus, as tempting as it may be, we cannot readily dispense with the freedoms of assembly and petition here via a careful reading of the First Amendment's text.

Fortunately, the freedom of petition need not detain us long at all. This freedom encompasses primarily the right to seek redress of grievances from the government. It has been interpreted to extend beyond its literal text and extends to all branches of government.[17] Corporations have explicitly been held to possess this right.[18] As with any area of law, this subject has its controversies, but they do not implicate the subjects with which we here are concerned.[19]

More germane for our purposes is the freedom of assembly. This freedom has generally been understood to refer to the act of physically gathering together.[20] As corporations lack a material composition, they cannot physically assemble. With apologies to the medieval scholastics, there would seem to be an answer to the question "how many corporations can dance on the head of pin?": none, because corporations cannot dance.

That said, the issue can certainly be complicated by those who may wish to do so. For example, is not a corporation "present" when one of its agents is present? Is not a corporation "present" on the Internet via its website? Are not companies "present" at conventions, meetings, and other fora?[21] The common language we use to describe corporate conduct and interactions certainly suggests that corporations can indeed be "present," begging the question whether they can be present for purposes of the right to assembly.

This implicates the personification of groups. It touches upon the concept of corporate "personhood," which we addressed in our last chapter. As we discussed, via the concept of corporate personhood the courts have extended the constitutional rights of persons to the corporation. As we also discussed, this approach suffers from a lack of convincing theoretical justification and has encountered no small amount of criticism.

Although I have articulated a defense of corporate personhood vis-à-vis the postmodern corporation, it is important to explicitly acknowledge that I have not and shall not undertake a detailed inquiry into the personification of groups generally. Among other reasons, such an undertaking is not necessary here. For, as we shall find, the protections of the First Amendment have regularly been applied to groups and organizations to such an extent that calling this general practice into question would be of little value. Thus, there is very little debate over whether the First Amendment rights of individuals also apply to groups and organizations (they generally do). Rather, the critical question today (and for our purposes) is whether business corporations ought to be included in the collection of groups and organizations that can lay claim to such protections.

Unlike the freedom to petition, this question has not been squarely raised with regard to the freedom of assembly. Moreover, it does not appear likely to be raised in the future. John Inazu has called freedom of assembly the "forgotten freedom," and with good reason: this freedom has been encroached upon, if not practically eclipsed, by other First Amendment freedoms.[22] Thus, recourse to the freedom of assembly has increasingly been considered unnecessary.[23] Be it a cause or a consequence of this phenomenon, the freedom has also not been carefully delineated.[24] As a result, there are very few examples of corporations invoking the freedom of assembly; and most of the concerns raised by such an invocation nowadays could be raised by reference to other constitutional rights.[25]

The most relevant historical commentary on the freedom of assembly, for our purposes, hails from the U.S. Supreme Court case *Thomas v. Collins*.[26] *Thomas* concerned a Texas statute regulating labor unions that, among other things, required the credentialing of labor organizers. The question of freedom of assembly was raised and, consistent with Inazu's observations, the case was decided on other grounds. That said, the Court offered a few thoughts on freedom of assembly and the First Amendment more broadly that we would do well to consider.

The Court labeled freedom of assembly as "inseparable," although "not identical," with freedom of speech, press, and petition.[27] "It was not by accident or coincidence," the Court wrote, that these "cognate rights . . . are united in the First Article's assurance."[28] Significantly, the Court rejected the argument that "the First Amendment's safeguards are wholly inapplicable to business or economic activity."[29] The Court proceeded as follows:

> [I]t does not resolve where the line shall be drawn in a particular case merely to urge, as Texas does, that an organization for which the rights of free speech and free assembly are claimed is one "engaged in business activities" or that the individual who leads it in exercising these rights receives compensation for doing do. Nor, on the other hand, is the answer given, whenever what is done is an exercise of those rights and the restriction a forbidden impairment, by ignoring the organization's economic function, because those interests of workingmen are involved or because they have the general liberties of the citizen, as appellant would do.
>
> These comparisons are at once too simple, too general, and too inaccurate to be determinative. . . . [I]n our system where the line can constitutionally be

> placed presents a question this Court cannot escape answering. . . . And the answer, under that tradition, can be affirmative, to support an intrusion upon this domain, only if grave and impending public danger requires this.[30]

For the reasons discussed above, freedom of assembly does not furnish a particularly worthwhile object of examination for our purposes. Notwithstanding that, the Supreme Court's opinion in *Thomas*, authored almost seventy years ago, underscores a central theme of this book: that the applicability of First Amendment rights ought not be determined via rules of thumb that are "too simple, too general, and too inaccurate."

FREEDOM OF THE PRESS

As David Anderson explains, "'Freedom of the press' has less legal significance than meets the eye."[31] For much of what the press engages in would constitute speech and thus be protected as such via the First Amendment's freedom-of-speech protections. As Anderson explains further: "The press is protected from most government censorship, libel judgments, and prior restraints not because it is the press but because the Speech Clause protects all of us from those threats."[32] When boiled down, freedom of the press refers primarily to a fairly specific collection of rights and privileges that go beyond the simple protection of speech. Among these would include the right to keep one's sources of information confidential and special protections against discriminatory taxation.[33]

Of particular relevance to us is not so much the substantive rights protected by freedom of the press, but rather how "the press" is defined. There are two schools of thought on the subject, from each of which we can draw a lesson.

Some insist that "the press" is limited to the institutional media. Others, such as Eugene Volokh, have argued persuasively that the "the press" refers not to a fixed body of actors, but rather to anyone who employs the "technology" of public communication.[34] Without attempting to resolve this debate, let us consider the relevant implications of each approach.

The broader approach, exemplified by Volokh, posits that the First Amendment's freedom-of-the-press clause protects certain conduct, not certain persons. Anyone communicating information or ideas to the public falls within its purview. This perspective appears to comport well with the common law understanding of the term, along with courts at the time of the amendment's framing. A typical formulation can be found in an opinion of the Supreme Court of Pennsylvania, construing its state constitution in 1788: "The true liberty of the press is amply secured by permitting every man to publish his opinions."[35] According to Volokh, this broad approach was rather uniformly taken across the United States for nearly two centuries and, with the exception of a hiatus of confusion starting in the 1970s, has been confirmed by the Supreme Court as recently as 2010 (in *Citizens United v. FEC*).[36]

If Volokh's interpretation is correct, it could influence our reading of those First Amendment freedoms that we are focusing upon: speech, religion, and association. Although freedom of the press is certainly a freedom distinct from these other freedoms, its inclusion in the same amendment certainly suggests that we at least entertain the possibility of taking a common approach to interpreting all of them. Plainly put, such an approach would have us disregard the corporate status of a First Amendment claimant and instead concentrate upon the claimant's conduct to ascertain whether it falls within those protections recognized by the First Amendment. It would matter not that a particular claimant was organized as a corporation—what would matter is whether the claimant was engaged in activity that could be characterized as speech, free exercise, or association.

Let us consider the repercussions of adopting the narrower approach to the freedom-of-press clause, pursuant to which "the press" refers only to the institutional media. In a speech given in 1974, Justice Stewart referred to "the press" as: "the daily newspapers and other established news media" and "newspapers, television networks, and magazines."[37] Once updated to take into account the "new media" of the Internet era, Justice Stewart provides as good a definition of "the press" as any.

Significantly, even under this narrow definition, an entity's status as a "corporation" plays no role in the analysis of its First Amendment right. So long as the claimant is a member of the institutional media ("the press"), the fact that it happens to be a business corporation is irrelevant. Even in the days prior to *Citizens United*, before the Supreme Court held that the free speech protections of the First Amendment applied to all corporations (and speakers) equally, it was well understood that "media corporations" were fully protected by the freedom-of-press clause.[38] Thus, the fact the *New York Times* is a business corporation in no way hampers the assertion of its rights under the freedom-of-press clause.

It would seem, therefore, that under both common interpretations of the Press Clause, corporate status is simply not relevant to the operation of this First Amendment freedom.

THE FOURTEENTH AMENDMENT

Before moving on, a quick word regarding the Fourteenth Amendment is necessary. By its terms, the First Amendment applies only to the federal government. Indeed, the whole purpose of the Bill of Rights was to restrict the powers of the federal government, thereby preserving the rights of the people and of the states. Today, of course, the First Amendment, and much of the Bill of Rights, applies to state governments as well. As indicated in our last chapter, the reason for this is the Fourteenth Amendment and the doctrine of "incorporation."

Incorporation is itself a doctrine fraught with controversy. It stems from the Fourteenth Amendment's demand that

> [n]o State shall make or enforce any law which shall abridge the privileges or immunities of citizens of the United States; nor shall any State deprive any person of life, liberty, or property without due process of law; nor deny to any person within its jurisdiction the equal protection of the laws.

Some interpret this language as requiring that state governments recognize and honor all the rights contained within the Bill of Rights. With this approach, the Fourteenth Amendment is said to "incorporate" the entirety of the Bill of Rights, making its provisions applicable against the states. Others believe that the Fourteenth Amendment does not necessarily incorporate the Bill of Rights in its entirety, but rather, selectively. To them, each provision of the Bill of Rights must be independently assessed before it can be deemed incorporated by the Fourteenth Amendment and thereby made applicable to the states. Finally, some assert that the Fourteenth Amendment does not "incorporate" any of the first ten amendments at all. Rather, it simply prohibits states from infringing upon fundamental rights and freedoms. To the extent that these rights and freedoms find expression in the Bill of Rights, that is simply an understandable coincidence.[39]

Fortunately, for our purposes, there is little serious doubt that the freedoms of speech, religion, and association apply as equally to state governments as to the federal government.[40] Thus, we may proceed, certain in the knowledge that the First Amendment rights and protections examined herein are fully applicable to state governments and need not particularly concern ourselves with the debate over incorporation.

NOTES

1. U.S. CONST. amend. I.
2. Robert Sprague & Mary Ellen Wells, *The Supreme Court as Prometheus: Breathing Life into the Corporation Super Citizen*, 49 AM. BUS. L. J. 507, 519 n.68 (2012) (quoting ADOLPH A. BERLE JR., STUDIES IN CORPORATE FINANCE 15 (1928)).
3. *See* Sprague & Wells, *supra* note 2, at 519 n.68 (quoting 4 JOSEPH STANCLIFFE DAVIS, ESSAYS IN THE EARLIER HISTORY OF AMERICAN CORPORATIONS 8 (1917)

("Prior to 1801 over 300 charters were granted for business corporations, ninety percent of them after 1789.")).

4. *See* chapter 1.
5. *See* RICHARD LABUNSKI, JAMES MADISON AND THE STRUGGLE FOR THE BILL OF RIGHTS 10 (2006).
6. AKHIL REED AMAR, THE BILL OF RIGHTS xi (1998).
7. *See* LABUNSKI, *supra* note 5, at 9–10.
8. FEDERALIST NO. 84 (Alexander Hamilton) (*quoted in* LABUNSKI, *supra* note 5, at 9–10).
9. *See* LABUNSKI, *supra* note 5, at 10–11, 19–20, 38, 41–42.
10. *See id.* at 113, 161–62, 198, 215.
11. *See id.* at 191, 199.
12. *See* AMAR, *supra* note 6, at 20–45.
13. *See* JAMES E. LEAHY, THE FIRST AMENDMENT, 1791–1991 223 (1991).
14. *See* Note, *The Meaning(s) of "The People" in the Constitution*, 126 HARV. L. REV. 1078, 1089 (2013).
15. *See* Darrell A. H. Miller, *Guns, Inc.: Citizens United, McDonald, and the Future of Corporate Constitutional Rights*, 86 N.Y.U. L. REV. 887, 903–904 (2011).
16. *See id.* at 910.
17. *See* California Motor Transp. Co. v. Trucking Unlimited, 404 U.S. 508, 511–12 (1972).
18. *See* Citizens United v. Fed. Elec. Comm'n, 558 U.S. 310, 355 (2010); Charles H. Moellenberg Jr. & Leon F. DeJulius Jr., *Second Class Speakers: A Proposal to Free Protected Corporate Speech from Tort Liability*, 70 U. PITT. L. REV. 555, 558–63 (2009).
19. *See* LEAHY, *supra* note 13, at 199–215.
20. *See id.* at 216–22.
21. *See* Amanda D. Johnson, *Originalism and Citizens United: The Struggle of Corporate Personhood*, 7 RUTGERS BUS. L. J. 187, 202–203 (2010).
22. *See* John D. Inazu, *The Forgotten Freedom of Assembly*, 84 TUL. L. REV. 565, 566–67 (2010) (decrying the common contention that "the right of assembly has been subsumed into the rights of speech and association").
23. *See id.*
24. *See id.* at 566.
25. A rare example of the right of assembly being attributed to a corporation, albeit in dicta, is provided by *Savoy v. Graham Memorial Auditorium Ass'n, Inc.*, 329 S.W.2d 352, 354 (Tex. App. 1959).
26. 323 U.S. 516 (1945).
27. *Id.* at 530.
28. *Id.*
29. *Id.* at 531.
30. *Id.* at 531–32.
31. *See* David A. Anderson, *Freedom of the Press*, 80 TEX. L. REV. 429, 430 (2002).
32. *See id.* at 431.
33. *See id.* at 431.
34. Eugene Volokh, *Freedom for the Press as an Industry, or for the Press as a Technology? From the Framing to Today*, 160 U. PA. L. REV. 459, 462 (2012).
35. Respublica v. Oswald, 1 Dall. 319, 325 (Pa. 1788) (commenting upon freedom of the press as contained in the state constitution of Pennsylvania) (*quoted in* Volokh, *supra* note 34, at 466).

36. *See* Volokh, *supra* note 34, at 516.
37. Potter Stewart, *"Or of the Press,"* 26 HASTINGS L.J. 631, 631, 636 (1975) (*quoted in* Anderson, *supra* note 31, at 436).
38. *See* Anderson, *supra* note 31, at 455.
39. *See* Akhil Reed Amar, *The Bill of Rights and the Fourteenth Amendment*, 101 YALE L.J. 1193, 1194–95 (1992).
40. *See* LAURENCE H. TRIBE, AMERICAN CONSTITUTIONAL LAW 772; Robert C. Wigton, *American Political Parties under the First Amendment*, 7 J.L. & POL'Y 411, 419 (1999).

CHAPTER 6

The First Amendment

Freedom of Speech

In 2010, to both great acclaim and tremendous criticism, the U.S. Supreme Court decided the case *Citizens United v. FEC*.[1] In *Citizens United*, the Court held that the First Amendment's free speech protections applied regardless of the speaker, thereby protecting business corporations as definitively as individuals.

At first blush, based upon a reading of the First Amendment's text, it would seem that the Court's ruling was entirely correct. The First Amendment's "majestic guarantee" of freedom of speech is, after all, as sweeping as it is famous.[2] The amendment boldly declares that Congress shall "make no law... abridging the freedom of speech." In light of this, one could be forgiven for believing that the question of corporate speech is a rather simple, straight-forward one. The amendment appears to strictly forbid any governmental abridgment of speech whatsoever, corporate or otherwise.

Of course, things are not so simple. This is underscored by the fact that the *Citizens United* opinion was not a unanimous one, but rather the 5–4 result of a closely divided court. For the First Amendment's protections have been interpreted in ways that are both broader, and narrower, than one might initially surmise. Indeed, the phrase "freedom of speech," if not the very word "speech," is a term of art for First Amendment purposes.[3]

Herein I shall suggest a transformation of the question of corporate speech as it is usually formulated. To ask whether corporations should enjoy the protections of the First Amendment is not sufficiently precise. What we ought to be asking is whether corporations are capable of engaging in "speech" as that term is understood under the First Amendment. If so, the First Amendment's prohibitions on the abridgment of speech ought to apply with fullness of force. If not, then government regulation of corporate communications should pose little problem under the First Amendment.

This hearkens back to a concept introduced with regard to the freedom of the press in our previous chapter: that the protections of the First Amendment are centered upon specific conduct and activity and not upon specific actors per se.[4] Such a reformulation of the question may also point us toward the best way to interpret *Citizens United*. I contend that the *Citizens United* decision is not wrong insomuch as it is overly broad. For, as I hope to demonstrate, certain corporations are capable of engaging in "speech" (as understood for First Amendment purposes), whereas others are not. As has been previewed, the dividing line would be the distinction between a "postmodern corporation" and a "modern corporation." If my suggestion is correct, the holding of *Citizens United* should be limited to protecting the communications of the former group of corporations but not the latter. This would provide the fullness of the First Amendment's protections to communications of those corporations most deserving of such protections given the purpose of, and values embodied in, the First Amendment; it would withhold the fullness of the First Amendment's protections from communications of those corporations least deserving of such protections.

WHAT IS "SPEECH"?

When I contend that a particular corporation is more versus less deserving of free speech protections, the touchstone I employ is the concept of "speech" under the First Amendment. As mentioned, "speech" as per the First Amendment is a term of art. Not every sound, utterance, or communication constitutes speech.

Consider, for example, a parrot sitting in a tree on a street corner. To the extent that the parrot mimics the words and sounds it hears throughout the day, is it engaging in "speech" that ought to be protected by the First Amendment? Consider further that the parrot overhears some electioneering and begins to squawk out, on a regular basis, "vote for Lincoln"—now is it engaged in speech? Further still, consider that the parrot was trained, by its owner, to squawk out "vote for Lincoln" and dutifully does so throughout the day. In this third hypothetical, do we have First Amendment speech?

Some may object that in all cases, the speaker is not human and therefore there is no "speech" protected by the First Amendment. This cannot be correct. Substitute for a trained parrot a robot that has been programed to deliver a speech. Substitute for the robot an electronic billboard flashing political messages. In all three cases, we do not have a human being engaging in real-time communications, but in all cases I propose we most certainly have "speech," as that term would be understood under the Constitution.

These examples illustrate a couple of important and related points. The first is the complexity of the concept of "speech" for First Amendment purposes. The second is the importance of context in assessing whether a communication is speech or not. Although, as discussed, the ordinary focus is on the purported speech itself, and not on the speaker per se, the nature of the speaker serves to contextualize the purported speech, and in this way contributes significantly to the analysis.

This is why the question of corporate speech is so difficult to assess. At first blush, it would appear as though corporations engage in speech frequently, if not with regularity. Corporations run commercials, take out newspaper ads, and even have official "spokespersons." Like a parrot, however, the corporation is itself not a human being. This complicates our assessment of the speech in question.

Further, we must also bear in mind that not every communicative act of even a human being constitutes "speech." Pointlessly yelling "fire" in a crowded theater is certainly an act of speaking, yet, based on well-established judicial precedent, does not qualify for the protections of the First Amendment. Conversely, and to complicate matters even further, there are activities that are not readily described by the ordinary definition of "speech" yet have been protected via recourse to freedom of speech principles under the First Amendment: activities such as burning a flag[5] and dancing topless.[6]

Ordinarily, a good place to start interpreting any provision of the Constitution is the text itself and the framers' original intent.[7] Unfortunately, neither is particularly availing when it comes to the freedom of speech.

With regard to the text, the word "speech" has a variety of potential meanings, from formal addresses, to excited utterances, to lies. The amendment does not clearly identify what exactly is intended to be protected. "Freedom of speech" has never been read to mean an "unlimited license to talk," for it always coexisted with laws that simultaneously forbade a broad swath of communications, such as "libel, slander, misrepresentation, obscenity, perjury, false advertising, solicitation of crime, complicity by encouragement, [and] conspiracy."[8]

Similarly, recourse to the framers' original intent is of little help. As Stanley Brubaker has found, "[t]he debates in Congress concerning the speech and press clauses shed scant light on the question of meaning.... Nor do we find enlightening comments in the state legislatures that considered the amendments or the local newspapers or pamphlets of the time."[9]

As a result, courts (particularly the Supreme Court) and commentators have needed to formulate their own theories of the First Amendment, pretty much from whole cloth. To properly assess the applicability of the First Amendment to the phenomenon of corporate speech, we need to consider these theories.[10]

THEORIES OF THE FIRST AMENDMENT

Attempts to interpret the First Amendment have inspired no fewer than four theories of prominence, each of which will be presented in turn. Our purpose here is not to resolve the debate over which theory is most sensible. Indeed, many commentators critique all four and find that the best explanation of the First Amendment lies in some combination of these theories, if not altogether elsewhere.[11] Rather, our purpose is to identify the degree to which these various theories support, or undermine, the corporation's claim to freedom of speech.

The theories in question will be referred to as (1) The Marketplace of Ideas, (2) Political Speech, (3) Listener Autonomy, and (4) Self-Realization. It will be shown that these theories pose serious challenges to the question of speech rights when the claimant in question is a modern corporation. Conversely, these theories are generally supportive of speech rights when the claimant in question is a postmodern corporation.

The Marketplace of Ideas and Political Speech

Two thousand years ago, Pontius Pilate asked, "*Quid est veritas?*"[12] Western liberal philosophy has championed the notion that the free exchange of thought and opinion furnishes society with the best means of discovering the truth and thereby answering that fundamental question.[13] This notion was expressed poignantly in John Milton's *Areopagitica*:

> And though all the windes of doctrin were let loose to play upon the earth, so Truth be in the field, we do injuriously by licencing and prohibiting to misdoubt her strength. Let her and Falshood grapple; who ever knew Truth put to the wors in a free and open encounter?[14]

In ordinary prose (if Justice Holmes's writing can be considered as such), this notion was more recently expressed in *Abrams v. United States*:

> Persecution for the expression of opinions seems to me perfectly logical. If you have no doubt of your premises or your power and want a certain result with all your heart you naturally express your wishes in law and sweep away all opposition. To allow opposition by speech seems to indicate that you think the speech impotent, as when a man says that he has squared the circle, or that you do not care whole-heartedly for the result, or that you doubt either your power or your premises. But when men have realized that time has upset many fighting faiths, they may come to believe even more than they believe the very foundations of their own conduct that the ultimate good desired is

> better reached by free trade in ideas—that the best test of truth is the power of the thought to get itself accepted in the competition of the market, and that truth is the only ground upon which their wishes safely can be carried out. That at any rate is the theory of our Constitution.[15]

Pursuant to this line of thinking, efforts to curb or censor speech generally inhibit society's efforts to discern the truth. Scholars debate whether "the truth" here represents an objective reality, or is rather, by definition, equivalent to whatever consensus society happens to reach.[16] This question, as interesting as it may be, need not detain us. For under each possible answer, speech is deemed to further public discourse and the ascertainment of truth, thereby serving the common good.

Closely related to the "marketplace of ideas" conceptualization of the First Amendment is the "political speech" conceptualization. Indeed, the notion that the First Amendment exists primarily to protect political speech can fairly be categorized as an offshoot if not a subset of the marketplace of ideas conceptualization.

Perhaps no one expressed the political speech theory of the First Amendment as well and as forcefully as Alexander Meiklejohn, whose thoughts on the subject remain influential. In his own words, "[t]he First Amendment does not protect a 'freedom to speak.' It protects freedom of those activities of thought and communication by which we 'govern.' "[17] This theory prioritizes political speech over all other forms and makes political speech the focus of the First Amendment's protections.

Narrowly construed, Meiklejohn's approach would protect *only* political speech—communications of an explicitly political nature. Perhaps foreseeing the inevitable criticism that this would invite, Meiklejohn took pains to explain that his theory would protect other cherished forms of expression as well, forms that he identified as relating to the "dignity of the individual."[18] He tied protection of such forms into his overall theory by arguing that they contribute to the creation of political speech and the act of governance. As he explained: "Self-government can exist only insofar as the voters acquire the intelligence, integrity, sensitivity, and generous devotion to the general welfare that, in theory, casting a ballot is assumed to express."[19] The acquisition and development of these traits, in turn, requires freedom in four general areas: "education," "philosophy and the sciences," "[l]iterature and the arts," and "[p]ublic discussions of public issues."[20]

By linking speech to truth and public discourse, these two theories readily allow for the regulation of certain communications. Communications that are objectively and patently false, or that serve in no way to inform or persuade, could be abridged as they fail to contribute toward the ascertainment of truth. For practically all other intentional communicative efforts, however, the marketplace-of-ideas theory would counsel against abridgement.

Under these two theories, however, there would initially seem to be little reason to distinguish the communications of individuals from the communications of corporations. Regardless of the speaker, or the speaker's motivations, information and advocacy are protected for their own sake. The protection stems from recognition that information and advocacy serve a salutary function per se, without regard to their source.

That said, many have argued that the identity of the speaker is indeed relevant. More specifically, they have argued that the communications of business corporations should not be given equal footing in the marketplace or the political sphere. The reasons given for this distinction are generally twofold.

The Problem of Profit Maximization

The first reason is that modern business corporations are oriented toward profit maximization.[21] Consequently, corporate communications are similarly directed. Thus, corporate speech does not contribute to the ascertainment of truth because corporate speech is not designed to contribute to the ascertainment of truth—it's designed to further the narrow economic interests of the corporation itself.[22] For similar reasons, corporation participation in the political process is deemed problematic.

The assertion that all corporate speech is self-interested is not entirely accurate. Certainly most corporations can be characterized as self-interested in that they seek to maximize profits. I have referred to these as "modern corporations," and it is indeed likely that their communications are directed toward their profit-maximizing end. In fact, it would arguably be a dereliction of duty for those who command such corporations to employ their speech for any other purpose. Thus, we can fairly and reasonably presume, for the reasons set forth in our discussion of the modern corporation in chapter 2, that the speech of the modern corporation is undertaken primarily (if not strictly) to further its narrow, economic interests.

However, as has been discussed, other business corporations balance their pursuit of profits with other, nonfinancial goals.[23] These entitles I have referred to as "postmodern" corporations. They employ their speech for purposes that are not necessarily related to profit maximization. Consider, for example, Chick-fil-A, a fast food company that has donated money in the past to groups advocating a particular definition of marriage.[24] Such acts of corporate expression do not serve to maximize the company's profits (indeed, they may have economically damaged the company in light of the boycott they provoked[25]). This is not a fact that should be overlooked or disregarded, as it goes to, and undermines, the very core of this particular argument against corporate speech. It would be wrong to treat these two types of corporations, the modern and the postmodern, which are significantly and relevantly different, identically for purposes of the First Amendment. Thus, if a restriction on First Amendment corporate rights is to be predicated upon corporate profit maximization, it ought to be limited only to those businesses that embrace profit maximization and not extended to those businesses that do not.

Even with such a qualification, however, this argument against corporate speech rights remains vulnerable to criticism. For any objection to protecting speech that is of a self-interested nature can readily be applied to the speech of a large number of individual human beings as well. Common is the person who puts his or her interests before those of others and whose communications are crafted for that very purpose. All of us are certainly aware of people, be they public figures or simply friends and family, who say and do things not out of genuine conviction, but rather out of a concern with how they will be perceived or with some other motive in mind—unconcerned with the truth and honesty of their statements.

On a related note, economic and financial interests, in particular, appear to dominate the thinking of many individuals. (Who can forget the Clinton era's contribution to our political lexicon: "It's the economy, stupid"?). It may indeed be psychopathic for an individual to fixate upon the maximization of their wealth to the same extent that many corporations fixate upon profits, but even psychopaths are not categorically excluded from the protections of the First Amendment.

Complicating matters further is the observation that an individual or entity's self-interest and the truth need not be mutually exclusive. An actor's private good and the common good can often be aligned. A homeowner who advocates for lower property taxes may very well be articulating the best public policy for society, his or her personal bias notwithstanding. A company that sells energy-efficient light bulbs and other "green" products just might be correct in its assessment of global warming.

Thus, reference to self-interest, individual or corporate, as a means to disqualify certain speakers from the protections of the First Amendment poses a fundamental problem. Indeed, this objection arguably strikes at the heart of the "marketplace of ideas" rationale used to defend freedom of speech. A central tenet of the marketplace conceptualization, and its focus on political speech, is that the free flow of information and ideas helps society sort the good from the bad. Through the exchange of points and counterpoints, an argument's strengths and weaknesses are discerned. In making this assessment, the source of information is likely to be considered as well, thereby lending (or detracting) weight from its credibility and influence. The overall contribution that corporate speakers can and do make to the marketplace of ideas was captured well by Martin Redish and Howard M. Wasserman:

> Who, one reasonably could ask, has a greater interest in what actions the government takes with regard to the economy than corporations, whose very survival may well turn on the success or failure of those actions? Who possesses

> more firsthand knowledge and expertise on issues relevant to potential government regulation of private economic activity? To exclude corporate expression from the scope of the free speech clause, then, would be unwisely to shut from public debate a substantial amount of relevant, provocative, and potentially vital information and opinion on issues of fundamental importance to the polity.[26]

In light of the preceding, it would seem difficult to justify treating self-interested corporate speech differently under the Constitution than self-interested individual speech. There is, nevertheless, at least one defensible rationale for doing so.

Recall that even within the broad "marketplace of ideas" approach to speech, objectively false communications may be restricted. This follows naturally from the purpose of speech under the marketplace approach: the ascertainment of truth. As falsehoods in no way contribute to that end, their restriction serves, rather than undermines, the marketplace of ideas.

The law generally follows this approach and in so doing treats corporate and individual speech similarly. An individual's prevarication is actionable under the law just as a corporation's.

Building upon this, it would be reasonable to label disingenuous speech similarly unhelpful and thereby not deserving of First Amendment protection. By "disingenuous speech" I refer to communications that are rendered without regard to truth or falsity, but rather simply to further some particular end. Pretextual speech, for which truth would be merely coincidental.

Again, the law already does this to a degree. Consider the treatment of "commercial speech." Commercial speech does not receive the same protections as noncommercial speech. The law understands that speech undertaken for the purpose of selling a particular product is ordinarily qualitatively different from other forms of speech—especially political speech. Although there can certainly be an eerie similarity in a business's selling of a product and a candidate's campaigning for political office, at least in the case of the latter the focus is on ideas and policies.

Tellingly, and appropriately, the inferior treatment afforded to commercial speech under the Constitution applies regardless of whether the speech is that of an individual or a corporation. Similarly, logic would dictate that disingenuous speech, if carved out from the full protections of the First Amendment, ought to be left unprotected if spoken by either an individual or a corporation. That would not only be consistent with the approach the law takes with regard to false speech and commercial speech but would serve to underscore, once again, the critical focus of inquiry: the character of the speech itself, rather than the speaker. Indeed, on a theoretical level, it would be difficult to justify disparate treatment here, by which disingenuous corporate speech could be deemed unprotected by the First Amendment while disingenuous individual speech would be. Nevertheless, on account of compelling practical reasons, disparate treatment can indeed be justified.

It is ordinarily quite difficult to discern the genuineness of an individual's speech, especially in light of the fact that much speech contains an admixture of purpose and principle. The degree to which a statement of purported political opinion is primarily one of authentic belief, versus self-serving pretense, is perhaps impossible to measure.

With regard to the modern corporation, however, we can readily and plausibly presume that the speech in question is pretextual. As explained, the profit-maximizing modern corporation does not engage in genuinely political, ideological, religious, expressive speech, but rather uses its speech to further its commercial ends. Its speech is not genuinely expressive in that it does not flow from any genuine convictions or principles. As such, it is wholly unlike the political speech that individuals are capable of.

Thus, whereas the political speech of an individual *might* be pretextual, and not a true expression of his or her beliefs and opinions, the political speech of a modern corporation *must* be pretextual, undertaken strictly in furtherance of the corporation's economic interests. The inability to accurately distinguish between an individual's authentic versus pretextual speech precludes us from limiting his or her First Amendment rights; our ability to safely presume the nonexpressive character of the modern corporation's speech allows us to justifiably limit its First Amendment protections. In contradistinction, the postmodern corporation more closely resembles the individual in this regard, as its rejection of strict profit maximization similarly prevents us from justifiably presuming that its speech is inauthentic, disingenuous, or otherwise pretextual. As with the individual, the postmodern corporation's speech can be the result of a complicated interplay of concerns, difficult to accurately disentangle.

Anti-Distortion Rationale

A second common argument leveled against corporate speech is that it threatens to overwhelm the marketplace of ideas, given the wealth of some corporations. Corporate participation in civil discourse, they argue, undermines speech's truth-seeking function and subverts democratic government because of the disproportionate influence that corporations can bring to bear upon the dialogue.[27] This argument is often referred to as the "anti-distortion rationale." This argument, in turn, consists of two components.

First, corporate speech is deemed problematic because corporate wealth and power enable the corporation to monopolize the marketplace of ideas, thereby crowding out the speech of others. Second, and more perniciously, corporate speech distorts societal discourse because its volume is not commensurate with its level of popular support.

The first half of the anti-distortion argument is not particularly convincing. In principle, it was rejected by the Supreme Court decades ago, when in *Buckley v. Valeo* the Court declared that "the concept that government may restrict the speech of some elements of our society in order to enhance the relative voice of others is wholly foreign to the First Amendment."[28]

Further, the argument is predicated upon a supposition of questionable accuracy. Far from every corporation has the wealth or power to monopolize anything—let alone political discourse. Perhaps the typical corporation has more disposable assets than the typical individual, but there are certainly a large number of impoverished corporations and a large number of wealthy individuals. Oprah Winfrey, Bill Gates, and Warren Buffett, for example, have far more wealth than the vast majority of corporations. To carve out corporate speech from the protections of the First Amendment strikes me as an incredibly imprecise means of addressing one's concern over the influence of money in politics, especially given the Supreme Court's admonition that "[i]ndependent expenditures constitutes expression 'at the core of our electoral process and of the First Amendment freedoms.'"[29]

The argument also rings especially hollow in the modern era, where the ability to distribute and access information has never been greater. When a very simple home movie entitled "Charlie Bit My Finger—Again!" is one of the all-time most viewed videos on YouTube, it's difficult to maintain that corporate speech precludes individuals from getting their messages out to the public.[30]

More potent is the second half of the anti-distortion argument: that corporate speech influences society and the political process disproportionately, well beyond the degree to which it should. The problem identified here lies in the relative quantity of corporate speech. Simply put, arguments pushed by corporations proliferate beyond their level of popular support. Justice Brennan captured the argument well when he authored the Supreme Court's decision in *Federal Election Commission v. Massachusetts Citizens for Life, Inc.*:

> Direct corporate spending on political activity raises the prospect that resources amassed in the economic marketplace may be used to provide an unfair advantage in the political marketplace. Political "free trade" does not necessarily require that all who participate in the political marketplace do so with exactly the same resources. Relative availability of funds is after all a rough barometer of public support. The resources in the treasury of a business corporation, however, are not an indication of popular support for the corporation's political ideas. They reflect instead the economically motivated decisions of investors and customers. The availability of these resources may make a corporation a formidable political presence, even though the power of the corporation may be no reflection of the power of its ideas.[31]

In response, a couple of observations are in order. As with my prior critique of anti-distortion rationale arguments, Justice Brennan's more sophisticated gloss fails to consider the logical extension of his argument to human beings. Just as the political speech of a corporation to advance its political priorities might bear no resemblance to its level of popular support, the same could as readily hold true for the political speech of Winfrey, Gates, and Buffett. Indeed, Congress (and state legislatures) features a number of members whose campaigns were self-financed and as such had access to personal funds well beyond their popular level of support. If the operative principle is that the arguments advanced in the marketplace of ideas/political sphere ought to somehow reflect their relative popularity per capita, restrictions on corporate political speech present, once again, quite a roughly hewn solution.

The inadequacy of the purported solution is exacerbated by a second observation. Justice Brennan assumes a strict divide between a customer's (and an investor's) economic decisions and his or her political beliefs. As discussed, developments over the past few decades call this assumption into serious doubt. Although Justice Brennan's assumption may hold with regard to the modern corporation, it does not hold with regard to the postmodern corporation. As has been explained, investors and customers increasingly view their investment and purchasing decisions as political decisions as well. Consequently, many gravitate toward postmodern corporations precisely because of the politics and values of these corporations.[32] Thus, it is not so clear today (if, indeed, it has ever been genuinely clear) that a corporation's wealth bears no relation to its political agenda (should it choose to adopt one). Indeed, for the postmodern corporation, its wealth would appear to be significantly related to its values and agenda.

Listener Autonomy

A relatively recent interpretation of the First Amendment holds that speech is to be protected in order to respect the autonomy of its audience.[33] This limits the power of government from paternalistically interfering with messages directed to the individual. When it comes to speech, it is for the individual listener, not the government, to separate the wheat from the chaff.

The listener autonomy approach nevertheless begs the question: listen to *what*? We are once again confronted with the difficulty of separating speech from nonspeech under this particular interpretation of the First Amendment.

No such separation is explicitly made under the listener autonomy approach. Instead, we are asked to consider the justifications for any curtailment of speech. It is not the nature of the speech that matters so much as the legitimacy of the grounds upon which the speech is being abridged.[34] To assess this legitimacy, we are asked to apply the "Millian Principle." The principle's name is a nod to John Stuart Mill, whose book *On Liberty* remains a pillar of Western liberal thought. The Millian Principle has been articulated by Thomas Scanlon as follows:

> There are certain harms which, although they would not occur but for certain acts of expression, nonetheless cannot be taken as part of a justification for legal restrictions on these acts. These harms are: (a) harms to certain individuals which consist in their coming to have false beliefs as a result of those acts of expression; (b) harmful consequences of acts performed as a result of those acts of expression, where the connection between the acts of expression and the subsequent harmful acts consists merely in the fact that the act of expression led the agents to believe (or increased their tendency to believe) these acts to be worth performing.[35]

In other words, the Millian Principle precludes government from attempting to protect people from "erroneous" or heterodox beliefs. An individual must assess a message's truth, falsity, wisdom, and folly, and government should not interfere with this assessment. The subject matter of the speech in question is not specifically bounded, but rather extends to anything over which individuals could potentially disagree.

The Millian Principle does not prevent government from regulating speech in order to protect against harms that are unrelated to the speech's content. As such, under the principle, the government would apparently be justified in attempting to "bar the use of loudspeakers because they are too noisy" or "ban all parades because they disrupt traffic and cause litter."[36] Recognizing obvious objections to such regulations, Scanlon suggests further analysis of such rules would be needed and that the resulting solution would most likely come in the form of a balancing test of some kind.[37]

It appears that pursuant to the listener-autonomy approach, there would be little basis for infringing the speech of any corporation, modern or post-modern. For the approach specifically precludes abridgments of expression designed to protect individuals from harms consisting of "coming to have false beliefs as a result of those acts of expression." Such harms are essentially the very harms that motivate calls for restrictions upon corporate speech. Recall that the problems typically identified with corporate speech center around the ability of that speech to distort the public discourse, via its disproportionately persuasive effects. At its heart, this "distortion" is little more than the widespread adoption of "false beliefs."

Nevertheless, as with the marketplace-of-ideas approach, efforts to distinguish corporate speech from individual speech persist under listener-autonomy theory as well. The persuasiveness of these attempts varies with regard to the corporation in question. This is because the strongest argument in favor of treating corporate speech differently than individual speech lies in demonstrating that such speech is in fact different. Once again, therefore, the divide between the modern corporation and the postmodern corporation becomes paramount.[38] Whereas the speech of the former entity does not resemble individual speech, the speech of the latter entity (the postmodern corporation) in many important respects does.

Self-Realization

A widely recognized theory of the First Amendment is that its protections exist to protect human expressivity in general and thus an individual's right to "self-realization."[39] This venerable theory arguably has the deepest philosophical roots, which can be traced to Aristotle's identification of man as a "social animal."[40]

The previous approaches to the First Amendment we have considered largely treat freedom of speech as instrumental: valued insofar as it contributes to the art of self-governance or the ascertainment of truth. The self-realization approach (and, arguably, the listener-autonomy approach to a degree as well[41]) views freedom of speech as intrinsically valuable. Pursuant to this perspective, freedom of speech is protected as a natural right upon which government cannot encroach because of its centrality to human dignity.[42] This perspective was articulated by Justice Brandeis in *Whitney v. California*, in which he wrote:

> Those who won our independence believed that the final end of the State was to make men free to develop their faculties.... They valued liberty both as an end and as a means. They believed liberty to be the secret of happiness and courage to be the secret of liberty.[43]

It is perhaps this understanding of freedom of speech that appears, initially, to pose the greatest challenge to corporate free-speech claimants. For this understanding is tethered to, primarily, the interests of the speaker. This does not permit us to sidestep the question of a corporation's nature via a focus on the speech and/or audience. Rather, this understanding forces us to squarely confront the question of the corporation's nature in order to ascertain how best to characterize its "speech."

This confrontation is vividly illustrated by the 1978 Supreme Court case *First National Bank of Boston v. Bellotti*.[44] In *Bellotti*, a divided Court struck down a Massachusetts criminal statute that restricted corporate campaign expenditures. How the two sets of justices (those in the majority versus those in the dissent) described the First Amendment is telling.

The majority opinion drew upon Meiklejohn and the listener-autonomy theory in its characterization of the First Amendment. In so doing, it rather easily concluded that the statute in question was unconstitutional, as it represented a paternalistic attempt to shield the public from corporate political speech. The Court's majority declared:

> [T]he people in our democracy are entrusted with the responsibility for judging and evaluating the relative merits of conflicting arguments. They may consider, in making their judgment, the source and credibility of the advocate. But if there be any danger that the people cannot evaluate the information and arguments advanced by appellants, it is a danger contemplated by the Framers of the First Amendment.[45]

In contrast, the dissenting justices described the First Amendment in self-realization terms. Such an understanding of the First Amendment calls into question the propriety of permitting a corporation to lay claim to its protections on a level equal to that of an individual. Justice White, who authored the dissent, reasoned as follows:

> There is now little doubt that corporate communications come within the scope of the First Amendment. This, however, is merely the starting point of analysis, because an examination of the First Amendment values that corporate expression furthers and the threat to the functioning of a free society it is capable of posing reveals that it is not fungible with communications emanating from individuals and is subject to restrictions which individual expression is not. Indeed, what some have considered to be the principal function of the First Amendment, the use of communication as a means of self-expression, self-realization, and self-fulfillment, is not at all furthered by corporate speech. It is clear that the communications of profitmaking corporations are not "an integral part of the development of ideas, of mental exploration and of the affirmation of self." They do not represent a manifestation of individual freedom or choice.[46]

Justice White's dissent echoes, in an important respect, Justice Brennan's majority opinion in *Federal Election Commission v. Massachusetts Citizens for Life, Inc.*, quoted earlier. Each justice presumes that corporate speech must be invariably profit-oriented and devoid of any authentically derived political or ideological content. The justices adopt a false dichotomy, failing to consider the possibility of corporate speech that is *both* profit-oriented *and* authentically political. Is it unthinkable that the publisher of libertarian-leaning books might actually embrace the ideals and principles espoused in its books? If, for example, such an entity were to support the elimination of taxes on the sale of books, would not such efforts reflect both its business and ideological interests?

Further, neither Justice seems capable of imagining the existence of the postmodern corporation: a corporation with a distinctive, genuinely political, ideological, or religious persona.[47] Whether they can be faulted for this during their own times (a few decades ago) is perhaps questionable. As has been discussed in chapter 3, however, recent developments in both law and society make such corporations an unmistakable reality in our times. This undermines the notion that corporations can "not at all" serve as a vehicle for the First Amendment speech and expression.

Thus, under a self-realization approach to the First Amendment, the divide between the modern and postmodern corporation is its most significant. For the very factors and characteristics that make up this divide also compel disparate treatment for these two entities under the First Amendment. The modern corporation, as we have seen, is not genuinely expressive, but rather narrowly focused on generating shareholder profits. As per Justice White, protecting the activities of such an entity is not the purpose of the First Amendment. Conversely, a postmodern corporation is capable of genuine expression. It exists, in part, to give individuals a vehicle through which they can engage in self-realization.

Finally, we cannot ignore the repeated references to the "individual" in Justice White's dissent. These references leave the impression that First Amendment rights protect only individuals. Such is not the case. From churches, to newspaper publishers, to political parties, it is well established that groups and organizations may lay claim to First Amendment rights and have standing to vindicate those rights in court as need be. White's dissent, therefore, should not be read literally. Rather, it should be read as a philosophical exposition of the First Amendment and on those grounds represents a well-respected point of view. Namely, that the purpose of the First Amendment is to protect the freedom of individuals.[48] That such is so does not conflict with affording groups and associations rights. Indeed, a desire to fully protect the rights of individuals leads naturally to the recognition and protection of groups and associational rights. For, as was discussed in chapter 1, associations are indispensable vehicles through which an individual's rights and freedoms are exercised.

COMMERCIAL SPEECH

There is no clear definition of "commercial speech." That said, the term has generally been used to cover what one might expect it to cover: communications that are commercial in nature, usually "made as part of an effort of a for-profit enterprise to induce purchase of specific commodities or services."[49] As mentioned, the dividing line between speech that is commercial versus that which is noncommercial can and is oftentimes blurred.[50] For reasons that will become apparent, that problem need not detain us.

Views on the applicability of the First Amendment to commercial speech have shifted over time, and nowhere is this more obvious than at the U.S. Supreme Court. A complete recitation of the amendment's jurisprudential history in this regard is unnecessary and can readily be found elsewhere.[51] In sum, the movement has been toward affording such speech more First Amendment protection over time.[52]

That said, speech of a commercial nature remains subject to diminished protection under the First Amendment. One could say that communications that are commercial in nature are not considered true "speech" for purposes of the First Amendment, or at least not to the same degree as those forms that receive the fullest First Amendment protection. Tom Bennigson summarizes the inferior protections received by commercial speech as follows:

> Specific differences in the treatment of commercial speech include less tolerance of false or misleading speech, more readily allowing speech to be compelled, the inapplicability of overbreadth doctrine, greater tolerance of prior restraints, and, most controversially, less rigorous standards for allowing truthful speech to be regulated to achieve other government ends.[53]

Related to commercial speech is what can be called "regulatory speech." With this term I refer to those disclosures that regulated entities are required to make, along with those communications that such entity may be precluded from making. There have been few challenges to regulatory speech on First Amendment grounds, and thus the Amendment's applicability in this context has not been well explored. Generally, it has been assumed that the rules governing commercial speech apply to regulatory speech as well, but increased scholarly attention upon this subject is calling that into question.[54]

Although commercial and regulatory speech is often associated with corporate speech, conceptually they are not necessarily connected. The linkage lies in the fact that corporate entities are so often engaged in commercial speech and are also so often subject to communications that are regulated by one or more regulatory agencies. Subject to a few exceptions, however, the status of the speaker as corporate or noncorporate is irrelevant.

The commercial speech doctrine addresses all communications of a commercial nature, regardless of the speaker. A woman hawking her used car should be subject to the same diminished First Amendment protections as Toyota Corporation when it comes to advertising materials and the like. The same holds true with regard to regulatory speech. Whether it be the question of labels on food packaging or certain postings in places of employment, what frequently matters is not the corporate identity of the regulated entity, but rather its regulated activities. Thus, the doctrine of commercial speech (including regulatory speech) is not truly relevant to our assessment of corporate speech of a political or expressive dimension.

CORPORATE SPEECH

Our review of the various approaches to freedom of speech allows us to draw a few significant conclusions regarding corporate speech, many of which have already been suggested.

First, to the extent that the corporate speech in question is neither political nor expressive but merely commercial, it would not receive the full protections of the First Amendment. This is not due to anything particular about the corporation or the corporate form, but rather due to the nature of the speech as commercial.

Second, regardless of the theory employed, the First Amendment's guarantee of freedom of speech protects only "speech." Thus, whether "corporate speech" should receive protection under the First Amendment should not turn on the speaker's identity as a corporation, but rather on the existence of genuine "speech." This, in turn, requires us to consider whether corporations are capable of engaging in "speech."

No clear definition of what exactly constitutes "speech" has been established. At a minimum, based upon the various theories regarding the First Amendment, it would seem as though communications contending for the categorization of "speech" should have some expressive component. What should be clear, however, is that the mere fact of an entity's incorporation, by itself, should not be dispositive. Put differently, the question of corporate freedom of speech should not be resolved identically for all corporations. With regard to the modern corporation, the argument against recognition of First Amendment free speech rights is very strong. The caricature of the modern corporation that opponents of the *Citizens United* decision paint is rather accurate and not one that lends itself to "speaking" as envisioned by the First Amendment. The modern corporation exists to produce profits in order to maximize shareholder wealth. Its acts of "speech" are instrumental to that narrow end. Thus, when the modern corporation purchases a political advertisement or throws it support behind a particular candidate or issue, it takes a position that, ideologically speaking, not a single one of its constituents might genuinely support. Although, as discussed, under certain theories of the First Amendment this could arguably be protected as speech, by all accounts it certainly approaches (if not crosses) the limits of the amendment's rationale. One would be hard pressed to find utterly no meaningful distinction between genuine articulations of beliefs and positions on the one hand and statements of beliefs and positions that are not genuinely held on the other (even if the latter should be afforded protection on prophylactic grounds).

None of this, however, fairly applies to the postmodern corporation. As explained in chapter 3, the postmodern corporation, unlike the modern corporation, represents a genuine Tocquevillian Association. As such, it serves as a vehicle for individual expression of values, beliefs, and priorities. When the postmodern corporation engages in acts of expression or political advocacy, it serves to amplify the voice of its various constituencies. It uses their pooling of efforts and resources to promote values that they themselves have decided to support. This would constitute protected speech under any theory of the First Amendment.

NOTES

1. 558 U.S. 310 (2010).
2. LAURENCE H. TRIBE, AMERICAN CONSTITUTIONAL LAW 785 (2d ed. 1988).
3. *See* Thomas Scanlon, *A Theory of Freedom of Expression*, 1 PHIL. & PUB. AFFAIRS 204, 206–207 (1972).
4. *See* chapter 4; *see also* TRIBE, *supra* note 2, at 795 ("[T]he first amendment protects speech whether or not it protects the particular speaker").
5. *See* United States v. Eichmann, 496 U.S. 310, 312 (1990).
6. *See* Doran v. Salem Inn, 422 U.S. 922, 932–33 (1975).
7. As this project is not primarily one of hermeneutics, I shall eschew the question of how best to interpret the Constitution. *See generally, e.g.*, ANTONIN SCALIA, A MATTER OF INTERPRETATION (1997). Rather, in this chapter and the foregoing, I shall proceed directly to a consideration of particular schools of thought and their merits.
8. Konigsberg v. State Bar, 366 U.S. 36, 49 n.10 (1961) (*quoted in* Alexander Meiklejohn, *The First Amendment is an Absolute* 5–6 (1961), *in* FREE SPEECH AND ASSOCIATION (Philip B. Kurland ed., 1975)).
9. Stanley C. Brubaker, *Original Intent and Freedom of Speech and Press, in* THE BILL OF RIGHTS 85 (Eugene W. Hickok Jr. ed., 1991) (*quoted in* R. George Wright, *What Counts as "Speech" in the First Place? Determining the Scope of the Free Speech Clause*, 37 PEPP. L. REV. 1217, 1221 (2010)).
10. *See* Lawrence B. Solum, *Freedom of Communicative Action: A Theory of the First Amendment Freedom of Speech*, 83 NW. U. L. REV. 54, 60 (1989).
11. *See id.* at 82–86; TRIBE, *supra* note 2, at 788–89.
12. John 18:38 (Clementina Vulgata).
13. *See* Solum, *supra* note 10, at 68–69.
14. J. MILTON, AREOPAGITICA 51–52 (J. Hales ed., 1917) (1st ed. London 1644), (*quoted in* Harry H. Wellington, *On Freedom of Expression*, 88 YALE L. J. 1105, 1129 (1979)).
15. *See* Solum, *supra* note 10, at 68 (quoting Abrams v. United States, 250 U.S. 616, 630 (1919)) (Holmes, J., dissenting).
16. *See* Solum, *supra* note 10, at 69.
17. *See* Meiklejohn, *supra* note 8, at 11.

18. *Id.*
19. *Id.*
20. *Id.* at 12–13.
21. *See* chapter 2.
22. *E.g.*, Wayne Batchis, Citizens United *and the Paradox of "Corporate Speech": From Freedom of Association to Freedom of the Association*, 36 N.Y.U. REV. L. & SOC. CHANGE 5, 49–50 (2012).
23. *See* chapter 8.
24. *See Chick-fil-A Has Record Setting Sales on Appreciation Day*, ABC NEWS (Aug. 2, 2012), http://abcnews.go.com/Politics/OTUS/chick-fil-record-setting-sales-appreciation-day/story?id=16912978.
25. *See id.*
26. Martin H. Redish & Howard W. Wasserman, *What's Good for General Motors: Corporate Speech and the Theory of Free Expression*, 66 GEO. WASH. L. REV. 235, 235 (1998).
27. *E.g.*, J. Skelly Wright, *Money and the Pollution of Politics: Is the First Amendment an Obstacle to Political Equality?*, 82 COLUM. L. REV. 609, 636 (1982).
28. 424 U.S. 1, 48–49 (1976) (per curiam).
29. Fed. Elec. Comm'n v. Massachusetts Citizens for Life, Inc., 479 U.S. 238, 251 (1986) (quoting Williams v. Rhodes, 393 U.S. 23, 32 (1968)).
30. Jake Heller & Patrice Howard, "YouTube's 10 Most Watched Videos Ever," THE DAILY BEAST (Apr. 23, 2013), http://www.thedailybeast.com/articles/2013/04/23/youtube-s-10-most-watched-videos-ever.html.
31. 479 U.S. at 257–58.
32. *See* chapter 8.
33. *See* Solum, *supra* note 10, at 77–78.
34. *See* Scanlon, *supra* note 3, at 209.
35. *Id.* at 213 (*quoted in* Wellington, *supra* note 14, at 1121). It must be noted that Scanlon has backed away from the Millian Principle as he originally formulated it. *See* T. M. Scanlon Jr., *Freedom of Expression and Categories of Expression*, 40 U. PITT. L. REV. 519, 531–32 (1978).
36. *See* Willington, *supra* note 14, at 1122.
37. *See* Scanlon, *supra* note 3, at 223.
38. It should be noted that Scanlon asserts that limitations on campaign spending are "in principle compatible with freedom of expression." He compares these limits to "limits on the length of speeches in a town meeting." This echoes, to a degree, a noncontent-based concerns of the anti-distortion rationale: namely, the concern that absent regulation, the speech of some might crowd out the speech of others. Commendably, however, Scanlon does not carve out corporate campaign spending for special treatment, but rather focuses on the root of the problem: money's influence in politics, without regard to speaker.

    Nevertheless, I do not find Scanlon's analogy particularly persuasive: a town meeting is of a limited duration, and there may very well be more interested speakers than there is time to accommodate. By contrast, in the twenty-first century, the avenues by which an individual may engage in political speech via campaign spending are legion. When one considers the possibility of creating and funding one's own websites in order to further one's viewpoints or expression, there is practically no limit to how much speech an individual or entity can engage in nowadays should he, she, or it choose to do so. A more apt analogy to the limitations of the town meeting would be the broadcasting of political advertisements on AM or FM radio stations, given the limitations of available bandwidth and air time. Here one could plausibly compare limits on the amount of money expendable on such advertising to limits on the amount of time one would be permitted to speak during a town meeting.

Regardless, Scanlon is quick to add that although such limitations would be justifiable in principle, he nevertheless finds them highly problematic. He rightly finds it difficult to properly segregate "campaign speech" from "other expression on political topics," and fears the potential overbreadth of any such regulation. *See* Scanlon, *supra* note 35, at 540.

39. *See* Solum, *supra* note 10, at 79–81.
40. *See* ARISTOTLE, POLITICS, *in* 2 THE COMPLETE WORKS OF ARISTOTLE 1253a1 (J. Barnes ed., 1984) (cited in Solum, *supra* note 10, at 79).
41. *See* Laurent Sacharoff, *Listener Interests in Compelled Speech Cases*, 44 CAL. W. L. REV. 329, 379 (2008).
42. *See* STEVEN J. HEYMAN, FREE SPEECH AND HUMAN DIGNITY 7–12 (2008).
43. 274 U.S. 357, 375 (1927) (Brandeis, J. joined by Holmes, J., concurring) (*quoted in* TRIBE, *supra* note 2, at 788).
44. 435 U.S. 765 (1978).
45. *Id.* at 791–92 (citations omitted).
46. *Id.* at 804–805 (White, J., dissenting) (citations omitted).
47. Although Justice Brennan has come close. *See* chapter 7, text accompanying note 82.
48. With regard to the Establishment and Free Exercise Clauses, however, there are reasons to believe that the framers intended for "the church" to be protected from the state in the aggregate—as a societal institution. *See* Richard W. Garnett, *Do Churches Matter? Towards an Institutional Understanding of the Religion Clauses*, 53 VILL. L. REV. 273, 274 (2008).
49. Victor Bradley, *The First Amendment and Commercial Speech*, 53 B.C. L. REV. 1153, 1154 (2012).
50. Perhaps no greater example of this can be provided than that presented in *Kasky v. Nike*, 45 P.3d 243 (Cal. 2002). Accused of relying upon overseas sweatshop labor, Nike issued a series of communications in defense of its practices and products. *See* Tom Bennigson, *Nike Revisited: Can Commercial Corporations Engage in Non-Commercial Speech?*, 39 CONN. L. REV. 379, 381–82 (2006).
51. *See* TRIBE, *supra* note 2, at 890–904.
52. *See id.*
53. Bennigson, *supra* note 50, at 386–87.
54. *See, e.g.*, Henry N. Butler & Larry E. Ribstein, *Corporate Governance Speech and the First Amendment*, 43 U. KAN. L. REV. 163 (1994).

CHAPTER 7

The First Amendment

Freedom of Religion

Although the question of corporate free speech rights has received sustained attention for decades, the same cannot be said with regard to corporate free exercise rights. Throughout the course of American history, business corporations rarely invoked America's "First Freedom"—the freedom of religion as set forth in the First Amendment.

All that changed in 2012, when a handful of business corporations filed suit to block implementation of a government requirement that employee health insurance plans include coverage of sterilization, abortifacients, and birth control. This requirement, known as the "contraceptive mandate," was adopted by the Department of Health and Human Services in response to the Patient Protection and Affordable Care Act of 2010.[1] Certain corporations argued that the requirement conflicted with the religious principles upon which they operated and predicated their lawsuits upon the First Amendment's Free Exercise Clause (and the Religious Freedom Restoration Act). With little judicial precedent to go on, many of the courts grappling with the contraceptive mandate cases readily admitted that the cases presented matters of first impression and have rendered conflicting decisions.[2] The U.S. Supreme Court granted *certiorari* in two of these cases to consider the issue and resolve the split among the circuit courts in 2013 and is expected to render a decision in 2014.

As with the courts, commentators have weighed in on both sides of the issue. Given the lack of precedent on the issue, it presents itself as one fraught with great difficulty. That said, we are fairly well equipped to analyze the issues presented. The Free Exercise Clause has a rich history which can be drawn upon to discern the scope of religious freedom that its framers most likely intended. Although case law precisely on point is indeed sparse, there is significant precedent on related matters, enabling us, with a little extrapolation, to piece together the way forward.

As with freedom of speech, I contend that the critical question with regard to religious freedom is not the status of the claimant as a for-profit corporation. Rather, the critical question is the nature of the claimant's conduct. Just as freedom of speech demanded that we identify whether "speech" was being abridged, freedom of religion similarly demands that we identify whether the "free exercise of religion" is being abridged. And as with freedom of speech, the inquiry comes full circle insofar as we are inevitably confronted with the question: are corporations capable of engaging in the "exercise of religion" as that term is understood under the Constitution?[3]

FREE EXERCISE CLAUSE BACKGROUND

"Congress shall make no law respecting an establishment of religion, or prohibiting the free exercise thereof."[4] So begins the first sentence of the First Amendment to the United States Constitution, setting forth what has come to be known as the "Establishment" and "Free Exercise" clauses. Especially for its time, the First Amendment was "an absolutely unique constitutional provision for a nation."[5]

The backdrop of the First Amendment was the religious "strife and intolerance" that marked the Old World, and particularly England.[6] For most of the seventeenth century, the era of America's colonization, England was marked by an established, state church (the Church of England), and other faiths were, to a greater or lesser degree, generally suppressed. Interestingly, England's American colonies did not all follow suit. Some (such as Virginia) retained the Church of England as the established faith. Others (particularly the colonies of New England) continued to observe an established faith, but substituted other denominations for the Church of England. Four colonies (Rhode Island, New Jersey, Pennsylvania, and Delaware) lacked an established religion altogether.[7]

Coupled with this historical experience was the intense religiosity of the founding generation. According to Michael McConnell's impressive review of the historical record, the commitment to nonestablishment and religious liberty enshrined in the First Amendment was not simply a product of deistic or rationalistic Enlightenment-era thinking (as is commonly supposed). Rather, the commitment was especially championed by the "most intense religious sects" of the time, sects which suffered the most from their minority status.[8] They saw nonestablishment as essential to the health of religion generally, their religions in particular, and necessary to prevent religion's subordination to the state.[9] This view was well captured by James Madison, who famously declared:

> It is the duty of every man to render to the Creator such homage and such only as he believes to be acceptable to him. This duty is precedent, both in order of time and in degree of obligation, to the claims of Civil Society. Before any man can be considered as a member of Civil Society, he must be considered as a subject of the Governour of the Universe: And if a member of Civil Society, do it with a saving of his allegiance to the Universal Sovereign. We maintain therefore that in matters of Religion, no man's right is abridged by the institution of Civil Society and that Religion is wholly exempt from its cognizance.[10]

Rationalists and deists generally joined with the religiously fervent in support of Madison's robust approach to religious liberty.[11] (Thomas Jefferson, for example, favored a vigorous Free Exercise Clause coupled with a vigorous Establishment Clause.[12]) Curiously, a sizeable number of rationalists and deists took the opposite approach and believed that the state should play a role in regulating (and supporting) religion. Pursuant to this approach, neither the Establishment Clause nor the Free Exercise Clause was to be interpreted and applied vigorously. According to this perspective, religion was simply too important to a democratic republic to be left to its own devices. As John Adams remarked, "We have no government armed with power capable of contending with human passions unbridled by morality and religion. Our constitution was made only for a moral people and a religious people. It is wholly inadequate for the government of any other."[13]

As McConnell explains, this created a rather interesting paradox:

> The paradox of the religious freedom debates of the late eighteenth century is that one side employed essentially secular arguments based on the needs of civil society for the importance of religion, while the other side employed essentially religious arguments based on the primacy of duties to God over duties to the state in support of disestablishment and free exercise.[14]

Ultimately, what resulted was a nation that lacked an established faith and vigorously protected religious liberty.

As an aside, the history of the Free Exercise Clause highlights the fact that one need not be religious, or have a particularly favorable view of religion, in order to grasp the wisdom of a robust conceptualization of religious liberty. "Religious liberty does not view religion as a good thing to be promoted, nor as a dangerous force to be constrained."[15] Regardless of one's thoughts about religion, it is sensible for society to afford generous protections to religiously motivated behavior "because attempts to suppress religious behavior will lead to all the problems of conflict and suffering that religious liberty is designed to avoid... [since] religious behavior is as likely as religious belief to be of extraordinary importance to individuals."[16] As Douglas Laycock points out, "beliefs about religion are often... important enough to die for, to suffer for, to rebel for, to emigrate for, to fight to control the government for."[17] Freedom to "adopt religious beliefs and engage in religious practices... is one vital aspect of personal autonomy."[18] Common sense dictates that such suffering, and conflict, be avoided if at all reasonably possible. Thus, for purely secular reasons, reasons that have to do with the maintenance of public order and peace, it would seem sensible to protect religious conduct from encroachment or prohibition to the broadest extent reasonably possible.[19]

James Madison offers a view cut from the same cloth in *Federalist Paper 51*. Here, Madison explains that the security of rights, both religious and civil, depends on the "multiplicity" of interests and sects.[20] A robust approach to religious liberty is self-perpetuating, as it promotes this "multiplicity of sects" and inhibits the rise of a potentially rights-destructive hegemony.[21] Paradoxically, therefore, the more a society is marked by a vibrant religious pluralism, the less likely it is that government and public policy will be dictated by any one particular religious perspective. In more ways than one, therefore, freedom *of* religion contributes to freedom *from* religion.[22]

"TOLERANCE" VS. "LIBERTY"

A proper understanding of the First Amendment's approach to religious freedom must be careful not to conflate "religious liberty" with "religious tolerance." The Lockean ideal of religious freedom, which weighed heavily in the minds of the framers, was predicated precisely upon the notion of tolerance. For the peace of society, "sweeping toleration toward religious dissenters" was the best policy according to Locke.[23] Not surprisingly, therefore, early drafts of some state constitutions contained clauses proclaiming religious "tolerance." These approaches were, however, soundly rejected when it came to the federal Constitution.[24]

"Tolerance," as James Madison and others pointed out, implies "an act of legislative grace."[25] As per the American Declaration of Independence, rights as fundamental as religious liberty are not granted by the state, but rather were endowed to each individual "by their Creator." Constitutions and bills of rights merely give recognition to this fact.[26] As Thomas Paine remarked: "Tolerance is not the opposite of intolerance, it is the counterfeit of it. Both are despotisms. The one assumes to itself the right of withholding liberty of conscience, and the other of granting it."[27]

Thus, in place of language establishing religious "tolerance," Virginia's influential constitution was ultimately drafted to guarantee "the full and free exercise of religion."[28] This language, in large part, carried over into the U.S. Constitution.[29] As Laycock eloquently explains:

> The religion clauses represent both a legal guarantee of religious liberty and a political commitment to religious liberty. The religion clauses made America a beacon of hope for religious minorities throughout the world. The extent of religious pluralism in this country, and of legal and political protections for religious minorities, is probably unsurpassed in human experience. Religious liberty is one of America's great contributions to civilization.[30]

This foray into the historical backdrop of the Free Exercise Clause is helpful because it sheds much-needed light on many issues that are today contested. It suggests an approach to religious liberty that errs on the side of magnanimity, rather than one that is narrowly circumscribed.

And much concerning the Free Exercise Clause is fiercely disputed. Indeed, one of the only things upon which there exists broad consensus is that religious belief, per se, is inviolable. There is universal agreement among scholars that the Free Exercise Clause, at its irreducible minimum, absolutely prohibits the government from interfering with an individual's religious beliefs.[31] Indeed, this proposition is buttressed by the Establishment Clause, which prohibits the federal government from demanding citizen support of some official state religion, be that via tax dollars or otherwise.[32] Beyond that, the consensus breaks down.

Some would read little else into the Free Exercise Clause than simply this protection of individual conscience or belief. Others, however, would read much more into the amendment's scope.[33] Recourse to the historical background recounted above supports this latter interpretation, as the minimalist approach appears difficult to credit in light of the colonial record. Anemic indeed would be a version of religious liberty so restricted, and this is not what the amendment's framers had in mind. Even Elizabethan England, with its legendarily cruel and severe persecution of Catholics and non-Anglican dissenters, arguably permitted as much as freedom of private belief.[34] The same can be said of ancient Rome: "The faithful were seldom persecuted in Rome for *believing* in Christianity, they suffered oftenest for *acting* it."[35] Thus, to many, any understanding of religious liberty that claims to be consistent with the intent of the Constitution's framers must extend such liberty not merely to religious thought but to religiously inspired conduct as well. This is the conclusion that Noah Feldman reached in his acclaimed book *Divided by God*: "the Free Exercise Clause gave special protection to religious activity, greater than the protection available to nonreligious conduct."[36]

CONDUCT PROTECTED

Although, I suggest, it is easy to conclude that the Free Exercise Clause protects not merely religious belief but religious conduct as well, determining the scope of such conduct to protect is indeed a difficult task.

As a threshold matter, the clause explicitly protects the free exercise of "religion," thus the conduct in question must be religious in nature.[37] Distinguishing conduct that is religiously inspired from that which is not religiously inspired can be a daunting task, especially because "religion permeates the life of devout individuals and influences so many of their decisions."[38] One approach to this problem would be to equate religious conduct to little more than worship. Thus, aside from worship at one's temple, church, mosque, or home, religious individuals (and institutions) would have scarcely cognizable religious liberty rights before the government.[39]

For all its narrowness, such an approach is not without its proponents. In the United States, federal officials have, for example, increasingly substituted the phrase "freedom of worship" for "freedom of religion" in their public pronouncements. Whether this is merely a change in nomenclature, or whether it amounts to a substantive policy shift, is not yet entirely clear.[40]

More problematic is the lack of clarity concerning the line separating religiously motivated conduct that constitutes worship from religiously motivated conduct that does not constitute worship. As Laycock points out, "it is illusory to distinguish the right to worship from the right to engage in other religious practices."[41] Many if not most religions circumscribe a code of behavior that is completely integrated into their system of beliefs—a code of behavior that could be considered an extension of their "worship."[42] Temple services most obviously constitute worship, but what about grace before meals? What about sacrificial dietary restrictions, or manners of dress? Could not these, too, be considered acts of worship, defined by the dictionary as "reverent honor and homage paid to God"?[43]

In any event, few interpret the Free Exercise Clause as covering simply "worship" per se; most commentators (and all courts) interpret the clause as covering a much broader range of activity. Moreover, the broader approach comports better with both the American understanding at the time of the Constitution's adoption, and even the understanding of the modern, developed world insofar as is was accurately captured by the 1948 United Nation's Universal Declaration of Human Rights.

Regarding the American experience, the phrase "free exercise of religion" was generally understood (at the time of its inclusion in the Bill of Rights) to encompass more than simply religious "worship." It was understood to extend to essentially any religiously grounded conduct that was dictated by conscience and conviction.[44] As John Witte explains:

> Though eighteenth century writers, or dictionaries, offered no universal definition of "free exercise," the phrase generally connoted various forms of free public religious action—religious speech, religious worship, religious assembly, religious publication, religious education, among others. Free exercise of religion also embraced the right of the individual to join with like-minded believers in religious societies, which religious societies were free to devise their own modes of worship, articles of faith, standards of discipline, and patterns of ritual.[45]

The Universal Declaration of Human Rights, adopted in 1948, hews to this eighteenth-century understanding of religious liberty, defining freedom of religion as a person's freedom "either alone or in community with others and in public or private, to manifest his religion or belief in teaching, practice, worship and observance."[46]

However, even if we may agree on what constitutes religiously motivated conduct, and even if we may agree that such conduct ought generally to be protected from governmental encroachment, certain limits must inevitably apply. For there are limits to every freedom enumerated in the Bill of Rights, as such is necessary for an orderly society. Even the fiercest defender of religious freedom is unlikely to support its application to protect, for example, the practice of human sacrifice so infamously featured in the Aztec religion. The jurisprudence of the Free Exercise Clause reveals the courts' difficulties in setting these limits. From a review of precedent and commentary, three separate approaches to the Free Exercise Clause can be distilled. I shall refer to them as the "narrow approach," the "discretionary approach," and the "broad approach."

The Narrow Approach

Under the narrow approach, the First Amendment only protects religiously motivated conduct that is targeted for abridgment by the government specifically on account of its religious nature. Running afoul of this approach, for example, would be a government prohibition not on headwear in general, but rather only on headwear worn for religious reasons (such as a yarmulke, headscarf, or mantilla). There is near universal consensus that such a prohibition would give rise to a free exercise claim. The claim would be resolved via recourse to the stringent "compelling government interest/least restrictive means" test. Pursuant to this test, the challenged law or regulation would pass constitutional muster if and only if the government were able to demonstrate that the provision in question was "[1] justified by a compelling [government] interest and [2] narrowly tailored to advance that interest."[47] The test is a demanding one, and most government efforts subjected to it would fail. Of course, some would pass master. Legislation that simultaneously allowed an individual's heart to be removed for the purpose of transplantation, but not for the purpose of some religious ritual, would not be found unconstitutional. Although the law was aimed at prohibiting a specifically religious practice, it would readily find justification under even the heightened compelling government interest/least restrictive means test given the state's compelling interest in protecting human life.

For all other legislation and regulation, such as generally applicable laws that infringe upon religious conduct only by happenstance, and not by design, the free exercise claimant is unlikely to prevail. Thus, a law that makes it illegal to ingest peyote under any circumstances would not give rise to a free exercise claim on the part of those individuals who might ingest peyote as part of a religious ritual.[48] This is because the law does not target religious behavior in particular for circumscription. In such situations, the standard by which the law is assessed is the lenient "rational basis" standard: the law "need only be rationally related to a legitimate governmental interest in order to survive a constitutional challenge."[49] This is not a difficult hurdle for the government to clear.

The Discretionary Approach

What I term the "discretionary approach" builds upon the narrow approach. Pursuant to the discretionary approach, the Free Exercise Clause protects religious beliefs and conduct as previously discussed, but also permits Congress and the states, in their discretion, to promulgate exemptions to generally applicable laws for religious individuals and groups, otherwise known as "religious accommodations."[50] Such is the regnant standard, as embraced by the U.S. Supreme Court in its 1990 decision *Employment Division, Department of Human Resources of Oregon v. Smith*.[51] Absent such an accommodation, even an individual is not relieved of his or her obligation to follow a generally applicable law, and the "narrow approach" articulated above applies.[52] Quoting approvingly from precedent, the Court in *Smith* held:

> The mere possession of religious convictions which contradict the relevant concerns of a political society does not relieve the citizen from the discharge of political responsibilities.... To permit this would be to make the professed doctrines of religious belief superior to the law of the land, and in effect to permit every citizen to become a law unto himself.[53]

When a generally applicable law is challenged by a free exercise claimant, if no legislative accommodation has been granted, the standard by which the law's constitutionality is assessed is the lenient "rational basis" standard articulated previously.

An additional facet of the discretionary approach is that a law or regulation that would otherwise appear to be "generally applicable" loses that designation if it contains a "system of individual exemptions" attached to it.[54] In such cases, failure to provide for a religious exemption (via the crafting of a comparable accommodation for religious individuals) could cause the law to run afoul of the Free Exercise Clause. By exempting some from the law for nonreligious reasons but refusing to exempt others from the law on account of religious reasons, the lawmaker can be said to have specifically targeted religiously motivated conduct for circumscription, in violation of even the narrowest reading of the Free Exercise Clause. If challenged, the absence of a religious exemption under such circumstances would be subject to the compelling government interest test: the government would need to demonstrate a compelling reason for failing to extend its list of exemptions to the religious claimants.[55] Harkening back to the peyote example: imagine that the government were to generally ban the ingestion of peyote, but permit its ingestion in certain limited circumstances. In that case, failure to permit the ingestion of peyote for religious purposes would subject the ban to the compelling government interest test with regard to those who would ingest it for religious purposes.

The Broad Approach

The broad approach to the Free Exercise Clause would subject any law or regulation that abridged the free exercise of religion to the compelling government interest test, even a law of general applicability. In other words, all religiously motivated conduct would be strictly protected, even conduct that was not specifically targeted for circumscription on account of its religious motivation. It must be recalled that even such strict protection has its limits; it is not absolute. The primary difference between this approach and the previous two, therefore, is largely the applicable standard against which government infringements upon religious conduct are to be assessed. Whereas the prior approaches utilized the rational basis test as the default standard by which to adjudicate alleged infringements upon religiously motivated conduct, the broad approach would instead turn to the stringent compelling government interest test in all such situations (not reserving it for only select infringements, such as the specific targeting of religious conduct for circumscription, or the failure to include an exemption for religious believers where exemptions for nonbelievers have been promulgated).

According to the dissenting Justices in *Smith*, this broad approach was the traditional approach to the Free Exercise Clause in the United States before *Smith*'s majority changed things:

> This Court over the years painstakingly has developed a consistent and exacting standard to test the constitutionality of a state statute that burdens the free exercise of religion. Such a statute may stand only if the law in general, and the State's refusal to allow a religious exemption in particular, are justified by a compelling interest that cannot be served by less restrictive means.[56]

The broad approach also appears to comport best with the framers' generous approach to religious liberty, as previously discussed.[57] A ban on infant circumcision, for example, infringes upon traditional Jewish practices regardless of whether the ban was enacted generally versus enacted only against circumcisions undertaken solely for religious reasons. Ignorance of and insensitivity toward religious practices can create a society nearly as inhospitable toward religion as one that lacks the First Amendment's guarantees of religious freedom altogether. The First Amendment's framers were aware of this. Although by today's standards, America's founding generation might appear religiously homogeneous, such appearances are misleading. Colonial America was marked by profound religious differences, and the framers of the First Amendment understood that religious liberty would not be sufficiently protected if subject to majoritarian whims via the promulgation of discretionary exemptions and accommodations from laws of general applicability.

Hybrid Claims

Before proceeding, a potentially significant wrinkle to the prevailing understanding of the Free Exercise Clause must be mentioned. In order to account for precedent in which claimants were granted an exemption to a law of general applicability under the Free Exercise Clause, the Supreme Court in *Smith* recognized and distinguished certain "hybrid situation[s]."[58] As the Court explained, these situations implicated both the Free Exercise Clause and other constitutional rights:

> The only decisions in which we have held that the First Amendment bars application of a neutral, generally applicable law to religiously motivated action have involved not the Free Exercise Clause alone, but the Free Exercise Clause in conjunction with other constitutional protections, such as freedom of speech and of the press . . . or the right of parents . . . to direct the education of their children. . . . And it is easy to envision a case in which a challenge on freedom of association grounds would likewise be reinforced by Free Exercise Clause

> concerns. *Cf. Roberts v. United States Jaycees*, 468 U.S. 609, 622, 104 S.Ct. 3244, 3251–52, 82 L.Ed.2d 462 (1984) ("An individual's freedom to speak, to worship, and to petition the government for the redress of grievances could not be vigorously protected from interference by the State [if] a correlative freedom to engage in group effort toward those ends were not also guaranteed").[59]

This "aside" of hybrid situations is an interesting one, but not something in which courts since *Smith* have shown much interest. Indeed, some have characterized it as mere dicta.[60] Scholars, too, have not lavished much attention on the exception (indeed, most of the commentary hails from student notes).[61] Because the exception may be of relevance to corporate free exercise rights, however, it merits our attention. Indeed, as one scholar who studied the *Smith* decision has noted, the "distinguishing feature in those cases" listed by Scalia as presenting hybrid claims "was generally the presence of a corporation (or some other associative entity) making a property claim."[62]

The circuits have split over their approach to free-exercise hybrid-rights claims. The Sixth and Second Circuits refuse to recognize hybrid-rights claims altogether.[63] The Ninth and Tenth Circuits, along with most other lower courts in general, do recognize hybrid-rights claims.[64] Within these circuits, "where a party asserts a 'colorable,' or arguable, hybrid rights claim, then strict scrutiny applies in evaluating the party's free exercise claim."[65] A "colorable" claim is a showing that presents a "fair probability" that (1) religiously motivated conduct and (2) some other fundamental right has been infringed.[66]

Initially, the hybrid-rights claim appears entirely redundant: why couple a free exercise claim with another alleged rights violation instead of simply litigating the other alleged rights violation? Indeed, the standard as articulated has given rise to a considerable amount of confusion. Adding my voice to the cacophony of perspectives, it appears as though the benefit (to the claimant) in a hybrid-rights claim is as follows: the claimant is relieved of the obligation of having to demonstrate that this other fundamental right has actually been violated. Instead, the claimant can require the government to meet its burden of "strict scrutiny" with regard to the challenged law or regulation by simply *alleging* a "colorable" violation of some other fundamental right (coupled with a demonstration that his or her religiously motivated conduct is being substantially burdened).[67] Of particular relevance for our purposes would be the well-established freedom of association.[68] Were a corporation to qualify for this particular freedom (as will be discussed in chapter 8), it should be able to invoke the hybrid-rights theory, triggering the strict scrutiny standard with regard to its free exercise claim. The corporation's argument would be predicated upon a law or regulation that allegedly burdened both its religious free exercise and their freedom of association. Rather than having to litigate each of these claims, the hybrid-rights exception would enable the corporate claimant to invoke the generous "strict scrutiny" standard vis-à-vis their free exercise cause of action.

The Religious Freedom Restoration Act

No discussion of religious liberty in America would be complete without a review of the Religious Freedom Restoration Act. For within three years of the *Smith* decision, Congress attempted its overturn via the Religious Freedom Restoration Act (RFRA). The act's stated findings recount much of what has been previously discussed:

> The Congress finds that—
>
> (1) the framers of the Constitution, recognizing free exercise of religion as an unalienable right, secured its protection in the First Amendment to the Constitution;
>
> (2) laws "neutral" toward religion may burden religious exercise as surely as laws intended to interfere with religious exercise;
>
> (3) governments should not substantially burden religious exercise without compelling justification;
>
> (4) in *Employment Division v. Smith*, 494 U.S. 872 (1990) the Supreme Court virtually eliminated the requirement that the government justify burdens on religious exercise imposed by laws neutral toward religion; and
>
> (5) the compelling interest test as set forth in prior Federal court rulings is a workable test for striking sensible balances between religious liberty and competing prior governmental interests.[69]

The act declared that its purpose was to restore the "pre-*Smith*" case law standard for adjudicating free exercise claims and set forth its understanding of that standard in the act's operative section, which reads in its entirety as follows:

> (a) In general
>
> Government shall not substantially burden a person's exercise of religion even if the burden results from a rule of general applicability, except as provided in subsection (b) of this section.
>
> (b) Exception
>
> Government may substantially burden a person's exercise of religion only if it demonstrates that application of the burden to the person—
>
> (1) is in furtherance of a compelling governmental interest; and
>
> (2) is the least restrictive means of furthering that compelling governmental interest.

(c) Judicial relief

> A person whose religious exercise has been burdened in violation of this section may assert that violation as a claim or defense in a judicial proceeding and obtain appropriate relief against a government. Standing to assert a claim or defense under this section shall be governed by the general rules of standing under Article III of the Constitution.[70]

RFRA was endorsed by a broad array of public advocacy groups, from the ACLU on the left to religious groups on the right.[71] In prescient remarks, Nadine Strossen, head of the ACLU, remarked that "[i]n the aftermath of the *Smith* decision, it was easy to imagine how religious practices and institutions would have to abandon their beliefs in order to comply with generally applicable, neutral laws." She declared that "[a]t risk were such familiar practices as . . . permitting religiously sponsored hospitals to decline to provide abortion or contraception services."[72] Not surprisingly, RFRA passed Congress with overwhelming bipartisan support and was signed into law by President Clinton in 1993.

RFRA was challenged in the courts and upheld as applied to federal legislation and regulation, but struck down as applied to state action on the theory that it exceeded Congress's powers under the Fourteenth Amendment.[73] This, in turn, spawned the promulgation of "state RFRAs": state-level legislation enacted to secure the free exercise protections contained in RFRA for those individuals whose religiously motivated conduct is impaired by state law or regulation.[74]

Finally, it should be noted that a separate debate has erupted over whether for-profit corporations should be considered "persons" for the purpose of RFRA.[75] This debate is one of statutory construction, centering on the meaning of "person" as that word is used in RFRA. As must be readily apparent, my concerns in this book are broader, largely invoking the normative question of what entities should or should not enjoy the protections of religious liberty. That said, given the legislative history of RFRA, it seems wisest to interpret its text as broadly as that of the First Amendment itself. There is no evidence whatsoever that RFRA was intended to curtail, in any way, the reach of the First Amendment as it had been interpreted prior to the *Smith* decision. Thus, whether a for-profit corporation has free exercise standing under the First Amendment, or can assert the protections of RFRA, should be answered together and consistently.

Religious Liberty Summarized

As a result of *Smith* and RFRA, the religious liberty rights of Americans are protected by different laws in different contexts. Some of these protections are the result of legislative action such as RFRA, and some can be traced directly to the First Amendment. This patchwork of protections can be summarized as follows:

- A law challenging religious belief is "never permissible" under the First Amendment.
- If a person's religiously motivated conduct is specifically targeted for circumscription by law, the First Amendment requires that it must be struck down unless it is "justified by a compelling [government] interest and ... narrowly tailored to advance that interest."
- If a federal law of general applicability "substantial[ly] burdens" a person's religiously motivated conduct, there is no relief afforded under the First Amendment other than the requirement that the law be "rationally related to a legitimate governmental interest."[76] However, under RFRA, the government will bear the burden of proving that the law "(1) is in furtherance of a compelling governmental interest; and (2) is the least restrictive means of furthering that compelling governmental interest" in order for it to be upheld.
- If a state law of general applicability "substantial[ly] burdens" a person's religiously motivated conduct, there is no relief afforded under the First Amendment other than the requirement that the law be "rationally related to a legitimate governmental interest."[77] RFRA would be inapplicable, thereby affording no additional relief. That said, if the state in question is one of the many that has enacted its own version of RFRA, then such a law would be struck down if it fails to comply with the standard set forth in its own version of RFRA (which generally follow the compelling government interest/least restrictive means standard of the federal RFRA).
- Finally, if a state law of general applicability "substantial burdens" a person's religiously motivated conduct in a state that has not adopted its own version of RFRA, then the person's ability to challenge such law will be dependent upon the religious liberty protections contained in his or her state's constitution (if any).

THE ASSOCIATIONAL DIMENSION OF RELIGIOUS LIBERTY

The breadth of what "free exercise" can encompass cuts in favor of the corporate claimant. As discussed in chapter 3, Americans are increasingly looking for ways to live integrated lives. For many religious Americans, this entails a career and work environment congruent with their religious principles. As such, the decision to start, invest in, work for, or patronize a particular corporation can accurately be characterized as, for some individuals, the exercise of religion. Supporting this perspective is the well-recognized associational dimension of religious liberty.

There are certainly those who view religion as a wholly private matter. Consider, for example, Jefferson's remark that "religion is a matter which lies solely between a man and his God."[78] Although this may be the case for certain individuals and certain religions, it is not the case for all. Indeed, for most faiths religion "connotes a community of believers,"[79] and as such includes an important communal dimension.[80] Indeed, "[m]ost religions cannot be exercised in a proper manner if the believers are deprived of the possibility to act collectively."[81] It can be fairly said, therefore, that for most religions, "individual freedom of religion cannot be guaranteed unless there is a collateral guarantee for the freedom to found and operate a church or other religious community."[82]

Consequently, a vision of religious liberty that fails to protect religiously inspired, collaborative, and associational conduct would be quite a parsimonious one. Under such a vision, few religious individuals would be able to live out their lives in a manner satisfactorily consistent with their beliefs and obligations.

For most religious individuals, religious associational activity will take place within a particular parish or congregation. For some, it will extend to charitable organizations and perhaps to faith-based clubs and interest groups. To this point there is no real disagreement.

Matters get interesting when individuals take their religious associational activity beyond the traditional confines of church and charity. As indicated, for some today religious belief and practice might manifest itself in one's choice of associates in the world of commerce and one's chosen place of employment. This, in turn, gives rise to and fosters corporate entities that embody certain distinctive religious values and beliefs. Finally, these entities themselves turn to such values and beliefs to guide their conduct. To the extent that the law impedes such religiously guided corporate conduct, we have a potential free exercise claim.

Many resist extending the protections of religious liberty to such conduct. Their objection generally parrots the core objection to corporate political speech: namely, that corporations cannot serve as a vehicle for genuine expression, let alone religious belief. They instinctively balk at the notion that a corporation can genuinely "believe" anything—let alone a set of religious teachings.

One reason for this reticence is the view that only flesh-and-blood human beings can have beliefs, not organizations. Putting aside the philosophical merits of this proposition, it must be readily admitted that our society already accepts the notion of organizational beliefs. Religious communities themselves, from individual temples to archdioceses, are frequently structured as incorporated entities, and few would question their ability to possess beliefs (at least under the law). A step removed, religiously grounded nonprofits and charities are also commonly understood to embrace certain beliefs. Thus, the concept that morally relevant beliefs can be attributed to organizations is fairly well established. With regard to the contraceptive mandate cases mentioned previously, no one has seriously challenged the existence of genuine religious beliefs when asserted by those claimants that are nonprofit corporate entities. Indeed, the Obama administration has indicated a willingness to entertain certain modifications to the mandate with regard to its imposition on "religiously affiliated universities, hospitals and charities."[83] To the extent that the matter has been litigated by these particular groups, the litigation has turned on whether the beliefs of these entities permit them to disregard a law of general applicability, as per the standards of the free exercise clause and RFRA. The government has not challenged the ability of these groups to possess genuine religious beliefs, nor their substantive right to defend these beliefs via recourse to the Constitution and RFRA. All seem to generally concede that, for legal and constitutional purposes at least, organizations can indeed possess authentic beliefs and values. The question of an organization's ability to believe only commonly arises when the organization in question is a for-profit business corporation.

Here we tread ground that has now become quite familiar. Those who would carve the for-profit corporation out from the common treatment of organizations do so on the supposition that its for-profit status fundamentally alters its ability to genuinely embrace, embody, and express noneconomic values. As has been pointed out repeatedly, this supposition holds true for many corporations, but not all, giving rise to an important difference between those companies that I have demarcated as "modern" versus "postmodern." Although this supposition is valid with regard to the typical modern corporation, it is not valid with regard to the postmodern corporation. For the reasons discussed in chapter 3, the postmodern corporation can constitute a genuine association, including a genuine religiously expressive association. It can serve as the focal point of religious fellowship and activity in very much the same way as religious nonprofits, charities, and perhaps even certain churches themselves. As Justice Brennan wrote in 1987, "it is . . . conceivable that some for-profit activities could have a religious character."[84] The religiously expressive, for-profit business corporation simply gives concrete form to this possibility.

It would seem, therefore, that a postmodern corporation's claim to religious liberty could be a compelling one. If the claim were predicated upon federal law, it would appear as though the generous provisions of RFRA would apply. If the claim were instead predicated upon state law, RFRA would not apply, but rather the First Amendment's Free Exercise Clause would need to be invoked.

In the latter case, relying wholly on the protections of the First Amendment post-*Smith*, a corporate free exercise claim (as with most free exercise claims) may be viewed as unlikely to succeed. This is due to the rational basis test that ordinarily applies to the challenge of a law of general applicability. It would be a mistake, however, to conclude that the right to bring such a claim is therefore valueless. For even the right to bring a weak claim is superior to no right at all.

Further, recognition of corporate free exercise rights would allow the corporation to bring some rather strong claims in certain situations. If, for example, corporate religious activity were specifically targeted for regulation, on account of its religious nature, then the much more substantial compelling government interest test would apply even under *Smith*'s interpretation of the Free Exercise Clause.

Although this may seem difficult to imagine, consider the actions of New Jersey and Oregon, which have enacted the Worker Freedom from Employer Intimidation Act and Worker Freedom Act (respectively).[85] These acts make proselytization in the workplace, if conducted by an employer other than a religious organization, an intentional tort.[86] (Although not defined in the statutes, "religious organization" has been interpreted to cover only nonprofit entities and therefore would not protect the for-profit claimant.) Were religiously expressive corporations held to possess free exercise rights, statutes such as these would be difficult to defend if challenged on First Amendment grounds by such corporations. For under this legislation, employers (corporate or otherwise) are restricted from engaging in conduct precisely because of its religious nature, thereby implicating the stringent compelling government interest test.[87]

Finally, if the postmodern corporation constitutes a genuine association and consequently can invoke the freedom of association, it could also potentially avail itself of the favorable "hybrid-rights" treatment articulated in *Smith*, as addressed above. Recall that pursuant to this, the corporate claimant could enjoy the more robust protections of the compelling government interest test in the adjudication of its free exercise claim, so long as it could simultaneously assert a colorable infringement of its freedom of association rights as well.

DISTINGUISHING BETWEEN THE INDIVIDUAL'S RIGHT AND THAT OF THE ASSOCIATION

Often lost in the discussion of corporate free exercise rights is the acknowledgment that failure to recognize such rights amounts, ultimately, to a restriction on the religious liberty of individuals as well. By depriving corporations of religious liberty, society would simultaneously be depriving individuals of the right to freely exercise their religion by means of a for-profit, corporate undertaking. It relegates the career choices of countless individuals to the nonprofit world and restricts the opportunities they might otherwise have to invest in and patronize establishments that are wholly consistent with their most deeply held principles and beliefs.[88] Worst of all, such an approach also falls into the error of limiting the free exercise right to "what the state views as religious or worthwhile" versus its intended scope: "what the believer views as his duty toward God."[89] Thus, conceptually, there is significant overlap between solicitude of corporate rights and individual liberty.

In the eyes of the law, however, important differences exist between individuals asserting a First Amendment right within an associational context and an association's assertion of that same right. For a variety of reasons, this issue is not a particularly salient one with regard to the questions of free speech and freedom of association. It becomes more germane, however, when we consider religious liberty.

Identifying a Right's Proper Claimant

Whenever a legal claim is asserted, First Amendment or otherwise, a threshold question is whether the party asserting the claim is properly situated to bring the claim, the legal term for which is "standing." With regard to claims concerning the freedom of speech, the standing issue is not particularly complicated, as there is a rather clear distinction between the speech of individuals associated with the corporation and the speech of the corporation itself. Corporate constituents have rarely (if ever) framed the question of corporate speech rights as somehow concomitant with their own individual free speech rights. For at the heart of the corporate speech issue is the expenditure of corporate funds to advance a position or support a candidate. No reasonable director, officer, or employee would assert a right to spend corporate money to advance his or her own personal political or expressive interests and, consequently, no one has plausibly asserted an independent, personal First Amendment right to do so. The speech of such individuals is certainly protected by the First Amendment—provided that it is their speech promulgated on their dime. As a result, when the speech in question consists of duly authorized corporate statements, sponsored by corporate funding, there is no reasonable question that the speech in question is that of the corporation and that any right to engage in such speech would need to be that of the corporation as well. If the right is recognized (as it has been under *Citizens United*), the corporation (and only the corporation) would have standing to vindicate it.

The freedom of association, in contrast, poses exactly the opposite problem. It is exceedingly difficult to distinguish the right of individuals to combine, form, and preserve a particular association and the right of the association itself to maintain the integrity of its membership and mission. The two concepts overlap significantly. The courts have not clarified whether any difference exists between the individual's versus the association's rights in this regard, perhaps failing to see a need to.[90] As things currently stand, all things being equal, it appears as though either an association's members, or the associational entity itself, could readily assert a freedom of association claim predicated upon the same operative facts.

Freedom of religion occupies a middle ground, in which the distinction between an individual's rights, and the organization to which he or she belongs, is neither obviously relevant nor obviously irrelevant. Consider, for example, a deeply religious individual who, through training, interest, and experience, has also become a successful businesswoman. At a certain point in her life she feels called to marry her faith with her career. She is like so many others who yearn for integrated living, as chronicled in chapter 3. Indeed, she interprets this yearning as her vocation and feels religiously obliged to pursue it.

She seeks out and finds a company that satisfies her objectives: one that shares her faith and values and offers her a position commensurate with her skills and abilities. Since such companies are relatively rare, it would be safe to assume that her choice involved a degree of sacrifice: the woman may have had to relocate her family and may have passed up more lucrative opportunities at other firms that sought her expertise.

Imagine the imposition of a law or regulation that would undermine that corporation's particular religious identity. Perhaps the law required the company to sell a product it found repulsive, or somehow prevented the company from sharing its religious beliefs with employees or customers. Either way, imagine that the law serves to somehow impede the corporation's religious identity. In so doing, a strong argument can be made that the law also infringes upon the businesswoman's ability to obey the dictates of her religiously informed conscience. By undermining the corporation's religious identity, the law narrows (if not eliminates) the opportunities of individuals (like the businesswoman in our example) to work at religiously distinct companies. To the extent that one feels religiously compelled to work at such companies, the law deprives these individuals of the ability to do so, thereby restricting their free exercise of religion. They could, therefore, challenge the law on free exercise grounds.

This raises the question: to what extent does the possibility of such individual challenges make the recognition of a corporate free exercise right redundant? Does the question of corporate standing to bring free exercise claims matter in light of the ability of individuals to bring them under the circumstances outlined above? For at least two reasons, it does matter.

First, the claim of one party might be stronger than the claim of another. Recall that a free exercise claimant, regardless of the circumstances, must demonstrate a substantial burden upon the exercise of religion. For the corporation, the regulation in question poses an existential threat to its religious identity. For the individual employee, however, other religiously fulfilling employment opportunities might be available in industries not subject to the regulations in question. This suggests that the corporate claimant's assertion of a substantial burden would not be the same as that of the individual's.

Second, consider further the prospect that the free exercise claim might only be cognizable if brought by the corporation itself.[91] The above-mentioned "contraceptive mandate" cases provide a good example. The mandate requires insurance coverage for practices and procedures repugnant to certain religious traditions. Pursuant to these religious traditions certain companies have been founded and operate. Assuming that the mandate is cost-neutral (either because insurers believe that it will pay for itself via a forecasted decrease in unintended pregnancies, or because the government pays for the additional coverage), it is difficult to see a compelling free exercise claim being brought by any individual affiliated with the corporation. No corporate constituency is being compelled to pay for the coverage: consumers and investors cannot claim that they are being forced to finance a product (the insurance plan) that violates their religious principles (through either higher prices or reduced profits); employees are not required to avail themselves of the coverage, and their work environment and conditions would seem largely unaffected. Certainly, these various individuals and constituencies could rightfully complain, just as the businesswoman in the hypothetical above, that the regulation undermines the character of the company they have chosen to support. In doing so, the government has deprived them of a choice: the choice of a company that faithfully comports itself with a particular set of religious values and principles. But the claim would appear to be attenuated and indirect. If a free exercise claim in such circumstances is to go forward, it would most strongly be brought by the corporation. For it is corporate conduct that is directly affected by the regulation in question, and it is the corporation that is being required to violate a particular set of religious principles.

NOTEWORTHY PRECEDENT

As previously mentioned, the Supreme Court in *Citizens United* has already announced that the First Amendment's free speech protections apply to corporations. In my critique of the decision, I found that it made sense as applied to postmodern corporations, but not as applied to modern corporations. With that caveat in mind, the logic of the opinion could readily be extended to freedom of religion. The Court noted in *Citizens United* that the amendment's proclamation that "Congress shall make no law... abridging the freedom of speech" applies *regardless of the speaker*, thereby covering corporations as well as individuals. Similarly, the amendment's proclamation that "Congress shall make no law respecting an establishment of religion, or prohibiting the free exercise thereof" could (and should, I suggest) be read as enjoining Congress from prohibiting any religiously motivated conduct, regardless of the actor. In both contexts, the primary focus is on the power of Congress; the nature of the actor is secondary, if not irrelevant. Congress cannot interfere with the exercise of religion, just as it cannot interfere with the freedom of speech. It matters not who (or what) is doing the acting or the speaking. The matter is not so much one of individual (or associational) rights, so much as the government's powerlessness to act in such a way.

Further, as we have seen, the "free exercise of religion" connotes a broader concept than "freedom of speech." The range of activities that qualify as "speech" are narrower than those that can qualify as the exercise of religion. Indeed, it could be said that in some situations, freedom of religion actually encompasses freedom of speech (consider, for example, the Christian exhortation to "preach the Gospel"). Consequently, it would seem incongruous to recognize a corporate right to speech but not to religion.

In terms of free exercise precedent, the Supreme Court has already clearly held that (1) profit-seeking sole proprietors and (2) nonprofit corporations each have standing to bring free exercise claims. To recognize corporate free exercise rights, therefore, the courts simply need to connect these two dots.

With regard to profit-seeking businesses, the Supreme Court has, on at least two occasions, recognized the standing of sole proprietors to bring free exercise claims challenging regulation that impacts their businesses. In *United States v. Lee*, an individual who was both a farmer and a carpenter had standing to raise a free exercise defense to his failure to pay social security taxes for the farmhands and carpentry shop assistants he employed.[92] The individual was Amish and "object[ed] on religious grounds to receipt of public insurance benefits and to payment of taxes to support public insurance funds." In *Braunfeld v. Brown*, Philadelphia "merchants" had standing to challenge that town's Sunday closing laws, claiming that it burdened their free exercise of religion.[93] The merchants were Orthodox, Sabbath-observing Jews, and as such were unable to work on Saturday. Inability to open their shops and do business on Sunday so as to compensate for this "impair[ed] the ability of all appellants to earn a livelihood" if they wished to remain faithful to their religious beliefs.[94] These cases stand for the unmistakable proposition that a sole proprietor has standing to raise a free exercise claim against a law or regulation that adversely affects his (or her) profit-seeking commercial enterprise if that law or regulation conflicts with the proprietor's religious beliefs and obligations.[95]

With regard to incorporated entities, the Supreme Court has consistently recognized their standing to bring free exercise claims, but to date, only insofar as these corporations were nonprofit.[96] This has been made abundantly clear in the body of law that comprises the "ministerial exemption," pursuant to which it has been repeatedly held that the free exercise clause grants religious *organizations* the right to make employment decisions free from the typical regulatory oversight that governs the employment decisions of most other groups (profit and nonprofit alike).[97] This was driven home most vividly by the Court's unanimous 2012 decision in *Hosanna-Tabor Evangelical Lutheran Church and School v. E.E.O.C.*, which recognized the standing of a religious school to bring Free Exercise and Establishment Clause claims.[98]

Although the Supreme Court has yet to connect these two strands of case law (and hold that for-profit corporations may bring free exercise claims), some lower courts have.

At least two federal district courts (the Eastern District of New York and the District of Nebraska) and one state court (the Court of Special Appeals of Maryland) have recognized, without discussion, a for-profit corporation's standing to bring a free exercise claim.[99] In *Commack Self-Service Kosher Meats v. Hooker*, the claimant, an incorporated "deli and butcher shop . . . that specializes in kosher foods," was permitted to raise a free exercise claim against New York State's kosher labeling and marketing regulations.[100] In *Womens Services, P.C. v. Thone*, the claimant, "a Florida corporation" that "provides facilities and support staff to physicians who perform abortions and other gynecological services on its premises," challenged Nebraska's law regulating abortions.[101] Curiously, the abortion provider itself raised a free exercise claim against the law, despite lacking any evidence that impediments to the procurement of an abortion would violate a "tenet of any religion."[102] This lack of evidence defeated the plaintiff's free exercise claim but, critically, the court did not question the ability of the plaintiff corporation to bring the free exercise claim per se.[103] In *Atlantic Department Store v. State Attorney for Prince George's County*, the claimant, "a corporation conducting retail business in Prince George's County," was permitted to bring a free exercise claim against that county's Sunday closing laws.[104] Unfortunately, in all three cases, the corporation's standing to raise the free exercise issue per se was apparently not challenged, and as such the issue of standing was not addressed by the court.

The Ninth Circuit Court of Appeals has come very close to recognizing the right of for-profit business associations to raise free exercise claims or defenses. In a pair of cases, the court granted for-profit business corporations standing to bring free exercise claims, but on the theory that the interests of the owners of the corporation and the corporation itself were indistinguishable, as the corporations were closely held.[105] Indeed, the courts were explicit in "declin[ing] to decide whether a for-profit corporation can assert its own rights under the Free Exercise Clause" and instead "examine[d] the rights at issue as those of the corporate owners."[106]

Similar reasoning was employed in a Minnesota case, concerning a for-profit health club that was pervasively Christian in its policies and practices.[107] In response to an action brought against it by the state's Department of Human Rights, the club defended its religiously driven employment practices with recourse to the Free Exercise Clause.[108] Significantly, the court found that the state's "conclusory assertion that a corporation has no constitutional right to free exercise of religion is unsupported by any cited authority."[109] That said, since the corporate veil had been pierced, and the club's individual owners were being held responsible for the actions of the club, the court held that "it is unnecessary to decide whether . . . a corporation[] has a first amendment right to free exercise of religion," as the club is essentially a stand-in for the individual owners.[110]

The Ninth Circuit and Minnesota cases were resolved via recourse to "associational standing" theory, in which the business entities were granted standing simply as a proxy for their owners.[111] In these particular cases, this was not difficult for the courts to do, as each concerned a closely held corporation in which the interests of the owners could clearly be ascertained. In such situations, the corporation's interests are largely indistinguishable from that of its owner(s).

Let us briefly dispense with the concept of associational standing before proceeding. As with the concept of commercial speech, associational standing is not directly applicable to the focus of our inquiry, but so closely related that we would be remiss in ignoring it altogether.

Associational standing is implicated when an association sues to vindicate the rights of its members under certain circumstances. It is not implicated when an association acts to vindicate rights of its own, nor does it preclude an association from acting to vindicate the rights of its own. As the Supreme Court has explained, whether associational standing exists turns on three factors:

> [A]n association has standing to bring suit on behalf of its members when: (a) its members would otherwise have standing to sue in their own right; (b) the interests it seeks to protect are germane to the organization's purpose; and (c) neither the claim asserted nor the relief requested requires the participation of individual members in the lawsuit.[112]

Associational standing is, therefore, largely a doctrine born of convenience and practicality. It enables associations to defend the rights of their members to the extent that those rights are relevant to the association's purpose and under circumstances when prudential to do so. It does not assist in determining which rights are properly those of the association *qua* association versus those of the association's individual members.

Associational standing will not work in many if not most corporate contexts, because corporations are commonly marked by a separation of ownership and control. Thus, a corporation's interests and policies would not necessarily be identical to that of its ownership, but rather a function of the needs and wants of its various constituencies. For corporations such as these, owners are not a proper proxy in free exercise litigation. Instead, recourse to statements in shareholder resolutions, the corporate charter, and similar documents, in addition to a review of corporate policies and practices, would be necessary to furnish the evidence needed to assess the corporation's free exercise claim. Unanimity among shareholders in such a situation is unlikely, but unanimity is not required even for associational standing to be recognized.[113]

Moving beyond these cases, the Eleventh Circuit acknowledged, albeit in dicta, the standing of for-profit corporations to bring suit in their own right without recourse to associational standing theory.[114] In the case *Primera Iglesia Bautista Hispana of Boca Raton, Inc. v. Broward County*, the Eleventh Circuit declared that "corporations possess Fourteenth Amendment rights of equal protection, due process, and, through the doctrine of incorporation, the free exercise of religion."[115] Since the plaintiff in that case was a religious corporation (a church), this broad language is dicta as applied to for-profit corporations. Nevertheless, the court's sweeping statement was not qualified and represents the clearest language in recognition of corporate free exercise rights in a published majority opinion to date.

Individual judges have expressed support for the idea of corporate free exercise standing in even bolder terms. In a dissent that turned on an issue other than standing, Ninth Circuit Judge Tashima proclaimed, "I assume, for purposes of the stay motion, that Stormans, as a [for-profit business] corporation, has a protectible free exercise right under the First Amendment."[116]

In another dissent, Judge Noonan of the Ninth Circuit offered the most extensive analysis of the issue yet to appear in a judicial decision.[117] The dissent was penned in the case of *EEOC v. Townley Engineering and Manufacturing Company*, one of the two Ninth Circuit cases (discussed previously) in which the court sidestepped the issue of whether a for-profit corporation had standing to bring a free exercise claim in its own right and decided, instead, to allow the corporation to bring suit on behalf of its owners.[118] Judge Noonan found this sidestepping unnecessary and was prepared to hold that the First Amendment's Free Exercise Clause makes no distinction between individuals and organization, and between profits and nonprofits.[119] Judge Noonan's remarks are cogent and insightful, and merit reproduction at considerable length:

> The First Amendment, guaranteeing the free exercise of religion to every person within the nation, is a guarantee that Townley Manufacturing Company rightly invokes. Nothing in the broad sweep of the amendment

puts corporations outside its scope. Repeatedly and successfully, corporations have appealed to the protection the Religious Clauses afford or authorize. Just as a corporation enjoys the right of free speech guaranteed by the First Amendment, so a corporation enjoys the right guaranteed by the First Amendment to exercise religion.

The First Amendment does not say that only one kind of corporation enjoys this right. The First Amendment does not say that only religious corporations or only not-for-profit corporations are protected. The First Amendment does not authorize Congress to pick and choose the persons or the entities or the organizational forms that are free to exercise their religion. All persons—and under our Constitution all corporations are persons—are free. A statute cannot subtract from their freedom....

Respect for the religious beliefs of others is particularly difficult when one does not share these beliefs. Judges are no more immune than congressmen from prejudices that are not only officious and overt but subtle and latent and incline one to take less than seriously notions of religious belief that depart markedly from one's own or some assumed norm. The First Amendment is an effort, not entirely forlorn, to interpose a bulwark between the prejudices of any official, legislator or judge and the stirrings of the spirit.

The [EEOC] and the court appear to assume that there must be a sharp division between secular activity and religious activity. Such a sharp division finds nourishment in one of our cases. But of course such a dichotomy is a species of theology. The theological position is that human beings should worship God on Sundays or some other chosen day and go about their business without reference to God the rest of the time. Such a split is attractive to some religious persons. It is repudiated by many, especially those who seek to integrate their lives and to integrate their activities. Among those who repudiate this theology is the Townley Manufacturing Company.[120]

The Chief Justice of the Minnesota Court of Appeals also must be added to the list of dissenting jurists who have expressed the belief that the Free Exercise Clause applies to corporations, at least closely held corporations.[121] He observed that the distinction "between institutional rights of free exercise and a corporation's assertion of the free exercise rights of its principals is a distinction without a difference when a corporation is closely held."[122] When the alleged harm or regulation befalls the corporate entity and failure to recognize availability of the free exercise clause to the corporate claimant would "effectively preclude[] [religious businesspeople] from entering the marketplace."[123] Chief Justice Popovich continued:

Can it be said that a professional person who incorporates a sole professional corporation loses all constitutional rights because of the incorporation? Such a result would be absurd. Individuals of strong religious convictions do not live in a vacuum or practice their faith only on their days of worship. Religious values should and do permeate a person's daily activities.[124]

Importantly, prior to the politically charged lawsuits against the 2010 Affordable Care Act's contraceptive mandate, very little has challenged this backdrop of precedent. Historically, in many if not most of the cases in which a for-profit corporation has asserted free exercise rights, that standing has been granted, usually justified via recourse to associational standing theory, as discussed above, but sometimes without discussion or qualification. In cases where a corporate free exercise claimant did not prevail, it was ordinarily not on the ground that the corporation did not possess standing to raise a free exercise claim as a matter of law, but for some other reason.[125]

Recent Developments

In the highly publicized contraceptive mandate cases, however, we see for the first time courts seriously questioning the notion of corporate free exercise rights. Struggling in these largely unchartered waters, courts have reached widely divergent conclusions on how best to interpret the First Amendment's applicability, with some proclaiming that the amendment does not protect corporate religious conduct.[126] This is unfortunate, given the fact that the most applicable judicial precedent, the best understanding of the First Amendment, and the advent of the postmodern corporation all point overwhelmingly in one direction—the direction favoring recognition of free exercise rights for qualifying companies. Given the timeliness and germaneness of these decisions, let us examine them at some length here. All of these decisions were handed down in 2013.

The Third, Sixth, Seventh, Tenth, and D.C. Circuits have each grappled with cases brought by business corporations challenging the contraceptive mandate.[127] The facts and procedural posture of these cases were substantially the same. Factually, each case concerned a business corporation that operated pursuant to certain religious principles, principles that the corporation would be forced to violate were it to offer the insurance coverage mandated by the Affordable Care Act. Procedurally, each plaintiff sought a preliminary injunction to block the enforcement of the act's contraceptive mandate, which was scheduled to take effect on August 1, 2012. In order to grant the injunction, the courts needed to find, among other things, that plaintiffs have a likelihood of success on the merits were the cases to be fully litigated.

The Seventh, Tenth, and D.C. Circuits agreed that plaintiffs were likely to succeed on the merits; the Third and Sixth disagreed. In reaching their conclusions, each of the circuits passed judgment on the question of corporate free exercise rights. The Tenth held that "as a matter of constitutional law, Free Exercise rights may extend to some for-profit organizations."[128] The Seventh rejected the government's assertion that "a secular, for-profit corporation cannot assert" a religious liberty claim, holding that "the corporate form is not dispositive of the claim."[129] The Third and Sixth Circuits, contrary to the Seventh and Tenth, held that "secular corporations cannot engage in religious exercise," and as such do not possess religious liberty rights.[130] The D.C. Circuit, although holding in favor of the free exercise claimants, did so only with regard to the owners of the closed corporation before them and explicitly held that free exercise rights do not extend to the corporate entity itself.[131] The two decisions that best set forth the arguments for and against corporate free exercise rights hail from the Tenth and Third Circuits, and to those decisions we shall now turn.

The Tenth Circuit, in *Hobby Lobby Stores, Inc. v. Sebelius*, made the now-familiar point that "[i]t is beyond question that associations—not just individuals—have Free Exercise rights."[132] The rationale for this, set forth by the Tenth Circuit, and explored previously here, is that recognition of associational freedoms is an "indispensable means of preserving other individual liberties."[133] The court proceeded to note that among those associations that enjoy the protections of the First Amendment are included those that have incorporated. The court noted further that, although such protections have not been explicitly extended to for-profit corporations by the Supreme Court, the Supreme Court has recognized that "individuals have Free Exercise rights with respect to their *for-profit businesses*."[134] As the Tenth Circuit summarized things:

> In short, individuals may incorporate for religious purposes and keep their Free Exercise rights, and unincorporated individuals may pursue profit while keeping their Free Exercise rights. With these propositions, the government does not seem to disagree. The problem for the government, it appears, is when individuals incorporate *and* [pursue a for-profit undertaking]. At that point, Free Exercise rights somehow disappear.[135]

The court proceeded to note that nothing in the text of the First Amendment precludes its applicability to business corporations, and then recounted the historical understanding of free exercise along lines similar to those recounted here. In his concurrence, Judge Hartz cited Justice Brennan's poignant admonition that the "State may [not] put an individual to a choice between his business and his religion."[136]

As mentioned, the Third Circuit reached a different conclusion. In *Conestoga Wood v. Secretary of the United States Department of Health and Human Services*, the court acknowledged, as it had to, that certain associations have free exercise rights. It limited this, however, to "churches and other religious entities" and stated that it need not add the for-profit, business corporation to this list.[137] This acknowledgment is difficult to square with the court's proclamation, elsewhere in its opinion, that it "cannot understand how a for-profit, secular corporation—apart from its owners—can exercise religion."[138] As the court explained:

> General business corporations do not, separate and apart from the actions or belief systems of their individual owners or employees, exercise religion. They do not pray, worship, observe sacraments or take other religiously-motivated actions separate and apart from the intention and direction of their individual actors.[139]

The earlier acknowledgment is difficult to square with this later proclamation and reasoning because the very same argument can be made against "churches and religious entities" for whom free exercise rights are readily invoked. That is, unless one wishes to delve into the most rarified heights of theology, an individual church, or a religious entity such as a school or hospital, does not "pray, worship, observe sacraments or take other religiously-motivated actions separate and apart from the intention and direction of [its] individual actors." The court was either unaware of or untroubled by this fairly profound inconsistency.

Further in its opinion, the court stressed the separate legal entity that a corporation obtains and how this prevents its owners from asserting free exercise claims through the corporation.[140] As the court concluded: "A holding . . . that a for-profit corporation can engage in religious exercise . . . would eviscerate the fundamental principle that a corporation is a legally distinct entity from its owners."[141]

Although the court is correct in identifying as a "fundamental principle" of corporate law that a "corporation is a legally distinct entity from its owners," it does not at all follow that this principle would be "eviscerate[d]" by a holding that "a for-profit corporation can engage in religious exercise." The court failed to appreciate the possibility of a corporation that is both separate of its owners and religiously expressive at the same time. As has been explained throughout this book, the postmodern corporation's status as an expressive entity (and a potentially religiously expressive entity) flows not simply from the wishes of its owners, but rather from the confluence of a multitude of constituencies. In fact, one could fairly posit that for a postmodern, religiously expressive corporation, it is not the corporation that takes its religious identity from the owners (its shareholders), but rather the shareholders who take their identity as "faith-based investors" from the religious identity of the corporation.

A close reading of *Conestoga* suggests that the plaintiffs did not press the argument that the corporate entity *itself* was religiously expressive. Rather, the plaintiffs appear to have stressed instead that corporate compliance with the contraceptive mandate would have infringed upon their own personal free exercise rights. In other words, as majority owners of this closed corporation, claimants maintained that they were morally responsible for its conduct. As plaintiffs in the similarly decided Sixth Circuit case *Autocam Corp. v. Sebelius* explained:

> They...believe that they become morally responsible for the use of contraception by others when they "directly pay for the purchase of drugs and services...in violation of [their] beliefs." This teaching is sometimes referred to by the plaintiffs as "material cooperation." In applying these teachings to their ownership and operation of Autocam, the Kennedys believe that they cannot direct their closely held company's health insurance plan to "provide, fund, or participate in health care insurance that covers artificial contraception, sterilization, and related education and counseling."[142]

Thus, *Conestoga* and *Autocam* apparently do not concern religiously expressive, postmodern corporations. Although the language employed by the courts is regrettably broad, encompassing all for-profit corporate claimants, the holdings rendered could arguably be limited to situations in which the corporate claimant is not a religiously expressive one. The courts' language could be constrained as unauthoritative dicta as applied to a genuine, religiously expressive corporation.[143]

That said, I do not mean to suggest that the claimants in *Conestoga, Autocam*, and similar cases ought to inevitably suffer defeat. Although such claimants could not legitimately proceed under the theory advanced in this book regarding the constitutional rights of postmodern corporations, they may indeed have a meritorious argument predicated upon other approaches. They may, for example, be entitled to assert associational standing, as discussed earlier in this chapter. Alternatively, drawing upon the unique nature of the closed corporation, the owners of these entities may be able to assert their personal free exercise rights via a partnership-based or property-based model of the organization. For within the context of the closed corporation, the distinction between the owners and the corporation itself can indeed become blurred—just as the distinction between partners and a partnership is largely illusory. The Third and Sixth Circuits, arguably, elevated form over substance, insisting that the fact of incorporation renders the company entirely independent of its owners—to the point of stripping away constitutional rights that would have existed had the business entity not chosen to avail itself of the protections of limited liability afforded by the corporate form. Such an approach would seem to implicate the doctrine against "unconstitutional conditions," pursuant to which the government "cannot grant [a] privilege subject to conditions that improperly 'coerce,' 'pressure,' or 'induce' the waiver of constitutional rights."[144] A strong argument could be made, therefore, that the government could not require a company to relinquish its free exercise rights in exchange for the benefits of limited liability that come with incorporating. Perhaps an appreciation of these principles, even if not explicitly expounded, is one of the reasons why, in almost all other cases concerning closed corporations, courts have found ways to permit the free exercise claims to proceed.

Although closed corporations per se are not the focus of this book, further consideration of the closed corporation will be set forth in chapter 9.

NOTES

1. *See* Newland v. Sebelius, 881 F. Supp. 2d. 1287, 1292 (D. Colo. 2012); O'Brien v. U.S. Dep't of Health & Human Servs., 854 F. Supp. 2d. 1149, 1154–55 (E.D. Mo. 2012); Hobby Stores, Inc. v. Sebelius, 870 F. Supp. 2d 1278, 1283–84 (W.D. Okla. 2012), *rev'd en banc*, 723 F.3d 1114 (10th Cir. 2013); Triune Health Grp., Inc. vs. U.S. Dep't of Health & Human Services, No. 12-CV-06756 (N.D. Ill. Filed Aug. 22, 2012). These cases are, in many respects, companion cases to the more widely publicized litigation brought by a group of forty-three diverse Catholic Church–affiliated entities against "the Department of Health and Human Services' sterilization, abortifacient and birth-control insurance mandate." *See* Mary Ann Glendon, *Why the Bishops Are Suing the U.S. Government*, WALL ST. J., May 22, 2012, at A17.
2. *Compare* Hobby Lobby Stores, Inc. v. Sebelius, 723 F.3d 1114, 1145 (10th Cir. 2013) (holding that for-profit corporation had standing to bring religious liberty claims against the contraceptive mandate under RFRA, but not reaching the question of whether the corporation had standing under the Free Exercise Clause) *with* Conestoga Wood Spec. Corp. v. Sebelius, 724 F.3d 377, 388 (3d Cir. 2013) (holding that for-profit corporation did not have standing to bring religious liberty claims against the contraceptive mandate under either RFRA or the Free Exercise Clause).
3. I originally presented my thinking on the religious liberty of business corporations in Ronald J. Colombo, *The Naked Private Square*, 51 HOUS. L. REV. 1 (2013).
4. U.S. CONST. amend. I.
5. *See* John T. Noonan Jr., *The End of Free Exercise?*, 42 DEPAUL L. REV. 567, 567 (1992).
6. *See* Michael W. McConnell, *The Origins and Historical Understanding of Free Exercise of Religion*, 103 HARV. L. REV. 1409, 1421 (1990).
7. Many conflate the question of religious liberty with the (dis)establishment of religion, but the two concepts are separate. State establishment and support of a specific religion need not necessarily be accompanied by suppression of other religions (Norway and Malta, for example, have established religions, and neither are considered religiously intolerant countries). Nor does the lack of an established religion necessarily entail religious liberty (China and Cuba come quickly to mind as examples of this point.). Thus, the colonial experience with religious liberty did not always track its experiments with nonestablishment. Some colonies (including those with established religions) generally extended religious liberty to all faiths, while others (including some that lacked an established religion) aggressively persecuted minority sects. The critical point is that

by the time of the Constitution's ratification, Americans enjoyed an experiment with disestablishment, and a taste of religious freedom, that few of their contemporaries in the Old World had ever experienced.

8. *Id.* at 1438.
9. *See id.*
10. JAMES MADISON, MEMORIAL AND REMONSTRANCE AGAINST RELIGIOUS ASSESSMENTS (1785) (*available at* http://religiousfreedom.lib.virginia.edu/sacred/madison_m&r_1785.html).
11. *See* Mark Movsesian, *Crosses and Culture: State-Sponsored Religious Displays in the US and Europe*, OXFORD J. L. & RELIGION 1, 15 (2012).
12. *See* John Witte, *From Establishment to Freedom of Public Religion*, 32 CAP. U. L. REV. 499, 501 (2004).
13. RICHARD JOHN NEUHAUS, THE NAKED PUBLIC SQUARE 94 (1984).
14. *See* McConnell, *supra* note 6, at 1421.
15. Douglas Laycock, *Religious Liberty as Liberty*, 7 J. CONTEMP. LEGAL ISSUES 313, 314 (1996).
16. *Id.* at 319.
17. *Id.* at 317.
18. KENT GREENAWALT, 1 RELIGION AND THE CONSTITUTION: FREE EXERCISE AND FAIRNESS 3 (2006).
19. *But see* David O. Conkle, *Religious Truth, Pluralism, and Secularization: The Shaking Foundations of American Religious Liberty*, 32 CARDOZO L. REV. 1755, 1778 (2011) (questioning whether the "secular case for religious liberty" provides an adequate justification for it).
20. Andrew A. Beerworth, Comment, *Religion in the Marketplace: Establishments, Pluralisms, and the Doctrinal Eclipse of Free Exercise*, 26 T. JEFFERSON L. REV. 333, 386–87 (2004).
21. *Id.*
22. Kathleen M. Sullivan, *Religion and Liberal Democracy*, 59 U. CHI. L. REV. 195, 197–98 (1992).
23. *See* McConnell, *supra* note 6, at 1432 (elaborating that Locke did not propose extending this toleration to Catholics or atheists, neither of which he believed could be trusted for different reasons).
24. *See id.* at 1443.
25. *Id.*
26. Declaration of Independence (1776).
27. *See* McConnell, *supra* note 6, at 1444.
28. *Id.* at 1443.
29. *See* U.S. CONST. amend. I.
30. Douglas Laycock, *The Religious Freedom Restoration Act*, 1993 B.Y.U. L. REV. 221, 222 (1993).
31. *See* NOAH FELDMAN, DIVIDED BY GOD 20 (2006); *see also* Marci A. Hamilton, *The Belief/Conduct Paradigm in the Supreme Court's Free Exercise Jurisprudence: A Theological Account of the Failure to Protect Religious Conduct*, 54 OHIO ST. L.J. 713, 792 (1993).
32. Caroline Mala Corbin, *Nonbelievers and Government Speech*, 97 IOWA L. REV. 347, 400 (2012).
33. *E.g.*, Brian Leiter, *Why Tolerate Religion?*, 25 CONST. COMMENT. 1 (2008).
34. *See* Michael W. McConnell, *Establishment and Disestablishment at the Founding, Part I: Establishment of Religion*, 44 WM. & MARY L. REV. 2015, 2160 (2003).
35. 1 JOHN P. DAVIS, CORPORATIONS 36 (1905).

36. Feldman, *supra* note 31, at 206. This position is not without its detractors, who challenge it on both normative and descriptive grounds. *See* Alan Brownstein, *Taking Free Exercise Rights Seriously*, 57 Case W. Res. L. Rev. 55, 60–61, and n.16 (2006).
37. Although courts have at times treated conscience in ways similar to religious belief for First Amendment purposes, a distinction nevertheless remains between religiously motivated and nonreligiously motivated conscience and conduct. *See* Marsh v. Chambers 463 U.S. 783, 812 (Brennan, J., dissenting) ("Under the Free Exercise Clause religiously motivated claims of conscience may give rise to constitutional rights that other strongly-held beliefs do not.").
38. *See* Brownstein, *supra* note 36, at 69.
39. *Id.* A colleague has suggested that this is the view of the Supreme Court as well in light of *Emp. Div., Dept. of Human Resources of Oregon v. Smith*, 494 U.S. 872 (1990). *Smith* will be discussed at length below. *See infra* text accompanying notes 50–55. In short, *Smith* held that religious practices must yield to laws of general applicability. *See Smith*, 494 U.S. at 890. This might seem the equivalent of arguing that religious liberty protects little more than freedom of belief and worship and does not extend to religiously inspired conduct in general. There is an important difference, however, in the Court's holding and the federal government's position. The Court explicitly acknowledged the appropriateness of promulgating exemptions from generally applicable laws in order to protect religious adherents. The Court identified such exemptions, crafted via the political process, as a part of our nation's religious liberty protections. The Court did not take a position on whether such exemptions should or should not be promulgated, but remained neutral on that political question. *See id.* The government, however, has taken a position on this question, one which generally rules out the accommodation of religious practices that conflict with its laws and policies. I posit that there is a difference between the Court's opinion of religious exemptions (which is one of neutrality) and the government's (which is one of general denial).
40. *See* O. Carter Snead, *Obama's Freedom Deficit*, First Things Mar. 2012, at 24.
41. *See* Douglas Laycock, *Sex, Atheism, and the Free Exercise of Religion*, 88 U. Det. Mercy L. Rev. 407, 427 (2011).
42. *See* Aryeh Kaplan, The Handbook of Jewish Thought 78 (1979) (noting that the commandments of Judaism "penetrate every nook and cranny of a person's existence, hallowing even the lowliest acts and elevating them to a service to God... the multitude of laws governing even such mundane acts as eating, drinking, dressing and business, sanctify every facet of life, and constantly remind one of his responsibilities toward God") (*quoted in* Samuel J. Levine, *Professionalism without Parochialism: Julius Henry Cohen, Rabbi Nachman of Breslov, and the Stories of Two Sons*, 71 Fordham L. Rev. 1339, 1352 n.85 (2003)).
43. "Worship," Webster's Encyclopedic Unabridged Dictionary of the English Language (Gramercy 1989). *But see* Brownstein, *supra* note 36, at 138 (noting that "[l]ocation can also be taken into account in developing doctrine to protect the free exercise of religion").
44. McConnell, *supra* note 6, at 1452. Of course, this general opinion was not shared by everybody; most notably embracing a more restrictive view was Thomas Jefferson. *Id.* at 1450–52. Indeed, Jefferson "espoused a strict distinction between belief... and conduct," and apparently would have preferred no protection for religious conduct that conflicted with generally applicable secular law. *Id.* at 1451. According to McConnell, however, Jefferson's position was "extraordinarily restrictive for his day," *id.*, and his compatriot James Madison, whose

views more closely aligned with those of most Americans of the time, prevailed in the drafting of the First Amendment. *Id.* at 1455.

45. John Witte, *The Essential Rights and Liberties of Religion in the American Constitutional Experiment*, 71 NOTRE DAME L. REV. 371, 395 (1996).
46. Universal Declaration of Human Rights, G.A. Res. 217(III) A, U.N. Doc. A/RES/217(III) (Dec. 10, 1948).
47. Church of the Lukumi Babalu Aye, Inc. v. City of Hialeah, 508 U.S. 520, 533 (1993).
48. Such are essentially the facts of *Employment Div., Dept. of Human Resources of Oregon v. Smith*, 494 U.S. 872 (1990).
49. Grace United Methodist Church v. City of Cheyenne, 451 F.3d 643, 649 (10th Cir. 2006). It should be noted that under existing precedent, a law that would otherwise appear to be "generally applicable" loses that designation if it contains a "system of individual exemptions" attached to it. *Id.* at 650. In such a case, the law "may not refuse to extend that system to cases of 'religious hardship' without compelling reason." *Id.*
50. *See* Ronald J. Colombo, *Forgive Us Our Sins: The Inadequacies of the Clergy-Penitent Privilege*, 73 N.Y.U. L. REV. 225, 236 (1998).
51. 494 U.S. 872 (1990).
52. *See id.* at 879.
53. *Id.* (citations omitted).
54. Grace United Methodist Church v. City of Cheyenne, 451 F.3d 643, 649–50 (2006).
55. *Id.*
56. Emp't Div., Dep't of Human Resources of Oregon v. Smith, 494 U.S. 872, 907 (1990) (Blackmun, J. dissenting).
57. *See* McConnell, *supra* note 6, at 1515–16. *But see* Philip A. Hamburger, *A Constitutional Right of Religious Exemption: An Historical Perspective*, 60 GEO. WASH. L. REV. 915, 947–48 (1992) (disputing the claim that the framers intended the Free Exercise Clause to cover exemptions).
58. 494 U.S. at 882.
59. *Id.* at 881–82 (citations omitted). The Court explicitly upheld (as a hybrid-rights situation) the special right of parents to resist laws of general applicability when it comes to questions of childrearing, preserving as good law the precedent of *Wisconsin v. Yoder*, 406 U.S. 205, 219–20 (1972). *See* B. Jessie Hill, *Whose Body? Whose Soul? Medical Decision-making on Behalf of Children and the Free Exercise Clause Before and After* Employment Division v. Smith, 32 CARDOZO L. REV. 1857, 1866–67 (2011). The Court also acknowledged an additional exception to its holding (that a law of general applicability does not yield to a free exercise claim) with regard to legislation or regulation that contains within it a set of recognized exceptions. *Smith*, 494 U.S. at 884. In such situations, a free exercise claim can be pursued on the grounds that the law's recognized exceptions fails to take into account a potential exception for religious believers who are disproportionately burdened by the law. *See id.* This enabled the Court to uphold its earlier decision in *Sherbert v. Verner*, 374 U.S. 398, 400–402 (1963). *See id.*
60. *Grace United Methodist Church*, 451 F.3d at 655.
61. A Westlaw search of articles on the Free Exercise Clause referencing "hybrid" in their title yields only twenty-three articles, many of which are student notes. *See* Steven H. Aden & Lee J. Strang, *When a "Rule" Doesn't Rule: The Failure of the Oregon* Employment Division v. Smith *"Hybrid Rights Exception,"* 108 PENN ST. L. REV. 573 (2003); Ryan M. Akers, *Begging the High Court for Clarification: Hybrid*

Rights under Employment Division v. Smith, 17 REGENT U. L. REV. 77 (2004); Frederick Mark Gedicks, *Three Questions about Hybrid Rights and Religious Groups*, 117 YALE L.J. POCKET PART 192 (2008); Ariel Y. Graff, *Free Exercise and Hybrid Rights: An Alternative Perspective on the Constitutionality of Same-Sex Marriage Bans*, 29 U. HAW. L. REV. 23 (2006); Murad Hussain, *Reweighting the Balance: Religious Groups, Mortal Threats, and "Hybrid Situations,"* 117 YALE L.J. POCKET PART 177 (2008); Ming Hsu Chen, Note, *Two Wrongs Make a Right: Hybrid Claims of Discrimination*, 79 N.Y.U. L. REV. 685 (2004); Bradley L. Davis, Comment, *Compelled Expression of the Religiously Forbidden: Pharmacists, "Duty to Fill" Statutes, and the Hybrid Rights Exception*, 29 U. HAW. L. REV. 97 (2006); William L. Esser IV, Note, *Religious Hybrids in the Lower Courts: Free Exercise Plus or Constitutional Smoke Screen?*, 74 NOTRE DAME L. REV. 211 (1998); Bertrand Fry, Note, *Breeding Constitutional Doctrine: The Provenance and Progeny of the "Hybrid Situation" in Current Free Exercise Jurisprudence*, 71 TEX. L. REV. 833 (1993); Shawn Gunnarson, Note, *No Constitutional Shelter: The Ninth Circuit's Reading of the Hybrid Claims Doctrine in* American Friends Service Committee Corp. v. Thornburgh, 7 BYU J. PUB. L. 413 (1993); William J. Haun, Comment, *A Standard for Salvation: Evaluating "Hybrid-Rights" Free-Exercise Claims*, 61 CATH. U. L. REV. 265, 265–66 (2011); Jonathan B. Hensley, Comment, *Approaches to the Hybrid-Rights Doctrine in Free Exercise Cases*, 68 TENN. L. REV. 119 (2000); Michael E. Lechliter, Note, *The Free Exercise of Religion and Public Schools: The Implications of Hybrid Rights on the Religious Upbringing of Children*, 103 MICH. L. REV. 2209 (2005); Hope Lu, Comment, *Addressing the Hybrid-Rights Exception: How the Colorable-Plus Approach Can Revive the Free Exercise Clause*, 63 CASE W. RES. L. REV. 257 (2012); James R. Mason III, Comment, Smith's *Free-Exercise "Hybrids" Rooted in Non-Free-Exercise Soil*, 6 REGENT U. L. REV. 201 (1995); Eric J. Neal, Note, *The Ninth Circuit's "Hybrid Rights" Error: Three Losers Do Not Make a Winner in* Thomas v. Anchorage Equal Rights Commission, 24 SEATTLE U. L. REV. 169 (2000); Timothy J. Santoli, Note, *A Decade after* Employment Division v. Smith: *Examining How Courts Are Still Grappling with the Hybrid-Rights Exception to the Free Exercise Clause of the First Amendment*, 34 SUFFOLK U. L. REV. 649 (2001); Benjamin I. Siminou, Note, *Making Sense of Hybrid Rights: An Analysis of the Nebraska Supreme Court's Approach to the Hybrid-Rights Exception in* Douglas County v. Anaya, 85 NEB. L. REV. 311 (2006); Peter M. Stein, Note, Smith v. Fair Employment and Housing Commission: *Does the Right to Exclude, Combined with Religious Freedom, Present a "Hybrid Situation" Under* Employment Division v. Smith?, 4 GEO. MASON L. REV. 141 (1995); Kyle Still, Comment, Smith's *Hybrid Rights Doctrine and the Pierce Right: An Unintelligent Design*, 85 N.C. L. REV. 385 (2006); Note, *The Best of a Bad Lot: Compromise and Hybrid Religious Exemptions*, 123 HARV. L. REV. 1494 (2010); John L. Tuttle, Note, *Adding Color: An Argument for the Colorable Showing Approach to Hybrid Rights Claims Under* Employment Division v. Smith, 3 AVE MARIA L. REV. 741 (2005).

62. Liam Séamus O'Melinn, *The Sanctity of the Association: The Corporation and Individualism in American Law*, 37 SAN DIEGO L. REV. 101, 153–54 (2000).
63. *See* Graff, *supra* note 61, at 32.
64. *See id.*
65. *See id.*
66. *See id.* at 33.
67. Aden & Strang, *supra* note 61, at 591–92, 594 n.193, 602 (2003).
68. Boy Scouts of Am. v. Dale, 530 U.S. 640, 648 (2000).
69. 42 U.S.C. §2000bb-1(a) (2006).

70. *Id.* §2000bb-1(a)–(c).
71. *See* Thomas D. Dillard, *The RFRA: Two Years Later and Two Questions Threaten Its Legitimacy*, 22 J. CONTEMP. L. 435, 435 (1996).
72. Kevin C. Walsh, *ACLU's President on Forced Provision of Contraceptive Services over Religious Objections—Circa 1992*, WALSHLAW (July 13, 2012), http://walshslaw.wordpress.com/2012/07/13/aclus-president-on-forced-provision-of-contraception-services-over-religious-objections-circa-1992/ (quoting *Religious Freedom Restoration Act of 1991: Hearing on H.R. 2797 Before the Subcomm. On Civil and Constitutional Rights of H. Comm. On the Judiciary*, 1029 Cong. 80–91 (1992) (statement of Nadine Strossen, President, American Civil Liberties Union, and Robert S. Peck, Legislative Council, American Civil Liberties Union)).
73. *See* City of Boerne v. Flores, 521 U.S. 507, 211, 536 (1997); Douglas Laycock, *Conceptual Gulfs in* City of Boerne v. Flores, 39 WM. & MARY L. REV. 743, 745 (1998); Nadia N. Sawicki, *The Hollow Promise of Freedom of Conscience*, 33 CARDOZO L. REV. 1389, 1412 (2012).
74. *See* Christopher C. Lund, *Religious Liberty after Gonzales: A Look at State RFRAs*, 55 S.D. L. REV. 466, 471–72 (2010).
75. *See* Steven J. Willis, *Corporations, Taxes, and Religion: The Hobby Lobby and Conestoga Contraceptive Cases*, 65 S.C. L. REV. 1, 9 (2013).
76. Grace United Methodist Church v. City of Cheyenne, 451 F.3d 643, 649 (10th Cir. 2006).
77. *Id.*
78. ROBERT VISCHER, CONSCIENCE AND THE COMMON GOOD: RECLAIMING THE SPACE BETWEEN PERSON AND STATE 34 (2010); *see also* Michael Newsom, *Pan-Protestantism and Proselytizing: Minority Religions in a Protestant Empire*, 15 WIDENER L. REV. 1, 21, 22 (2009) ("The fundamental affirmative principle of Protestantism is private judgment").
79. McConnell, *supra* note 6, at 1490. Indeed, an original (and rejected) draft of the First Amendment explicitly referred to freedom of "conscience," in place of "exercise." *See* Donald L. Beschle, *Does a Broad Free Exercise Right Require a Narrow Definition of "Religion"?*, 39 HASTINGS CONST. L.Q. 357, 381 (2012).
80. *See* Kent Greenawalt, *History as Ideology: Philip Hamburger's Separation of Church and State*, 93 CALIF. L. REV. 367, 392 (2005).
81. Francoise Tulkens, *The European Convention on Human Rights and Church-State Relations: Pluralism vs. Pluralism*, 30 CARDOZO L. REV. 2575, 2578 (2009) (internal quotation marks omitted).
82. *Id.* (internal quotation marks omitted). *See also* Richard N. Garnett, *Religious Liberty, Church Autonomy, and the Structure of Freedom, in* CHRISTIANITY AND HUMAN RIGHTS: AN INTRODUCTION 228 (John Witte Jr. & Frank S. Alexander eds., 2010).
83. Louise Radnofsky, *Contraceptive Opt-Out Offer*, WALL. ST. J., Feb. 2, 2103, at A3.
84. Corp. of the Presiding Bishop of Church of Jesus Christ of Latter-day Saints v. Amos, 483 U.S. 327, 345 n.6 (1987) (Brennan, J., concurring).
85. *See* Roger C. Hartley, *Freedom Not to Listen: A Constitutional Analysis of Compulsory Indoctrination Through Workplace Captive Meetings*, 31 BERKLEY J. EMP. & LAB. L. 65, 115 (2010); *see also* OR. REV. STAT. ANN. §§ 659.785 (West 2012); N.J. STAT. ANN. §§ 34:19-9 (West 2009). These acts contain exemptions rule for religious organizations (*see* OR. REV. STAT. ANN. § 659.785 (4)(d)), but fail to define a "religious organization."
86. *See* Hartley, *supra* note 85; *see also* OR. REV. STAT. ANN. §§ 659.785 (West 2012); N.J. STAT. ANN. §§ 34:19-9 (West 2009).

87. *See* Julie Marie Baworowsky, Note, *From Public Square to Market Square: Theoretical Foundations of First and Fourteenth Amendment Protection of Corporate Religious Speech*, 83 NOTRE DAME L. REV. 1713, 1720–21 (2008).
88. It must be acknowledged that a different balance with regard to corporate religious liberty rights could be struck, even among those who are sympathetic to religious liberty in general. Kent Greenawalt, for example, recognizes that "people should not lose their capacity to carry out a religious vision simply because they want to do so in commercial affairs." Kent Greenawalt, *Title VII and Religious Liberty*, 33 LOY. U. CHI. L.J. 1, 37 (2001). Greenawalt would not, however, extend the full protections of the Free Exercise Clause to the business corporation as would I. Rather, he would afford the corporation some lesser level of free exercise protection.
89. Michael W. McConnell, *Free Exercise as the Framers Understood It, in* THE BILL OF RIGHTS 54, 59 (Eugene W. Hickok Jr. ed., 1991).
90. *See* chapter 7.
91. It should be noted that even in the absence of free exercise standing, a corporate claimant might have other avenues available to vindicate its rights in such situations. *See* Church of Scientology of California v. Cazares, 638 F.2d 1272, 1280 n.7 (5th Cir. 1981) ("[E]ven if a corporation is not entitled to the protection of the free exercise clause of the First Amendment, it would nevertheless have standing to protect its economic and property rights").
92. 455 U.S. 252, 256 (1982).
93. 366 U.S. 599, 601, 606 (1961).
94. *Id.* at 601–602.
95. *See also* Jasniowski v. Rushing, 678 N.E. 2d 743, 749 (Ill. App. Ct. 1997), *vacated*, 685 N.E.2d 622 (Ill. 1997) (granting standing to a "secular, for-profit, subchapter S corporation engaged in the business of repairing and selling electric motors" because "[t]he nexus between the sole proprietor and his business is sufficiently compelling that [the company] can raise a free exercise challenge asserting the free exercise rights of its sole corporate officer and shareholder").
96. *See,* e.g., Bob Jones University v. U.S., 461 U.S. 574, 574; *see also* Cambodian Buddhist Soc'y of Connecticut, Inc. v. Planning & Zoning Comm'n, 941 A.2d 868 (Conn. 2008) (applying federal precedent to interpret state constitution's free exercise clause); Lee v. State, 869 F. Supp. 1491 (D. Or. 1994); Chosen 300 Ministries, Inc. v. City of Phila., No. 12-3159, 2012 WL 3235317, at *16 (E.D. Pa. Aug. 9, 2012) (standing presumed without discussion).
97. Natal v. Christian & Missionary Alliance, 878 F.2d 1575, 1577–78 (1st Cir. 1989).
98. 132 S. Ct. 694, 710 (2012). When I speak of an organization's standing to bring suit in the preceding cases, I refer to standing to bring suit in its own name, for an injury allegedly injuring it—as distinct from the recognition of "associational standing" to bring suit on behalf of the organization's members. *See* Cornerstone Christian Schs. v. Univ. Interscholastic League, 563 F.3d 127, 134 (5th Cir. 2009). "An association can have standing on the basis of direct injury against itself as an association" and "[u]nder certain circumstances, an association can also have standing on the basis of injury to its members." Contractors Ass'n of Eastern Pa., Inc. v. City of Phila., 945 F.2d 1260, 1264 (3d Cir. 1991). Thus, when it comes to an assertion of the Free Exercise Clause as either a claim or defense, "[t]here are two possible theories under which an institution might assert the free exercise clause . . . : (1) it has institutional rights of free exercise, or (2) it may assert the free-exercise rights of its principals." Blanding v. Sports & Health Club, Inc., 373 N.W.2d 784, 789 (Minn. Ct. App. 1985), *aff'd*, 389 N.W.2d 205 (Minn. 1986).

99. Commack Self-Serv. Kosher Meats v. Hooker, 800 F. Supp. 2d 405, 415 (E.D.N.Y. 2011); Womens Servs, P.C. v. Thone, 483 F. Supp. 1022, 1039-40 (D. Neb. 1979).
100. 800 F. Supp. 2d at 405.
101. 483 F. Supp. at 1022.
102. *Id.* at 1040.
103. The court, in a footnote, did advert to "[a]nother ground for standing," predicated upon associational standing theory. *Id.* at 1030 n.6.
104. 323 A.2d 617, 618–19 (Md. Ct. Spec. App. 1974).
105. *See* Stormans, Inc. v. Selecky, 586 F.3d 1109, 1120–21 (9th Cir. 2009); E.E.O.C. v. Townley Eng'g & Mfg. Co., 859 F.2d 610, 620 n. 15 (9th Cir.1988).
106. *Stormans*, 586 F.3d at 1120.
107. *See* State ex rel. McClure v. Sports & Health Club, Inc., 370 N.W.2d 844, 847 (Minn. 1985).
108. *See id.* at 850.
109. *Id.*
110. *Id.* at 850–51.
111. *See supra* note 98 (explaining the "associational standing" theory).
112. Ass'n of Am. Physicians & Surgeons, Inc. v. Texas Med. Bd., 627 F.3d 547, 550 (5th Cir. 2010) (quoting Hunt v. Washington State Apple Adver. Comm'n, 432 U.S. 333, 343 (1977)).
113. *See* Nat'l Ass'n of Coll. Bookstores, Inc. v. Cambridge Univ. Press, 990 F. Supp. 245, 251 (S.D.N.Y. 1997).
114. Primera Iglesia Bautista Hispana of Boca Raton, Inc. v. Broward Cnty., 450 F.3d 1295, 1305 (11th Cir. 2006).
115. *Id.*
116. Stormans, Inc. v. Selecky, 526 F.3d 406, 417 n.8 (9th Cir. 2008) (Tashmina, J., dissenting).
117. E.E.O.C. v. Townley Eng'g & Mfg. Co., 859 F.2d at 633 (Noonan, J. dissenting).
118. *Id.* at 619 (majority opinion).
119. *Id.* at 623 (Noonan, J., dissenting).
120. *Id.* at 623–25 (citations omitted).
121. Blanding v. Sports & Health Club, Inc., 373 N.W.2d 784, 798 (Minn. Ct. App. 1985) (Popovich, C.J., dissenting), *aff'd*, 389 N.W.2d 205 (Minn. 1986).
122. *Id.*
123. *Id.*
124. *Id.*
125. *See, e.g.*, O'Brien v. U.S. Dep't of Health and Human Servs., 854 F. Supp. 2d 1149, 1158 (E.D. Mo. 2012) ("Because this Court finds that the preventive services coverage regulations do not impose a 'substantial burden' on either Frank O'Brien or OIH, and do not violate either plaintiffs' rights under the Free Exercise Clause, this Court declines to reach the question of whether a secular limited liability company is capable of exercising a religion within the meaning of RFRA or the First Amendment."); Cap Santa Vue, Inc. v. Nat'l Labor Relations Bd., 424 F.2d 883, 881 (D.C. Cir. 1970) (explaining that a corporation was presumed to have free exercise standing, but claim did not prevail because the challenged legislation did not interfere with religious belief or practice).
126. *See* David L. Hudson Jr., *Along with Political Speech, Many Companies Also Claim They Have Religious Liberty Rights*, ABA JOURNAL (June 1, 2013, 2:30 AM), http://www.abajournal.com/magazine/article/along_with_political_speech_many_companies_also_claim_they_have_religious/; Joshua Alston, *7th Circ.,*

Others Shield For-Profits from Contraceptive Mandate, LAW 360 (Jan. 2, 2013, 8:41 PM), http://www.law360.com/articles/403911.

127. *See* Hobby Lobby Stores, Inc. v. Sebelius, 723 F.3d 1114, 1120–21 (10th Cir. 2013) (en banc); Grote v. Sebelius, 708 F.3d 850, 852–53 (7th Cir. 2013); Korte v. Sebelius, 735 F.3d 654, 660 (7th Cir. 2013); Conestoga Wood Specialties Corp. v. Sec. of U.S. Dep't of Health & Human Servs., 724 F.3d 377, 381–82 (3d Cir. 2013); Autocam Corp. v. Sebelius, 730 F.3d 618, 621 (6th Cir. 2013); Gilardi v. U.S. Dep't of Health & Human Servs., 733 F.3d 1208, 1210 (D.C. Cir. 2013).
128. *Hobby Lobby Stores, Inc.*, 723 F.3d at 1129.
129. *Grote*, 708 F.3d at 854.
130. *Conestoga*, 724 F.3d at 381; *accord* Autocam, 730 F.3d at 628.
131. *Gilardi*, 733 F.3d at 1215.
132. 723 F.3d at 1133.
133. *See id.* (quoting Roberts v. U.S. Jaycees, 468 U.S. 609, 618 (1984)).
134. *Id.* at 1138 (emphasis in original).
135. *Id.*
136. *Id.* at 1148 (Judge Hartz, concurring) (citing Braunfeld v. Brown, 366 U.S. 599, 611 (1961) (Brennan, J., dissenting)).
137. 724 F.3d at 385.
138. *Id.*
139. *Id.* (quoting Hobby Lobby Stores, Inc. v. Sebelius, 870 F. Supp. 2d 1278, 1291 (W.D. Okla. 2012), *rev'd en banc*; 723 F.3d 1114 (10th Cir. 2013)).
140. *Conestoga*, 724 F.3d at 386–87.
141. *Id.* at 389.
142. 730 F.3d at 622.
143. The same can be said with regard to the D.C. Circuit opinion in *Gilardi v. U.S. Dep't of Health & Human Services*, 733 F.3d 1208 (D.C. Cir. 2013).
144. Richard Epstein, *Unconstitutional Conditions, State Power, and the Limits of Consent*, 102 HARV. L. REV. 4, 6 (1988).

CHAPTER 8

The First Amendment

Freedom of Association

As rare as corporate invocations of the Free Exercise Clause have traditionally been, corporate invocations of the freedom of association have been rarer still. Nevertheless, given the current trajectory of First Amendment precedent, coupled with the observations I have made with regard to the freedoms of religion and speech, an increasing number of such invocations are foreseeable. The issue, therefore, merits our attention. In light of the ground we have already covered, this particular examination will proceed quickly.

DEVELOPMENT OF THE FREEDOM OF ASSOCIATION

Unlike the other First Amendment freedoms we have considered, freedom of association is not explicitly mentioned in the Constitution. In fact, the history of its development cannot be traced back much earlier than the 1927 case *Whitney v. California*. In that case, the U.S. Supreme Court affirmed a defendant's conviction under California's Criminal Syndicalism Act on the grounds that she was a member of the Communist Labor Party of California.[1] In so affirming, the Court concluded that the act did not violate "the right of free speech, assembly or association," thereby recognizing, in theory at least, freedom of association. It was not until the 1958 case *NAACP v. Alabama* that the Supreme Court would provide an explanation of the freedom and a holding predicated upon it.[2]

The issue before the Court in *NAACP v. Alabama* was the validity of a state judicial order requiring the National Association for the Advancement of Colored People (NAACP) to produce records "containing the names and addresses of all Alabama 'members' and 'agents' of the Association."[3] The NAACP refused to comply with the order, on at least two grounds. The first had to do with the order's relevance to the underlying litigation (the NAACP had been accused of conducting its activities in Alabama without first qualifying to do business in the state, and the association challenged the pertinence of its membership rolls). The second ground was that compliance with the order would potentially expose its members and agents to serious harm (as experience had shown). It was this second ground that raised the issue of freedom of association.

In a unanimous opinion authored by Justice Harlan, the Court observed that "[e]ffective advocacy of both public and private points of view, particularly controversial ones, is undeniably enhanced by group association."[4] The Court added that "[i]t is beyond debate that freedom to engage in association for the advancement of beliefs and ideas is an inseparable aspect of the 'liberty' assured by the Due Process Clause of the Fourteenth Amendment" (by which the freedoms enshrined in the First Amendment, which are framed as restrictions upon Congress, are made applicable to state governments as well).[5]

The Court then proceeded to recognize that "compelled disclosure of affiliation with groups engaged in advocacy may constitute [an] effective restraint on freedom of association."[6] Whether such a restraint was constitutionally valid would need to be determined by the "compelling government interest" test discussed previously.[7] This requires the government to demonstrate that the challenged law (or in this case, court order) is justified via a compelling state interest. As the Court found itself "unable to perceive that the disclosure of the names of petitioner's rank-and-file members has a substantial bearing" on the issues in the case, the Court held that the order amounted to an unconstitutional violation of the freedom of association.[8]

Thus, in *NAACP v. Alabama*, the Supreme Court clearly recognized the freedom of association as a First Amendment right and imbued it with specific substance: the right to maintain the privacy of one's affiliations.

The next important Supreme Court case to address freedom of association was *Roberts v. United States Jaycees*.[9] *Roberts* is particularly significant because it both expands the scope of freedom of association and introduces an important new term into the constitutional lexicon: "expressive association."

Roberts concerned the applicability of Minnesota's Human Rights Act to the U.S. Jaycees (Jaycees), a nonprofit membership corporation designed to pursue "such educational and charitable purposes as will promote and foster the growth and development of young men's civic organizations in the United States."[10] The Jaycees restricted membership to men and threatened to revoke the chapters of its local chapters in Minnesota for failing to abide by this policy. In response, the local chapters filed charges against the Jaycees' national organization, alleging sex discrimination in violation of Minnesota's antidiscrimination legislation. The Jaycees asserted that the legislation impermissibly violated its freedom of association.

As would be expected, the Court's analysis echoed many of the observations it made in *NAACP* regarding the importance of associations and the freedom to associate. Justice Brennan, who authored the Court's opinion, remarked that the Constitution protects "collective effort on behalf of shared goals" in order to "preserve political and culture diversity" and to protect "dissident expression from suppression by the majority."[11] He then proceeded to categorize associations into two explicit groups: "intimate associations" and "expressive associations." To fall within the protections of the First Amendment, an association must fit within one of these two groups. (Implicitly, therefore, the Court also recognized a third category: associations that are neither intimate nor expressive.)

The "intimate association" concerns close interpersonal relations, such as those within a family.[12] As the Jaycees' chapters were "large and basically unselective groups," they lacked "the distinctive characteristics that might afford constitutional protection" as an intimate association.[13] For the same reason, this is not the kind of association that most business corporations could potentially qualify for.[14]

The "expressive association" is characterized by individuals banding together "for the purpose of engaging in those activities protected by the First Amendment—speech, assembly, petition for the redress of grievances, and the exercise of religion."[15] As compared to the intimate association, most business corporations would have a stronger claim to this particular form of association, for the simple reason that most business corporations are not restricted to immediate family members. "The Constitution guarantees freedom of association of this kind as an indispensable means of preserving other individual liberties."[16] Significantly for us, the Court explicitly recognized the possibility of expressive associations created "in pursuit of . . . economic" purposes:

> [W]e have long understood as implicit in the right to engage in activities protected by the First Amendment a corresponding right to associate with others in pursuit of a wide variety of political, social, economic, educational, religious and cultural ends.[17]

The Jaycees easily passed muster as an expressive association, permitting the Court to advance to the next stage in the analysis: a consideration of the associational rights inuring to such an entity. In doing so, the Court went well beyond the right to keep its membership lists private, as articulated in

NAACP, recognizing an associational right to exclude would-be members from their ranks:

> There can be no clearer example of an intrusion into the internal structure or affairs of an association than a regulation that forces the group to accept members it does not desire. Such a regulation may impair the ability of the original members to express only those views that brought them together. Freedom of association therefore plainly presupposes a freedom not to associate.[18]

Therefore, once recognized as an expressive association, an organization acquires the constitutional right to limit its membership as it sees fit. But, as the court quickly added, "[t]he right to associate for expressive purposes is not... absolute."[19] The law or regulation in question may still be upheld and applicable if it passes the aforementioned compelling government interest test.[20] Recall that this test requires that the challenged law "serve compelling state interests" and "cannot be achieved through means significantly less restrictive" of the freedoms abridged.[21]

The Court in *Roberts* readily found that the state's interest in combating gender discrimination was compelling, thereby raising the question of whether Minnesota's antidiscrimination law was the "least restrictive means of achieving its ends."[22] This is where the Jaycees' assertion of freedom of association faltered. The Court found that the law was not substantially restrictive upon the Jaycees because "the Jaycees... failed to demonstrate that Minnesota's Human Rights Act imposes any serious burden on the male members' freedom of expressive association."[23] As the Court explained:

> There is... no basis in the record for concluding that admission of women as full voting members will impede the organization's ability to engage in [its] protected activities or to disseminate its preferred views. The Act required no change in the Jaycees' creed of promoting the interests of young men, and it imposes no restrictions on the organization's ability to exclude individuals with ideologies or philosophies different from those of its existing members.[24]

Thus, although the Jaycees was an organization designed to "promote and foster the growth and development of young men's civic organizations in the United States," the Court was not convinced that the admission of women, who themselves were ostensibly committed to these goals, would substantially impair the Jaycees' mission. This is admittedly an interesting finding of fact, but we should not let it distract us from what is most significant about *Roberts* for our purposes: the Court's acknowledgment that an economically oriented organization can be deemed an expressive association and that expressive associations can claim a constitutional right to exclude those who would "impair the ability of the original members to express only those views that brought them together."[25]

Before turning to the question of whether a corporation could qualify as an expressive association, we must consider one final Supreme Court freedom of association case: *Boy Scouts of America v. Dale*, decided in 2000.[26] For reasons that shall become apparent, *Dale* significantly brightened the prospects of such qualification.

Dale concerned the Boy Scouts' assertion that "homosexual conduct is inconsistent with the values it seeks to instill," and, relatedly, the Scouts' decision to revoke the membership of James Dale, "an avowed homosexual and gay rights activist."[27] The Scouts' expulsion of Dale conflicted with the antidiscrimination laws of New Jersey, making the case similar in many ways to that of *Roberts*.

Unlike *Roberts*, however, the Court in *Dale* held that application of the antidiscrimination laws to the group before it would be unconstitutional, thereby granting the Boy Scouts the victory that had eluded the Jaycees. In rendering its decision, the Court did not overturn *Roberts*, but rather distinguished the case factually.

Whereas the *Roberts* Court was unable to find that the admission of women would have interfered with the Jaycees' mission, the *Dale* Court was able to find that "a state requirement that the Boy Scouts retain Dale as an assistant scoutmaster would significantly burden the organization's right to oppose or disfavor homosexual conduct."[28] The Court essentially recognized that, as the saying goes, actions speak louder than words: to force the Scouts to include "an avowed homosexual and gay rights activist" within their ranks would undermine the message they were attempting to instill against "homosexual conduct." In response to the dissent's argument that "the public perception of homosexuality in this country has changed," the Court reminded the dissenting jurists that the First Amendment's freedoms are "crucial in preventing the majority from imposing its views on groups that would rather express other, perhaps unpopular, ideas."[29]

What makes *Dale* particularly important and relevant for us is not so much its application of law to the particular facts before it, but rather a few critical features in the decision that serve to broaden freedom of association.

First, the Court held that "associations do not have to associate for the 'purpose' of disseminating a certain message in order to be entitled to the protections of the First Amendment."[30] These protections are "not reserved for advocacy groups," the Court wrote, but rather extend to any group that engages "in some form of expression."[31] This is profound, as it signaled a shift away from an interpretation of *Roberts* that required a group to be initially identified as an expressive association in order to invoke the freedom of association.[32] In other words, the critical first question is not whether the group in question has been organized for the purpose of engaging in expression, but simply rather, at any given moment in time, is it choosing to engage in expression. As the Court explained: "An association must merely engage in expressive activity that could be impaired in order to be entitled to protection."[33] The decision to engage in expression apparently transforms any organization into an expressive association pursuant to *Dale*.

The profoundness of this shift is magnified by the Court's deferential approach toward assessing the question of expression. When an association asserts, in litigation, that it engages in certain expressive activity, "it is not the role of the courts to reject [the] group's expressed values because they...find them internally inconsistent."[34] Instead, the Court's review of the association's assertion must be "limited." The fact that it fails to "trumpet its views from the housetops, or that it tolerates dissent within its ranks" is of no moment.[35] Indeed, the Court appeared to accept the Boy Scouts' assertion, set forth in its litigation briefs, as conclusive.[36]

Further, the *Dale* Court afforded associations a wide degree of latitude in identifying the manner in which their expression occurs. In response to evidence that the Boy Scouts "discourages Scout leaders from disseminating views of sexual issues" (thereby undermining the claim that a scout's sexuality is a relevant membership factor), the Court noted that "the First Amendment protects the Boy Scouts' method of expression. If the Boy Scouts wishes Scout leaders to avoid questions of sexuality and teach only by example, this fact does not negate the sincerity of its belief."[37]

The Court also added that "the First Amendment simply does not require that every member of a group agree on every issue in order for the group's policy to be 'expressive association.'"[38] It is "sufficient for First Amendment purposes" that the group take an "official position."[39]

Finally, whereas *NAACP* was framed largely in terms of an *individual's* freedom of association rights (and, to a lesser extent, *Roberts* as well), *Dale* explicitly recognized the freedom of association as a freedom possessed by the association itself. As one scholar put it, *Dale* helped transform the "freedom of association" to "freedom of *the* association."[40]

THE POSTMODERN CORPORATION AND EXPRESSIVE ASSOCIATION

Dale liberalized the freedom of association. Post-*Dale*, the freedom of association can clearly be invoked by an association itself. The freedom encompasses not only the right to keep one's membership private but even permits the association to deny membership, in contravention of antidiscrimination laws, to those who would undermine its attempted expression. To qualify, an association need not be formed for the purposes of engaging in expression, but rather must merely be engaged in some form of expressive activity. In assessing the content of this expressive activity, courts are to be deferential to the association's articulation thereof.

The preceding would seem to open wide the door for recognizing business corporations as rightful claimants to the freedom of association. Similar to freedom of speech and religion, however, a critical threshold question must first be confronted: is the corporation an entity capable of engaging in "expressive activity" at all? Although precedent is clear that an organization need not be designed for the purpose of engaging in expression to invoke freedom of association, it must nevertheless be actually capable of such expression.

In her *Roberts* concurrence, Justice O'Connor attempted to articulate a standard by which to distinguish those groups that could qualify for "expressive association" status from those groups that could not, and this provides a natural starting point for our analysis.[41] She declared that an association's constitutional protections should be limited "when, and only when, the association's activities are not predominantly of the type protected by the First Amendment."[42] To this she added an important rule of thumb: if the association is a commercial entity, it cannot be deemed an expressive association.[43]

Justice O'Connor's approach never commanded a majority of the Court and would appear to be a dead letter after *Dale*. And for good reason. As Richard Epstein has persuasively argued, the divide that Justice O'Connor proposes "cannot be defended on either political theory or constitutional law grounds."[44] Among other deficiencies, this dichotomy fails to recognize that every association has expressive potential.[45] How would this approach treat an entity that was at one time primarily expressive, but ceases to be? Or an entity that was previously not expressive, but had suddenly become expressive? *Dale* avoids these problems by sidestepping an examination of the group's primary purpose and focusing instead on its present conduct.

Moreover, the Justice's assumption that commercial associations can never be "expressive" betrays quite narrow and unimaginative thinking. As I have explained, the line between "commercial" and "noncommercial" is oftentimes illusory and misleading.[46] It is also, as I have pointed out, to some extent ahistorical.[47] It is not difficult to envision a commercial entity that is strongly committed to a particular cause or set of values such that its expressive activity can fairly be said to predominate—indeed, companies such as this already exist, which I have labeled postmodern corporations.

Those who agree with Justice O'Connor's formulation argue that the corporation's profit motive belies any claim that the organization can be "predominantly" expressive.[48] Indeed, the argument has been made that the profit motive precludes a corporation from being expressive at all—an argument we encountered in our discussions of freedom of speech and religion. The argument posits that the business corporation is simply not an association capable of possessing genuine beliefs (let alone capable of genuine expression), but rather more akin to a robotic machine, fixated on profits.[49] Even though investors, officers, employees, and customers might influence a corporation to adopt a religious (or some other) persona, this persona is only legitimate to the extent that it is insincere—a ruse concocted to maximize profits. This must be so (the argument goes) because directors are duty-bound to maximize shareholder wealth and must not let ideology, religion, or anything else for that matter get in the way.[50] As such, the rights and protections of the First Amendment, which exist to protect "the individual's freedom to believe, to worship, and to express himself in accordance with the dictates of his own conscience," are simply inapplicable to such an entity.[51]

As has been explained repeatedly, these arguments are strong when applied to the modern business corporation, but not when applied to the postmodern corporation.[52] By definition, the postmodern corporation eschews limiting its objectives to profit maximization alone. By definition, it embraces an "expressive" element that draws together its various constituencies—an element beyond simply the maximizations of profits.

A postmodern corporation would, therefore, be capable of forming and expressing beliefs qualifying for First Amendment protection. Unlike a modern corporation, the structure and objectives of the postmodern corporation do not preclude this from being the case. Certainly no corporation is a human being, but neither is the NAACP, the Jaycees, nor the Boy Scouts, and each of those organizations undeniably possesses First Amendment rights, including the freedom of association.[53] Although those other groups might have greater cohesion than a corporation (even a postmodern corporation) when it comes to beliefs and values, *Dale* explicitly noted that an association's expression need not be uniformly endorsed by its members.

Of course, the simple capability of forming and expressing beliefs does not, in itself, trigger freedom of association. The freedom is triggered when an association actualizes this capability. An interesting question is whether this actualization requires some externalized manifestation of expression, or can be limited to expression that largely remains internal. Given that associations are "formative as well as expressive," I suggest that no external manifestation should be necessary. "Associations serve too complex a role in the infrastructure of public discourse to be reduced to mere megaphones.... To require an association to send a clear and articulable message... is to miss the point."[54] I agree with Paul Horwitz that the relevant question should be whether the organization lives by a set of values and norms of its own, rather than those dictated by the market.[55] Invoking the associational theory of Meir Dan-Cohen, James Nelson makes a similar point, arguing that what truly matters is not an entity's commercial or noncommercial nature, nor an entity's formulation of a "clear moral message on a particular issue." Rather, the critical question is whether the entity's membership "identifies" with the entity versus whether its membership remains "detached" from it (as discussed in chapter 1).[56]

Regardless of the approach taken, acknowledging an organization's entitlement to assert freedom of association does not grant the organization an ability to prescind from burdensome laws or regulations carte blanche. Rather, the freedom empowers the association to challenge only those laws or regulations that substantially undermine its "expression" (be that defined as a message articulated to the world or simply a coherent identity). Should it travel this far, the association may still fail in its challenge if the government can demonstrate a compelling interest in the law's applicability and that the interest has been furthered by means least restrictive to the association's constitutional rights (as was the case in *Roberts*). The critical point being made here is that certain for-profit corporations (namely, postmodern corporations) should simply have the right to assert expressive associational status and, as such, the potential protections afforded by freedom of association.

NOTES

1. *See* Wayne Batchis, *Citizens United and the Paradox of "Corporate Speech": From Freedom of Association to Freedom of the Association*, 36 N.Y.U. Rev. L. & Soc. Change 5, 14 (2012).
2. 357 U.S. 449 (1958).
3. *Id.* at 453.
4. *Id.* at 460.
5. *Id.*
6. *Id.* at 462.
7. *Id.* at 463.
8. *See id.* at 464–65.
9. 468 U.S. 609 (1984).
10. *Id.* at 612.
11. *Id.* at 622.
12. *Id.* at 618.
13. *Id.* at 621–22.
14. I write "most" because one could imagine a small, family-owned business that incorporated itself as a closed corporation. Such an entity might possibly be able to argue that, its commercial nature notwithstanding, it remained, essentially, a group tied together via close interpersonal relations.
15. *Id.* at 618; *see also* Erica Goldberg, *Amending* Christian Legal Society v. Martinez, *Protecting Expressive Association as an Independent Right in a Limited Public Forum*, 16 Tex. J. on C.L. & C.R. 129, 133–34 (2011).
16. Roberts, 468 U.S. at 618.
17. *Id.* at 622.
18. *Id.* at 623.
19. *Id.*

20. *See* chapter 6.
21. Roberts, 468 U.S. at 623.
22. *Id.* at 626.
23. *Id.*
24. *Id.* at 627.
25. *Id.* at 623.
26. 530 U.S. 640 (2000).
27. *Id.* at 643.
28. *Id.* at 659.
29. *Id.* at 648–49.
30. *Id.* at 655.
31. *Id.* at 648.
32. *See* ANDREW KOPPELMAN, A RIGHT TO DISCRIMINATE? xi (2009).
33. 530 U.S. at 655.
34. *Id.* at 651.
35. *Id.* at 656.
36. *Id.* at 651.
37. *Id.* at 655.
38. *Id.*
39. *Id.*
40. *See* Batchis, *supra* note 1, at 7.
41. *See* Roberts, 468 U.S. at 633 (O'Connor, concurring).
42. *See id.* at 636.
43. *See id.*
44. Richard A. Epstein, *The Constitutional Perils of Moderation: The Case of the Boy Scouts*, 74 S. CAL. L. REV. 119, 139 (2000) (*quoted in* Daniel A. Farber, *Speaking in the First Person: Expressive Associations and the First Amendment*, 85 MINN. L. REV. 1483, 1498). Epstein also remarked that "[o]nly the bold and foolhardy would claim that current law allows business associations . . . out from under the thumb of the anti-discrimination laws." *Id.* Those remarks strike uncomfortably close to home and as such prompt a response here. I am certainly not arguing that *all* business associations would be entitled to bring First Amendment claims, and I am not at all addressing the ultimate merits of such claims if brought against antidiscrimination laws. I am, instead, making the more modest argument that *some* business corporations ought to have standing to bring such claims, without passing judgment on how those claims would be resolved.
45. John D. Inazu, *The Unsettling "Well-Settled" Law of Freedom of Association*, 43 CONN. L. REV. 149, 176 (2010).
46. *See* chapter 3.
47. *See id.*
48. *See* Mark M. Hager, *Bodies Politic: The Progressive History of Organizational "Real Entity" Theory*, 50 U. PITT. L. REV. 575, 648–49 (1989).
49. Usha Rodrigues, *Entity and Identity*, 60 EMORY L. J. 1257, 1320 (2011).
50. *Cf.* Milton Friedman, *The Social Responsibility of Business Is to Increase Its Profits*, N.Y. TIMES, Sept. 13, 1970, §6 (Magazine), at 32, 33.
51. Wallace v. Jaffree, 472 U.S. 38, 48 (1985); *see also* Fed. Comm. Comm'n v. AT&T, 131 S. Ct. 1177, 1181, 1184–85 (2011) (concluding that although corporations are "legal persons," they do not possess "personal privacy interest" as that term is used in the Freedom of Information Act).
52. *See* chapter 3.

53. Certain nonprofit organizations are subject to restrictions on their ability to engage in political speech, and this might be invoked by some in support of limiting the First Amendment rights of the postmodern corporation. It is important to recognize, however, that these restrictions on certain nonprofits are imposed only by the Internal Revenue Service (IRS) as a condition to the preservation of their tax-exempt status. They do not, therefore, go directly to the question of the First Amendment rights of these organizations per se. Moreover, in light of the *Citizens United* decision, even these restrictions might be called into question as a violation of the prohibition on constitutional conditions. *See* chapter 7.
54. Paul Horwitz, First Amendment Institutions 223 (2013).
55. *See id.* at 228.
56. James D. Nelson, *Conscience, Incorporated*, 2013 Mich. State L. Rev. 1565, 1579–80 (2013).

CHAPTER 9

A Taxonomy of the Corporation

In the chapters that immediately preceded this one, we examined the freedoms protected by the First Amendment and considered the extent to which they should, or should not, be deemed applicable to the business corporation. In the chapters preceding those, we examined the history and nature of the corporation and demonstrated the rich variety of entities organized as corporations (both historically and in our own times). In this chapter, we shall pull these two threads together and map First Amendment constitutional rights onto particular corporate entities.

In doing so, we draw upon both precedent and recent practice. We start by recognizing that society's conceptualization of the corporation has changed over time as the corporation itself has changed over time. This, in turn, impacted the ways in which the corporation was regulated. This was both understandable and beneficial: the law did not generally persist in applying yesteryear's laws, based upon yesteryear's theories, to the evolving corporate entity. Instead, theory and law did its best to conform to the factual realities of the corporate enterprise.

Further, despite a general consensus over the nature of the corporation today as little more than a nexus of contracts, the practice of tailoring law to fit the realities of the corporation largely persists. As shall be shown below, the law does not treat all corporations similarly, but rather frequently takes into account key, relevant differences when regulating corporate entities.

Unfortunately, this has not been the case with regard to the question of corporate constitutional rights. As was recounted in chapter 4, constitutional law has not consistently kept pace with our evolving understanding of the corporation. Nor has it taken into consideration the fact that the corporations of today can vary dramatically from one another, calling into question a "one-size-fits-all" approach to the adjudication of corporate constitutional rights.

As has become clear by now, I suggest a different approach, one that considers the diversity of those entities we collectively call "corporations." An approach that draws upon the wisdom and practice of treating different corporations differently, and one that takes into account the most accurate theoretical conceptualization of a given corporation.[1] To do so requires a taxonomy of the corporation: an articulation of the different types of corporations and how they should be treated under the First Amendment.

We have been working toward such a taxonomy throughout this book, having identified and distinguished the modern corporation from the postmodern corporation, the closed corporation from the public corporation, and the religiously expressive corporation from the nonreligiously expressive corporation. Shortly, we shall pull these distinctions together and show how they can assist us in the adjudication of corporate constitutional rights. Before doing so, let us first pause to consider how corporate diversity is regularly taken into account in several other fields of law, thereby establishing that the proposal to treat different corporations differently for constitutional purposes is far from novel.

CORPORATE DIVERSITY

In chapter 2, we reviewed the unfolding historical conceptualizations of the corporation. Reviews such as this can have the unfortunate effect of marginalizing theories of the past. The effect is unfortunate because the insights of past conceptualizations remain more relevant today than is commonly acknowledged. Admittedly, these past conceptualizations have lost their positions of dominance, and their insights were gleaned in different times and under different circumstances. That said, some of the realities that animated their appearances have not entirely disappeared, making them far from irrelevant. To the extent that their insights go to features or characteristics that may mark certain corporate enterprises of our own time, these insights possess continued vitality and usefulness. Thus, although the contractarian conceptualization may best describe most corporations of today, it does not accurately describe all of them. Given the realities of most twenty-first-century corporations, contractarianism's theoretical dominance may be justifiable, but its monopoly is not.

Reviewing past corporate conceptualizations also serves to remind us that understandings and theorizations can and do change over time. Contractarianism is not etched in stone, and we ought to be open to the possibility that another evolutionary turn in corporate theory is upon us.

Finally, an awareness of the fluidity of corporate theory is particularly important as we confront the vexing question of corporate constitutional rights. For if it seems as though the recognition of First Amendments rights does not square with our prevailing understanding of the corporation, we have at least three potential responses. The first response is to reject the recognition of such rights. The second is to reconsider our understanding of the corporation. The third is to consider the possibility that perhaps different corporations ought to be conceptualized and treated differently under the Constitution. This third response, I suggest, offers the best path forward.

For corporations can vary quite dramatically from one another.[2] Corporations include entities as diverse as Microsoft, the American Red Cross, the *New York Times*, the Episcopal Diocese of Albany, the American Civil Liberties Union, the New Jersey Democratic Party, and the Jet Quick Lube Corporation of Hempstead, New York.[3] Some are large and international, others are small and local. Some are for profit, others are not for profit. Some are religiously oriented, others are politically oriented. Some are publicly traded, others are closely held.

As a result, some of today's corporations are best understood in terms of past conceptualizations. A small family owned and operated corporation, for example, would seem to be well described and understood under the aggregation theory of the 1800s—not contractarianism. A large pension fund—and, perhaps, mutual funds in general—might more accurately be envisioned in managerialist terms. A shell company, existing solely on paper and lacking constitutive human members, would appear to be the epitome of an artificial person—perhaps harkening back to concession-theory ideas of the corporation. In sum, although it may certainly be justifiable to adopt the contractarian model as the default conceptualization of the modern corporation, I suggest that previous conceptualizations be retained and employed as appropriate.

Fortunately, although academics and theoreticians have largely settled upon contractarianism, lawmakers and regulators do not appear wedded to a universal contractarian conceptualization of the corporation. As has become apparent to them, the fact that a particular entity is a "corporation" (and, as such, presumably a nexus of contracts) is in many cases neither particularly informative nor particularly noteworthy—other features and characteristics of the entity are far more important, depending on the context. Consequently, the manner in which corporations are ordinarily regulated largely reflects an appreciation of these salient distinctions. What we see time and again is not the law's deference to some overarching conceptualization of the corporation and whatever logical consequences would flow therefrom, but rather a tailoring of rules and regulations to the particular business entity before it. In the pages that follow, a few important examples of this practice are discussed.

To be clear, adoption of a uniform theory of the corporation does not mandate treating all corporations identically for all purposes; a weapons manufacturer would rightfully be subject to a different set of regulations than a toy manufacturer. Certain undertakings require heightened regulation and scrutiny compared to others, and these concerns would predominate over any consideration of a particular actor's status as a corporation versus some other business entity. Thus, it stands to reason that different industries require different regulations, and it comes as no surprise that a banking corporation would be treated differently under the law than an insurance corporation, and more differently still from a corporation engaged in the manufacturing of pharmaceuticals.

Accordingly, the examples that follow are as "content neutral" as possible with regard to the corporation's activities. Drawn from corporate law, securities law, and employment law, these examples show how corporations are frequently treated differently under the law even though they could very well be engaged in precisely the very same line of business. These examples are pertinent because they reveal the law taking into account differences that are constitutive in nature: differences that touch upon what the business enterprise *is* more than what the business enterprise *does*. As such, they drive home the point that merely identifying a particular business as a "corporation" is oftentimes inadequate for regulatory purposes—even if the regulation in question is not industry or activity specific.[4]

Corporate Law

Corporate law itself does not treat all corporations equally. Consider, for example, one of the defining characteristics of the modern business corporation: limited liability. Called "the greatest single discovery of modern times" ("even the steam engine and electricity are far less important than the limited liability corporation and they would be reduced to comparative impotence without it"),[5] limited liability permits a corporation's shareholders to partake in the upside potential of a business venture while risking only the limited sum of their invested capital.

Yet even this cornerstone of corporate law is not equally applicable across corporations. Pursuant to the doctrine of "piercing the corporate veil," a corporation's shareholders are more likely to be held liable for the debts of the corporation (beyond their total investment amount) if certain features characterize the corporation. These features primarily include (1) a shareholder's failure to observe corporate formalities, (2) a shareholder's domination of corporate affairs, and (3) inadequate corporate capitalization. When these features are present (and especially if they are present in combination), courts may discard the rule of limited liability and hold shareholders accountable for a corporation's debts.

The veil-piercing doctrine does not appear consistent with a contractarian view of the corporation, for a number of reasons. For example, veil-piercing clings to the notion that the corporation is a "thing" that is actually owned by somebody (the shareholders).[6] It also reads into the corporate enterprise contractual terms that are not necessarily justifiably inferred. The heavy handedness of this imposition harkens back, I suggest, to the concession theory of the firm more than any other. Regardless of the doctrine's propriety, however, the important point to be grasped is that veil-piercing handles different incorporated business entities differently. Veil-piercing is a good example of the law's ability to look beyond the mere nomenclature of a firm and into its substantive characteristics in assessing how best to treat that firm.

Another corporate law example is that of the "closed corporation." These entities share little in common with most other ("public") corporations, even though they are ordinarily incorporated under the same statutes of general incorporation. Most significantly, closed corporations "have only a small number (for example, fewer than thirty) of individual shareholders and their shares are not traded on a recognized securities exchange or on the over-the-counter market."[7] This lack of liquidity, coupled with the typically active management of the enterprise by its shareholders, gives rise to a host of characteristics at odds with the prevailing corporate paradigm, principally separation of ownership and control. In recognition of this, the law treats closed corporations differently than public corporations. It treats them more like partnerships, in ways that would be best justified under aggregation theories of the corporation. Not all the same corporate formalities need to be observed, restrictions on share transferability are more likely to be enforced, and even restrictions on director discretion have been upheld. Although this is largely a matter of case law, formal distinctions are also apparent in certain state codes as well.

Securities Regulation

Securities regulation, a close relative (if not a subset) of corporate law, also takes repeatedly into account the diversity that marks corporate entities.

Federal securities law distinguishes those corporations that are "public" (or "reporting") from those that are "nonpublic" (or "nonreporting"), and significant repercussions follow this categorization. Public companies are (subject to some exceptions) those corporations that (1) have made a public offering of securities; (2) have securities listed on a national stock exchange; or (3) have more than $10 million in total assets and more than 2,000 equity shareholders.[8] A public company (but not a nonpublic company) is subject to a panoply of disclosure requirements, including annual reports, quarterly reports, proxy statements, and other reports triggered by the occurrence of certain specified events.

An even more elaborate set of distinctions applies to issuers who wish to make a public offering of securities. The Securities and Exchange Commission divides these corporations into four different categories:

Unreporting issuers
Unseasoned issuers
Seasoned issuers
Well-known seasoned issuers[9]

A host of repercussions follow an issuer's categorization within the scheme set forth above.[10] As one moves from the first category ("unreporting issuers") to the fourth ("well-known seasoned issuers"), one moves from corporations that are not publicly traded, to corporations that are heavily capitalized capital-market veterans.[11] Along the way, one discovers greater privileges and flexibility being afforded to the issuing corporation in terms of required disclosures.[12] The logic behind this scheme is that the investing public needs greater disclosure when it comes to the securities of poorly known companies, and lesser disclosure when it comes to the securities of well-known companies.[13] Here we vividly witness the law's ability and tendency to look beyond the mere fact of incorporation and predicate its impositions upon other characteristics (in this case, social realities).

The JOBS Act of 2012 provides yet another example from the field of securities law.[14] The act liberalizes the initial public offering process for "emerging growth companies" (EGCs), which are defined as companies with gross revenues of less than $1 billion per year. EGCs may engage in communications with potential investors well beyond that permitted to non-EGCs. The S-1 registration statement, traditionally a public document, may be filed confidentially by an EGC and may remain confidential until the EGC's underwriters begin to actively promote the offering. The audited financial statements that must accompany an EGC's initial public offering need only go back two years and not the usual three. Finally, EGCs are relieved of some of the requirements set forth in the Dodd-Frank Wall Street Reform and Consumer Protection Act,[15] such as the need for periodic shareholder "say on pay" votes and limitations on the severance compensation available to executives. This stems from recognition that not all corporations can bear the burdens of U.S. federal securities regulation equally and that for some the costs of going public either exceed the benefits or are simply insurmountable. This is admittedly not the most profound of insights, but it nevertheless furnishes us with another illustration of policymakers taking corporate differences into account when fashioning regulation.

Employment Law

Title VII of the Civil Rights Act of 1964 prohibits any employer from discriminating against any employee on the basis of race, sex, color, or national origin.[16] Title VII defines an "employer" as[17]

> a person engaged in an industry affecting commerce who has fifteen or more employees for each working day in each of twenty or more calendar weeks in the current or preceding calendar year, and any agent of such a person, but such term does not include (1) the United States, a corporation wholly owned by the Government of the United States, an Indian tribe, or any department

> or agency of the District of Columbia subject by statute to procedures of the competitive service (as defined in section 2102 of Title 5), or (2) a bona fide private membership club (other than a labor organization) which is exempt from taxation under section 501(c) of Title 26, except that during the first year after March 24, 1972, persons having fewer than twenty-five employees (and their agents) shall not be considered employers."[18]

Observe how the definition turns not on whether the entity is incorporated, but instead primarily upon the entity's size ("fifteen or more employees").[19] Similarly, when it comes to punitive damages, Title VII requires the courts to consider the size and financial capacity of the defendant.[20] Further still, the act places statutory caps on the award of punitive damages based on the size and of the employer in terms of its number of employees.[21] Thus, when it comes to employment law, a business's size is what matters; the fact that a business may be incorporated or not is wholly irrelevant.[22]

A CONSTITUTIONAL TAXONOMY

Consistent with the law's practice in other areas, let us now construct a taxonomy of the corporation for constitutional purposes. As per my critique of the current approach to recognizing corporate constitutional rights, any attempt to evaluate the propriety of such rights should do so within the proper theoretical context. Consequently, throughout my explanation of this taxonomy, I shall consider the various theoretical conceptualizations of the corporation and how each theory supports or undermines the corporation's claim to constitutional rights.

The following chart summarizes the proposed taxonomy.

Type of Corporation	Best Theoretical Model(s)	Guiding Principle	Example	Freedom of Association?	Free Speech Rights?	Religious Liberty Rights?
Modern Corporation	Nexus of contracts	Profit maximization*	IBM	No	No	No
Postmodern Corporation	Real entity	Social/ethical concerns	Whole Foods	Yes	Yes	No
Religiously Expressive Corporation	Real entity	Religious convictions	Hobby Lobby	Yes	Yes	Yes
Closed Corporation	Aggregation; property model	Profit maximization	Cargill	Maybe	Yes	Maybe

* This is not necessarily the guiding principle of the corporation, but rather the objective of corporate investors and the guiding principle of the corporation's officers and directors.

"Type of corporation" is simply the name given to the category in question. Confusion may arise with regard to the religiously expressive corporation, as this is a subset of the postmodern corporation. In this case, these categories should be treated as mutually exclusive. Thus, to the extent that a corporation can be categorized as a religiously expressive corporation, it should bear this categorization and not that of the postmodern corporation for purposes of this taxonomy.

"Best theoretical model(s)" sets forth the corporate conceptualizations that best describe the category of corporation in question. Currently, the nexus-of-contracts conceptualization reigns supreme, and not surprisingly it serves to describe well the "modern corporation" for which it was designed to explain. Past theoretical conceptualizations, however, more accurately describe other types of corporations. "Guiding principle" sets forth the primary touchstone for corporate decision making. It is assumed that the corporation exists to supply some product or service, and thus the "guiding principle" serves to direct the means by which it goes about doing so.

"Example" sets forth an example corporation for each category.

"Free speech rights?," "free exercise rights?," and "freedom of association rights?" provide presumptive answers to the question of whether a corporation within a particular category can assert such rights.

The Modern Corporation

"Modern corporations" are probably what most individuals envision when they think of the corporation: large businesses, with securities that are publicly traded. Shareholders are multitudinous and remote, and rely upon the corporation's board and management to operate the corporation for their benefit. More specifically, shareholders expect to maximize their return on investment, and the corporation's board and management pledge themselves to that result. The other corporate constituencies, from employees to customers, are, primarily, means to this end. For purposes of public relations and corporate morale, most modern corporations will position themselves as good and wholesome. They may invest heavily in cultivating a positive image, and this investment may include decisions and policies of no small consequence. They may subscribe to the notion that businesses do well when they do good. Regardless, the corporation's leaders will consider themselves duty-bound to maximize shareholder profits, and this obligation will serve as their guiding star.

It is little surprise, therefore, that the nexus-of-contracts model has prevailed in the face of the modern corporation's ascendancy. The modern corporation does not consist of a community in the traditional sense, as each constituent ultimately puts himself or herself first and the collective second.

What the constituents share is a belief that their cooperation will lead to mutually beneficial outcomes—the foundational component of contracting. To the extent that better opportunities arise, many will sever their link to the corporation without much second thought. This holds true especially for shareholders, who view themselves (and are viewed) as primarily investors and not owners in any ordinary sense of that term. Indeed, a significant portion of shareholders will not be individuals at all, but rather other corporations, such as hedge funds and mutual funds that have seized upon the corporation in question as a wise investment opportunity. It holds true for employers and officers, who will ordinarily depart from the corporation if there are material incentives for doing so. It holds true for customers as well, who will often abandon their patronization of a particular company in response to changes in product or service pricing or value.

Given that the nexus-of-contracts understanding of the corporation reigns supreme today, and given its appropriateness in describing the modern corporation, let us consider how this conceptualization weighs upon our assessment of corporate rights. Not surprisingly, this is what leading corporate scholars have done (even if the Supreme Court has not).[23]

Unfortunately, among those who share the contractarian perspective, a consensus on the question of corporate constitutional rights has not been reached. According to some, "because the contractarian paradigm treats corporations as nothing more than a nexus of contracts among its constituents, it is a mistake to conclude that a corporation should be given the First Amendment protection given to individuals."[24] Applying political theory, Dan Greenwood has persuasively argued that if the corporation is a nexus-of-contracts (and even more so if it's a quasi-sovereign governed by peculiarly anti-democratic norms, as Greenwood characterizes it), it cannot claim to legitimately speak on behalf of anyone.[25]

An opposite perspective has been provided by scholars such as Larry Ribstein. As a "nexus of contracts," the corporation is, to him, a creature of private ordering—and not of government concession. This, in turn, weakens the government's claim to regulate the corporation—or strip it of its constitutional rights, for the government's regulation of contracts is ordinarily limited to "enforcing them."[26] Further, some have viewed contractarianism as essentially an offshoot of aggregation theory. As we shall see in a moment, aggregation theory is arguably quite supportive of corporate constitutional rights.[27] Viewed in this light, the contractarian corporation is merely an aggregation of individuals via contract and as such derives its constitutional rights from the rights of these individuals.

It seems to me that those scholars who read contractarianism as undermining corporate constitutional rights have the better of the two arguments. Contractarian rhetoric urges us to resist efforts to "reify" the corporation, insisting upon the corporation's fictional, abstract nature.[28] As such, it is difficult to see how the abstraction of a contractual nexus can lay claim to constitutional rights. It is difficult to comprehend how an abstraction can engage in speech, religion, or association as those terms are understood in constitutional jurisprudence.

Further, although individuals certainly have constitutional rights under the First Amendment, contracts per se do not. Whereas aggregation theory posits an aggregation of individuals, contractarianism more accurately posits an aggregation of contracts, thereby revealing a critical difference between the two. Unlike the aggregationist, who would claim that the corporation is little more than the sum total of its shareholders, the contractarian would not characterize the corporation as a collective at all. Under contractarianism, the corporation is not the mere grouping of any particular constituency (or even multiple constituencies), but rather a complicated web of explicit and implicit contractual arrangements. People are not central to the contractarian understanding of the corporation, legal obligations are.

Certainly, even the most vociferous contractarian opponent to corporate constitutional rights would readily concede that corporations must (as they have always) possess certain rights and privileges. Indeed, even in the bygone days of concessionary theory, pursuant to which the corporation owed its very existence to the discretionary will of the state, this was the case. However, as has been mentioned in chapters 2 and 4, before the advent of real entity theory, such rights and privileges were recognized out of mere convenience, in order to facilitate regulation and oversight, not to undermine it. This is incompatible with a genuine claim to First Amendment rights. According to its framers and judicial interpreters, the rights enshrined in the First Amendment are beyond the state's authority to bestow or deny: they must simply be recognized. Thus, conceding that certain corporate rights are important to acknowledge for prudential reasons (such as the right to own property, for example), does not commit one to conceding that corporations are inherently entitled to certain rights (or any rights whatsoever).

Conceptualizing the modern corporation as a nexus of contracts further undermines any claim that the entity might have classification as a Tocquevillian Association. Admittedly, Tocqueville's theory of the association explicitly covered commercial ventures. Further, few other entities can serve as effective a check on government expansion and power than the modern corporation, a factor Tocqueville mentioned in his discussion of associations. The critical criterion to Tocqueville, however, was the association's ability to serve as a vehicle through which individuals can work together for a common goal. Superficially, this might appear to be the case with the modern corporation, as all oars are supposed to be rowing in the direction of profit maximization. Upon closer inspection, however, as we have just noted, what we have instead is an assortment of individuals using the corporate entity (and one another) to further their own private gain. We do not have the reciprocal giving of selves (the constituents to the corporation, the corporation to the constituents, and the constituents to one another). Rather, we have a series of self-gratifying relationships, in which each party is using the other for its own personal advantage. Even the guiding principle of profit maximization overstates the degree of the modern corporation's cohesiveness. The investors are the only constituency that truly cares primarily about profit maximization: employees care more about higher salaries, and customers about lower prices. Directors and officers are arguably beholden to profit maximization by law, if not by those who have elected or appointed them. This calls into question whether their commitment is really the goal of profit maximization, versus a desire to avoid lawsuits alleging breach of duty and the security of their employment, positions, and compensation.

Indeed, if one takes the contractarian understanding of the corporation seriously, as we ought to, there is no "common good" of the corporation toward which all are striving, but rather countless individual, private concerns that motivate conduct. It is doubtful that this would qualify as the sort of common purpose about which Tocqueville wrote.

Still clearer, however, is that such an entity does not substantially further the values that animate the First Amendment's freedoms. The modern corporation is not genuinely expressive in the sense that would justify recognition of associational rights, and it is certainly not beholden to religious convictions that would justify free exercise rights. As for free speech rights, speaker-centered views of the First Amendment would not justify them, for, as mentioned, the corporation has no genuine expression of substance. Listener-centered views of the First Amendment are more complicated to assess, as was revealed in chapter 6. Even with regard to such theories, however, we discovered that a strong argument can be made that speech that is purely instrumental, such as the speech of the modern corporation, does not legitimately contribute to the marketplace of ideas. As such, some lesser level of protection, such as that afforded to commercial speech, might be more appropriate with regard to the modern corporation.

A final point regarding the modern corporation should be made explicit here. The problem with recognizing the First Amendment rights of the modern corporation should not be tied simply to its nature as a profit-seeking enterprise. Profit-seeking alone cannot strip a person or entity of its First Amendment rights—this the Supreme Court made clear as far back as 1952.[29] To hold otherwise would jeopardize the First Amendment rights of newspapers, radio stations, and most media outlets. Thus, the modern corporation cannot be denied the protections of First Amendment rights on account of its profit-seeking orientation alone. Rather, it is the modern corporation's unique nature as an entity beholden to profit maximization and only to profit maximization that poses an obstacle to the First Amendment's applicability. It is not the profit seeking per se that should give us pause, but rather the entity's understood *duty* to maximize profits. This particular feature is what helps transform the modern corporation into an entity very dissimilar to those entities that do (and should) receive First Amendment protections. For once this duty is imposed, the modern corporation is truly dehumanized, effectively deprived of the ability to balance profit-seeking against other values and concerns. This is something that those persons and entities that enjoy the protections of the First Amendment do, or at a minimum, have the potential of doing.

The Postmodern Corporation

As has become clear by now, the postmodern corporation is, in many ways, the antithesis of the modern corporation. The postmodern corporation explicitly eschews profit maximization as its only objective and may even consider profits secondary to other salient values and concerns. Whereas the modern corporation will adhere to certain norms and values to the extent that it remains financially feasible (or necessary) to do so, the postmodern corporation will only remain in business to the extent that it can do so in keeping with its principles. This level of commitment is what attracts a large number of the postmodern corporation's customers, investors, directors, officers, and employees. With regard to the company's directors, officers, and employees, evidence of commitment to the corporation's values will ordinarily drive their selection, hiring, and advancement. Individuals who fill these roles will oftentimes do so at levels of compensation lower than that which they could garner in similar positions at similar firms. This phenomenon mirrors that seen in the world of nonprofits and many religious schools, where individuals consciously opt for positions that pay less than comparable opportunities available to them elsewhere.

Unlike the modern corporation, the postmodern corporation is certainly an association in the Tocquevillian sense. Although an ideological component is not necessary for associational recognition, the presence of such a component contributes substantially to such recognition. The postmodern corporation, therefore, with its emphasis on values and principles, would appear to possess this component.

Further, the postmodern corporation represents the coming together of individuals around a shared goal much more clearly than the modern corporation. The presence of a guiding philosophy of business and of certain principles that guide corporate conduct create a bond of shared values among the corporation's various constituencies. This serves to diminish the degree to which the corporation is merely a collection of private interests and increases the degree to which the corporation's constituents are truly working toward a shared vision.

Admittedly, not every member of the corporate community is likely to share in its values and vision. This is not fatal, however. An association can remain an association even if some of its members find themselves apathetic to or in dissent of its principles. What matters, primarily, is the clear existence of these principles and continued attachment to the association by its members.

The insights of Meir Dan-Cohen, discussed in chapter 1, bear upon this point. According to him, the critical difference among organizations (for First Amendment purposes) is that regarding identification versus detachment. The members of the modern corporation are generally "detached" from the entity, neither forming an emotional attachment with it nor drawing their self-identification therefrom. This is to be contrasted with the situation of a "constitutive community," in which "individual members view their affiliation with the collective as a core aspect of their own identity." This is what led James Nelson to properly conclude that "nearly all" modern corporations lack the qualities of a constitutive community.[30]

It is important at this point to acknowledge that a "constitutive community" and an "association" are not one and the same. The former is a subset of the latter, and only the latter is necessary (I posit) for recognition of First Amendment rights. But to the extent that an entity is a constitutive community, it is, *a fortiori*, an association as well. Although not every postmodern corporation might be fairly characterized as a constitutive community, many, if not most, would. For these, there should be no doubt as to the applicability of the First Amendment's protections.

As an association, the postmodern corporation is poorly described by the prevailing contractarian conceptualization of the corporation. Instead, it is more accurately explained as a real entity. The bonds that hold its various constituencies together are not merely contractual, but rather are forged from the stronger metals of shared values and principles. Moreover, these bonds are transformative in the sense that all associational ties are transformative: they exert influences that serve to reinforce or otherwise affect those whom they tether together. As such, the postmodern corporation is both real and human, not fictitious and abstract.

Conceptualizing the postmodern corporation as a real entity reinforces its claim to constitutional rights. This should not be overstated, but acknowledged nonetheless. For, admittedly, constitutional rights do not ineluctably follow from an entity's status as "real." There are many "real entities" in this world, from tadpoles to trees, none of which enjoy constitutional rights (or constitutional personhood).[31] To ascertain whether a corporation conceived of as a "real entity" ought to enjoy the protections of the First Amendment, deeper reflection is needed. When undertaken, such reflection has generally lead real entity theorists to the view that the corporation was inherently entitled to certain rights.

As has been explained, real entity theorists essentially argue that the corporation is a genuine, naturally occurring human institution.[32] This does not mean that we can find references to corporate charters in prehistoric cave paintings. Rather, it reflects a belief that, given the perennial needs and desires that mark the human condition, and given the societal evolution of mankind, the development of the corporation is a natural occurrence not entirely unlike that of the family, the town, and the state. As such, real entity theorists link the business corporation to "drives and interests that the law might sometimes be obligated to respect."[33] Although it would probably be hyperbole to suggest that real entity theory requires the recognition of corporate constitutional rights, it can unquestionably be asserted that real entity theory supplies a powerful justification in support of such rights.

Finally, it should be acknowledged that the associational nature of the postmodern corporation might cause some to suggest the applicability of aggregation theory to the enterprise. Although this is understandable, the aggregation theory would be a poorer choice for the very reasons that the aggregation theory was largely discarded over a century ago: although not a modern corporation, the postmodern corporation still exhibits the separation of ownership and control that the modern corporation ushered in. It still exists as an entity that is distinct from its constituent parts, given the onset of professionalized management and a transformation of its owners from an analogue of partners to simple investors.

In sum, our assessment of the postmodern corporation brings us to a propitious confluence of theories. Real entity theory and Tocquevillian associational theory work together in mutual support of its assertion to constitutionally protected First Amendment rights.

The Religiously Expressive Corporation

Because the taxonomy's categories are intended to be mutually exclusive, the typical postmodern corporation's rights would not include the right to religious liberty. Religious liberty rights would turn on whether the corporation sincerely adhered to a set of religious principles or values. A corporation adhering to such religious principles or values should be identified as a special subset of the postmodern corporation: the religiously expressive corporation.

As indicated moments ago, what sets a postmodern corporation apart from a modern corporation is its commitment to values and principles beyond simply profit maximization. To the extent that such values and principles are religious in nature, the corporation should be considered a "religiously expressive corporation." As a postmodern corporation, the religiously expressive corporation ought to receive the same First Amendment protections as all other postmodern corporations discussed above. In other words, its associational and speech rights ought to be recognized. In addition to these, the religiously expressive corporation should be able to assert religious liberty rights as well.

As discussed in chapter 7, religious liberty is protected by a complicated patchwork of rights, drawn from the First Amendment's Free Exercise Clause and the Religious Freedom Restoration Act (RFRA), along with state constitutional and statutory provisions as well. These rights are all predicated upon a claimant's sincere adherence to religious beliefs, the observance of which is purportedly infringed upon by some government action. To be recognized as a religiously expressive corporation, therefore, a threshold question would be whether the corporation in question is indeed beholden to certain religious principles and values.

To some, the initial bias against recognition of a corporate entity in possession of religious beliefs is difficult to overcome. This should be quickly remedied, however, by the realization that our laws and society regularly credit and recognize the religious beliefs of corporations—insofar as they are nonprofit corporations such as Catholic Charities or the Presbyterian Church. So the only real question, therefore, is whether a *commercial* enterprise can possess religious beliefs.

The bias against such recognition is really no different from that expressed by Justice O'Connor in *Roberts v. Jaycees*: the bias that a business corporation cannot authentically lay claim to any values beyond profit maximization. As discussed at length, however, this presumption is conceptually, legally, and empirically incorrect. To the extent that an expressive corporation can be recognized, so can a religiously expressive association. The fact that the values in question are religiously grounded instead of predicated upon nonreligious principles should make no difference.

Arguably, it should be easier for a court to confirm the sincerity of a corporation's claim of adherence to religious principles over even an individual's given the paper trail that would probably be available. Statements of policy, board resolutions, and well-documented past conduct would, most likely, supply the evidence needed to ascertain the corporation's sincerity.

As with other religious liberty claimants, the corporate claimant would also need to demonstrate that government action somehow infringed upon the corporation's adherence to those beliefs, thereby prohibiting the free exercise of religion. Having done that, the claim's resolution is fairly complicated. As discussed in chapter 7, the applicable standard turns upon a variety of factors. Those need not be recounted. It should be noted, however, that nothing proposed here would disturb the traditional standards. The only modification to existing law would be an expansion of those parties permitted to bring such claims (an expansion that would now include religiously expressive corporations); the law governing such claims would remain substantively unchanged.

The Closed Corporation

The focus of this book has been on large, publicly traded corporations. An entirely different version of the business corporation exists as well, as has been referred to occasionally in this work: the closed corporation. This entity should not be excluded from the taxonomy.

Recall that the closed corporation is a corporation characterized by a small number of shareholders (ordinarily less than thirty) and stock that is not publicly traded. Such entities are not ordinarily governed with the same degree of formality as a public corporation, and state corporate law explicitly recognizes certain differences between the two.

Saliently, the separation of ownership and control that characterizes the modern corporation does not typically characterize the closed corporation. Quite frequently, its owners are simultaneously its controllers, with its board of directors and officer ranks populated by its shareholders. The important doctrine of limited liability, whereby a corporation's shareholders are not liable for the corporation's debts, is applied with somewhat less rigor when it comes to the closed corporation. In the context of a closed corporation, courts are far more likely to "pierce the corporate veil" and find that the corporate enterprise is little more than an alter ego of its owners and, consequently, hold its owners personally responsible for corporate liabilities.

All this suggests that when it comes to the closed corporation, the contractarian approach seriously misses the mark. The closed corporation in many ways resembles the corporation of a bygone era, when the differences between a corporation and a partnership were not as profound. With this comes the superior fit of a theoretical ancestor of the contractarian approach: the aggregation model of the corporation. For in many respects, the closed corporation is little more than the association of its shareholders, taking on employees and officers only as is necessary to assist the shareholder and supplement their efforts in running the business. And this is precisely what aggregation theory posits: that the corporation is essentially an aggregation of individuals—not unlike a partnership. The corporate identity, under aggregation theory, is merely a convenient means by which society can interact with this particular group of individuals.

Since the corporation described by aggregation theory is similar to a partnership, it would be instructive to examine the way partnerships are treated under the First Amendment. Although there is no clear guidance from the courts on the Constitution's applicability to partnerships in particular, most judges and commentators have generally understood partnerships, and virtually all noncorporate groupings of individuals, to possess the same First Amendment rights as the individuals within them.[34] For under the law, there is generally no distinction between a partnership and its members for a wide range of purposes.

Indeed, if one considers a primary argument against corporate First Amendment rights, one quickly discovers how inapplicable it is to the partnership. Recall the assertion that the separation of ownership and control makes the corporation an inappropriate rights-bearing entity for First Amendment purposes. Related to this is the notion that corporations are effectively on autopilot: lacking owner control, they are structured to narrowly purse profit maximization. Neither of these phenomena characterizes the partnership. Unlike a corporation, there is no separation of ownership and control in a partnership: the partnership's owners are its controllers. Consequently, there is no mandate to maximize profits and no structure erected to prevent deviation therefrom. Instead, one encounters a thoroughly human institution, with individual partners ordinarily taking personal responsibility over the direction of the firm. Certainly profits are typically pursed, but they are considered appropriately balanced by the moral principles and consciences of the individual partners. There is no mandate to cast aside such noneconomic concerns.

Thus, if conceptualized as an aggregation of individuals, the closed corporation has a far greater claim to First Amendment freedoms than the modern (public) corporation. For the mere fact of combining with others does not cause individuals to lose their constitutional freedoms. The mere fact that a combination has incorporated itself should also not alter the analysis. If anything justifies treating incorporated enterprises differently than unincorporated entities, it is the substantive changes that the entity undergoes upon incorporation. When these changes are marginal, as is often the case when a small business incorporates as a closed corporation, they ought not affect the entity's First Amendment rights.[35]

Alternatively, the closed corporation could be conceptualized under the property model of the corporation. Conceptualizing the corporation in this way would suggest the same result, however, for the owners of the corporation would be the very aggregation of shareholders upon which the aggregation model was based. The corporate apparatus and its personnel would serve as agents of the shareholder group, in which both ownership and control truly vest.

With regard to the freedom of speech, it would seem as though the closed corporation should clearly be able to avail itself of the First Amendment's safeguards. For if the corporation is merely an aggregation of shareholders, or the private property of such shareholders, why shouldn't its shareholders be permitted to make use of the corporation to further the expressive content of its choice? Just as a wealthy homeowner is free to instruct her staff to display a flag on her property conveying a political message, a corporate shareholder (under the property model of the corporation) should be able to instruct her corporation to display the very same flag atop the corporation's headquarters building. Or, more relevantly, to formulate and run a political advertisement. In both cases, we have a principal acting through her agent, and an individual does not ordinarily lose his or her constitutional rights simply because he or she decides to act through an agent.

With regard to the freedoms of association and religion, however, the question is less clear. For each of these latter freedoms requires a predicate showing that the claimant in question is engaging in expressive activity or in possession of sincerely held religious beliefs (accordingly). For the postmodern and religiously expressive corporation, these showings are clearly made (indeed, they're definitional). A closed corporation, however, could very well engage in no expressive activity whatsoever, nor susbscribe to any particular set of religious beliefs.

As discussed in chapter 7, this complicates matters when a closed corporation asserts free exercise or associational rights. To the extent that a closed corporation is genuinely expressive, it should be able to assert these rights to the same extent that a postmodern corporation can, and for the same reasons. The problem arises when the closed corporation is not an expressive entity, yet nevertheless wishes to assert free exercise or associational freedom claims. In this case, the basis of the claims would be the strongly held religious beliefs, or the associational ties, of the corporation's owners (its shareholders). Such claims could not, therefore, be justified by the arguments used to defend the First Amendment rights of postmodern and religiously expressive corporations throughout this book. Rather, they would need to be justified on other grounds.

It would seem as though ample justification could be found via recourse to either the aggregation or property model conceptualization of the closed corporation presented above. Under either approach, the requisite expressive entity (religious or otherwise) could be found to exist among the shareholders as a group. Given the conflation of ownership with control in the closed corporation, the other internal constituents of the corporation (its directors, officers, and employees) would all truly be the agents of this shareholder group. Thus, to the extent that the shareholder group constitutes an association engaged in expression as per First Amendment jurisprudence, or shares a set of sincerely held religious beliefs, it would seem as though the rights of this shareholder group should be exercisable by the closed corporation under their control.

Nevertheless, some insist on denying the closed corporation any First Amendment rights. From this perspective, a partnership would lose its First Amendment rights immediately upon incorporating—even if taking the form of a closed corporation and even if operating essentially as it had before. Upon what basis could this be so?

Such a perspective is ordinarily grounded on one (or both) of the following suppositions. The first is that the mere act of incorporation causes the entity to undergo a substantive (and constitutionally relevant) change. If this were factually correct, it would indeed justify treating the entity differently postincorporation. But, as explained, very little happens in terms of the substantive reality of the entity—the only change is "on paper" so to speak. As such, it would seem as though this entity should not be stripped of its First Amendment rights simply because it filed articles of incorporation.

The second supposition is that the act of incorporation bestows upon the entity certain privileges, and these privileges in turn justify a curtailment of First Amendment rights. The protection of limited liability is chiefly pointed to as an example of such a privilege. Although I argued in chapter 4 that with additional rights ought to come additional responsibilities, I do not endorse the notion that with additional rights should come a restriction on other rights. Indeed, such a perspective would seem to run afoul of the longstanding doctrine against "unconstitutional conditions," pursuant to which the government "cannot grant [a] privilege subject to conditions that improperly 'coerce,' 'pressure,' or 'induce' the waiver of constitutional rights."[36] As Lawrence Tribe explains, "[t]he notion that, whenever a privilege or benefit might be withheld altogether, it may be withheld on whatever conditions the government chooses to impose, has been repeatedly repudiated since the mid-Twentieth Century."[37] Thus it would seem as though the perspective that the mere fact of incorporation, without anything more, should affect an entity's constitutional rights is profoundly mistaken.

In response to the property model, opponents of corporate rights would be quick to point out that most shareholders are unable to direct the corporations they own in any way resembling a person's control over his or her private property. Under corporate law, as discussed, control and ownership are typically separated. For such corporations, the property model would be inapplicable. But by positing the appropriateness of the property model, I am presenting a type of corporation in which such control does indeed exist. For example, to the extent that the corporation happens to be privately held by only one shareholder, or a very small number of shareholders (such as a closed corporation), this might be possible. For these corporations, the property model, and with it First Amendments rights, are indeed appropriate.

Admittedly, for some entities, incorporation does indeed give rise to certain significant changes. Frequently, after incorporation, the number of shareholders grows, and outside investors may be added to the mix. With the ability to raise additional capital more easily, corporations often expand in size and outgrow their earlier management teams (which may have consisted entirely of the original shareholders).[38] The imposition of corporate law at this point actualizes the separation of ownership and control just spoken of, restricting the shareholders to powers so limited that they do not approximate owners in any typical sense of that word. The control that any particular shareholder could exercise (even a majority shareholder) would now be formally limited to a small number of avenues, such as the election of directors, the approval of mergers, and amendments to the corporate charter. Such changes undermine any plausible application of the aggregation or property models of the corporation, providing a point of departure from those theories.

For at this point, the enterprise takes on a character qualitatively different from that of a partnership. The admixture of outside investors and professionalized management transforms the entity into something other than an assemblage of "partners." Nor can the entity be considered the mere property of a select view: shareholder passivity (on account of reasons both practical and legal), transforms stockholder "owners" into investors not unlike any other (such as bondholders and other lenders). Roles and hierarchies develop, such that the enterprise can be said to take on a life of its own.[39]

But at this juncture, the corporation is no longer a closed corporation, and one should not expect the corporate theories applicable to the closed corporation to remain appropriate. For now we have either a modern or postmodern corporation. As has been discussed, for such entities, contractarianism and real entity theory (respectively) provide the best fit.

From Theory to Practice

Distinguishing the various kinds of corporations in theory is one thing, distinguishing them in practice is quite another. An articulation of key features and differences is of little practical use absent a way of authoritatively deciding among or acting upon them.

Broadly speaking, there are three ways in which the taxonomy set forth above can be realized: via self-designation, via government designation, and via judicial designation.

Self-designation would essentially amount to an "opt-in" or "check the box" regime. In the process of registering as a corporation, a business entity could be required to select a particular designation, and these designations would correlate with the types of corporations set forth in the taxonomy. A corporation could officially identify itself as a "religiously expressive corporation," for example, and with that designation receive the appropriate level of constitutional rights. Existing corporations would be able to make such a postincorporation designation as well.

Such an approach is neither novel nor difficult. Corporations already self-identify as nonprofit versus for-profit, and, as has been discussed, many states provide the option of identifying as a "benefit corporation" as well. Indeed, given the critical abandonment of strict profit maximization afforded by the benefit corporation form, this development, by itself, could serve as a means of implementing a self-designation regime. By deciding to pursue its business as a benefit corporation, a company could be comfortably designated as a postmodern corporation. By declining to seek such designation, a company could be comfortably designated a modern corporation. Although not every state offers the benefit corporation option, this is of little importance because businesses are free to incorporate in one state while conducting business in another.

The act of self-identifying as a modern versus postmodern corporation is important for reasons of corporate governance as well.[40] The simple fact of self-identification would signal to the markets (capital, labor, and consumer) how the business will be governed with respect to the question of profit maximization. It enables the business to attract those constituencies that prefer such a choice and enables those who disfavor it to steer clear.

As corporate regulation is primarily a matter of state law, the regime proposed above is state-based. However, the issue of First Amendment rights implicates federal (constitutional) concerns. Further, the question of a corporation's status as postmodern is one that may govern conduct of tremendous concern to states well beyond the state that the corporation incorporated in. Thus, it might make sense for any regime of self-identification to be federal in nature.

Regardless, once this self-identification has been made, the business would be treated in accordance with its chosen designation for purposes of the First Amendment. It is important to clarify what this would and would not entail.

If self-identified as a postmodern corporation, for example, the entity would have standing to assert the rights to freedom of speech, association, and religion (if it were a religiously expressive postmodern corporation) discussed throughout this book. The showing necessary to prevail in such assertions, however, would remain unaltered. This comes into play significantly with regard to the freedoms of association and religion. Each of these freedoms requires the claimant to demonstrate that government action infringes upon the claimant's expressive nature or religious liberty (respectively). Predicate to such a showing is the articulation of an expressive nature and/or religious character. Nor does an alleged infringement of associational or free exercise rights necessarily entail an actual infringement: the allegation will need to be put to the test, subject to the applicable standards of proof. The self-identification merely qualifies the entity in question to bring a First Amendment claim—it in no way influences the resolution of such claims.

Another approach toward effectuating the taxonomy would be to require corporations seeking rights-bearing designations such as (or equivalent to) "postmodern" and "religiously expressive" to apply for such designations with an appropriate government agency. Whether the application would be granted would be based upon the corporation's conformity with those characteristics essential to such designations. This would change the regime from one of "opting in" to one of "qualifying for." It would be similar in certain respects to the self-identification regime, but with the key difference that an entity's self-designation would not be dispositive. As with the "nonprofit" election of certain corporations, an entity's choice of a particular designation would be subject to certain objective criteria. The criteria in question would go to the appropriateness of a particular categorization based upon what has been discussed previously. They would concern matters such as the entity's approach to profit maximization and its articulation of and adherence to particular values and principles.

Finally, one could envision a judicial implementation of this taxonomy. In the absence of self-designation, or agency-designation, we could have court-designation. There would be no explicit, "official," ex ante categorization of corporations into a particular categories bearing upon their statuses under the First Amendment. Rather, it would be left to the courts to assess the nature of the corporate claimants before them, on a case-by-case basis, in order to determine the applicability of the First Amendment's protections. As discussed in chapter 7, for all its warts, this is something the courts already do in order to rule upon assertions of associational rights. We have seen how courts have scrutinized corporate claimants for evidence of expressiveness in order to determine the propriety of their invocation of freedom of association. Traditionally, however, this analysis has been limited to entities of a nonprofit nature. By discarding the formalistic and overly simplistic divide between nonprofit and for-profit corporations, and by opening up the inquiry more broadly (to encompass the freedom of speech and religion as well), the courts should be able to apply the same sort of scrutiny to business corporations too, thereby ascertaining the appropriate categorization of a given business corporation within the taxonomy and, *a fortiori*, its entitlement to particular First Amendment rights.

The preceding discussion was admittedly brief. Its purpose was merely to point the way forward or, more accurately, to suggest that ways forward do in fact exist. In short, once we acknowledge that different corporations ought to be treated differently, there are multiple ways of effectuating this acknowledgment.

NOTES

1. *Cf.* Eric W. Orts, *The Complexity and Legitimacy of Corporate Law*, 50 Wash. & Lee L. Rev. 1565 (1993) (discussing the complexity of corporate law and criticizing efforts to impose a uniform version of corporate law upon the corporation).
2. *See* Michael Novak, On Corporate Governance 4 (1997); Pamela H. Bucy, *Corporate Ethos: A Standard for Imposing Corporate Criminal Liability*, 75 Minn. L. Rev. 1095, 1123–27 (1991).

3. An independently owned automotive oil change facility on Long Island, N.Y., with a staff of one to four employees. *See* http://www.manta.com.
4. The examples that follow regarding the law's recognition of corporate diversity are largely taken from my previous article, Ronald J. Colombo, *The Corporation as a Tocquevillian Association*, 85 TEMP. L. REV. 1 (2012). I thank the *Temple Law Review* for granting me permission to reuse some of that material here.
5. *See* Daniel J. Morrissey, *Piercing All the Veils: Applying an Established Doctrine to a New Business Order*, 32 J. CORP. L. 529, 534–35 (2007) (quoting Columbia University President Nicholas Murray Butler).
6. *See* Stephen M. Bainbridge, *Abolishing Veil Piercing*, 26 J. CORP. L. 479, 515 (2001).
7. *See* ROBERT CLARK, CORPORATE LAW § 1.3, at 24 (1986).
8. If 500 shareholders are unaccredited, this too, combined with $10 million in assets, will trigger public company status. Jeff Schwartz, *The Twilight of Equity Liquidity*, 34 CARDOZO L. REV. 531, 558 (2012).
9. *See* Securities Offering Reform, Securities Act Release No. 8591, Exchange Act Release No. 52056, 70 Fed. Reg. 44,722, 44,734 (Aug. 3, 2005).
10. *See* MARC I. STEINBERG, SECURITIES LAW 117–18 (2009).
11. *See id.*
12. *See id.*
13. *See id.*
14. Jumpstart Our Business Startups Act, Pub. L. No. 112-106, 126 Stat. 306 (2012).
15. Pub. L. No. 111-203, 124 Stat. 1736 (2010).
16. *See* 3C KEVIN F. O'MALLEY, JAY E. GRENIG, & WILLIAM C. LEE, FEDERAL JURY PRACTICE & INSTRUCTIONS Ch. 171 Introduction (5th ed. 2000).
17. 42 U.S.C.A. § 2000e (West 2009).
18. *Id.*
19. *Id.*
20. 45C AM. JUR. 2D *Job Discrimination* § 2661 (2013).
21. 42 U.S.C.A. § 1981a (West 1991).
22. The same holds true with regard to the Patient Protection and Affordable Health Care Act (PPACA), Pub. L. No. 111-148, 124 Stat. 119 (2010), the applicability of which turns on the size of the business in question. *See* 1 RONALD J. COOKE, ERISA PRACTICE AND PROCEDURE § 1:101 (2d ed. 1996).
23. *E.g.*, Steven Bainbridge, *Citizens United, Corporate Personhood, and Nexus of Contracts Theory*, PROFESSORBAINBRIDGE.COM (Jan. 21, 2010), http://www.professorbainbridge.com/professorbainbridgecom/2010/01/citizens-united-corporate-personhood-and-nexus-of-contracts-theory.html.
24. Joseph F. Morrissey, *A Contractarian Critique of* Citizens United, 15 U. PA. J. CONST. L. 765, 819 (2013).
25. *See* Daniel J. H. Greenwood, *Essential Speech: Why Corporate Speech Is Not Free*, 83 IOWA L. REV. 995, 1030–31 (1998).
26. Larry Ribstein, *The Constitutional Conception of the Corporation*, 4 SUP. CT. ECON. REV. 95, 100 (1995).
27. *See* David Millon, *Theories of the Corporation*, 1990 DUKE L.J. 201, 203 (1990).
28. *E.g.*, Henry N. Butler & Larry E. Ribstein, *Opting Out of Fiduciary Duties: A Response to the Anti-Contractarians*, 65 WASH. L. REV. 1, 3 n.1 (1990).
29. Joseph Burstyn, Inc. v. Wilson, 343 U.S. 495, 502 (1952).
30. James D. Nelson, *Conscience, Incorporated*, 2014 MICH. STATE L. REV. (forthcoming 2014) (manuscript at 5) (*available at* http://ssrn.com/abstract=2247051).

31. *See* Charles I. Lugosi, *If I Were a Corporation, I'd Be a Constitutional Person Too*, 10 TEX. REV. L. & POL. 427 (2006).
32. *See* chapter 2.
33. Michael J. Phillips, *Reappraising the Real Entity Theory of the Corporation*, 21 FLA. ST. U. L. REV. 1061, 1097 (1994).
34. *E.g.*, Beechwood Restorative Care Center v. Leeds, 436 F.3d 147, 154 (2d Cir. 2006); *see* Carol R. Goforth, *"A Corporation Has No Soul"—Modern Corporations, Corporate Governance, and Involvement in the Political Process*, 47 HOUS. L. REV. 617, 654 n.186 (2010). The most glaring exception to this would be the Fifth Amendment right against self-incrimination, which has been consistently deemed a right wholly reserved for individual human beings. *See* Saru M. Matambanadzo, *The Body, Incorporated*, 87 TUL. L. REV. 457, 472 (2013).
35. Indeed, even opponents of extending the First Amendment's protections to business corporations in general have conceded that "it may not be appropriate to treat all speech by a partnership or closely held corporation" similarly to that of a typical corporation. Tom Bennigson, Nike *Revisited: Can Commercial Corporations Engage in Non-Commercial Speech?*, 39 CONN. L. REV. 379, 446 (2006).
36. Richard Epstein, *Unconstitutional Conditions, State Power, and the Limits of Consent*, 102 HARV. L. REV. 4, 6 (1988).
37. LAWRENCE H. TRIBE, AMERICAN CONSTITUTIONAL LAW 781 (1988).
38. *See* Lawrence E. Mitchell, *Close Corporations Reconsidered*, 63 TUL. L. REV. 1143, 1189 (1989).
39. *See* Phillips, *supra* note 33, at 1067–70.
40. Should such a regime be adopted, I do not imagine that the terms employed would be "modern" versus "postmodern," but rather something along the lines of "expressive" versus "nonexpressive," or "profit-maximizing" versus "non-profit-maximizing."

CHAPTER 10

The Problem of Discrimination

The prospect of recognizing corporate First Amendment rights, even if limited to strictly postmodern corporations, certainly raises some interesting and challenging concerns. Many of these concerns have been addressed over the course of the preceding chapters, either explicitly or implicitly.

One particular concern, however, has yet to be squarely confronted. Namely, that the rights advocated in this book would threaten to undo decades of civil-rights progress and to usher in a new era of exclusion. Given the obvious weightiness of this concern, I devote this last chapter to its consideration.[1]

Concerns regarding discrimination are certainly not without merit. After all, personnel is policy, and a postmodern corporation would certainly desire a freer hand than its modern counterpart in selecting and promoting those individuals who best suit its mission. The First Amendment's free exercise and associational rights would give postmodern corporations a freer hand.

With regard to religion alone, the rekindling of it in the workplace has, admittedly, sparked "a battle between what has long been a secular work world in the U.S. and the ever-increasing religiosity permeating our society."[2] As with any battle, there have been casualties. "The number of lawsuits claiming workplace religious discrimination . . . jumped by nearly 50% between 1997 and 2007 . . . according to the Equal Employment Opportunity Commission."[3] That is indeed problematic. Whether these lawsuits are equally meritorious, or rather reflect a reaction by some against an unwelcome infusion of religion in the working environment, remains unclear.

Paul Horwitz captured the situation well when he wrote:

> Freedom of association has benefits, but it also has a dark side—namely, the ways in which associations can resist the state's ability to vindicate equality and other important social goods. To conclude that the benefits outweigh the costs does not require us to deny that there are costs.[4]

Balanced against this, however, is the large number of employees for whom the workplace has become a more welcoming environment. From the proliferation of "workplace chaplains,"[5] to a greater willingness on the part of businesses to accommodate the religious practices of their employees,[6] workers are more empowered to be open about their faith and values than in yesteryear.[7] As one study on the issue thoughtfully concluded:

> There is little doubt that American society and its political and legal institutions are moving toward a more open, value-expressive environment that will put even greater pressure on companies to honor employees' requests for religious and spiritual accommodation. . . . Over the last 35 years, society has come full circle from advocating a workplace free of religion to encouraging a spiritually and religiously expressive one. There is little debate that many people desire this more individually relevant workplace. The challenge for managers is to make this environment work—legally, socially, and productively.[8]

Further, fears of discrimination should be tempered with our existing experience with such exemptions. Title VII of the Civil Rights Act of 1964, which forbids discrimination on the basis of "race, color, religion, sex or national origin," contains an exemption for "religious corporations."[9] It must be noted that the Title VII exemption is significantly more restrictive than that proposed here. What this book suggests is the recognition of a potential exemption from *any* law on the part of a qualifying postmodern corporation. Title VII's exemption only extends to the question of religious discrimination: the ability to take religion into account in employment decisions.[10] Further, Title VII's exemption has been narrowly construed as applicable to only nonprofit religious corporations (despite any such limitation in the text of the statute itself).[11]

Less on point, but also relevant, Title VII allows for employment discrimination on other (nonreligious) bases if needed as part of a "bona fide occupational qualification."[12] As with the exemption for a religious corporation, the bona fide occupational qualification exemption has also been narrowly construed,[13] although it has been extended in rare instances to for-profit corporations.

Having survived for nearly fifty years, it would appear as though the exemptions in Title VII have served our nation well, balancing a general prohibition against discrimination with exceptions in those rare situations where they might be warranted. The general success of Title VII arguably makes room for an expansion of exemptions thereto. Although one cannot deny the persistence of employment discrimination, one also cannot deny the tremendous progress that has been made since Title VII's promulgation. Much of the progress goes beyond mere compliance with laws prohibiting discrimination, but rather extends to attitudes and beliefs with regard to the (im)propriety of discrimination.

That this is so can be illustrated by a cursory review of the twenty-first-century marketplace. A company perceived as discriminatory will pay a steep price for that perception. As the experience of Chick-fil-A in the summer of 2012 demonstrates, adherence to traditional religious beliefs is quite unpopular in many quarters and can spark tremendous trouble for a business so inclined—even if those beliefs are not put into practice via company conduct that is discriminatory toward consumers or employees.[14] Thus, very few corporations could be expected to engage in conduct that would be rampantly unpopular, regardless of whether such conduct would be protected by the Free Exercise Clause. There would be tremendous market pressure against such actions, especially if the corporation was publicly traded and, as such, needed to concern itself with the capital markets as well as the consumer market. Even nonprofit corporations, such as the Boy Scouts, who prevailed in their right to restrict their membership to heterosexuals in *Dale*, eventually succumbed to public pressure and largely reversed this policy only thirteen years later in 2013.

There are other limiting principles as well. Only postmodern, expressive corporations (and, potentially, certain closed corporations) would qualify for associational rights. The majority of companies, being modern corporations, could not evade the prohibitions on religious discrimination contained in state and federal legislation.

Further, there would be important limitations on postmodern corporations as well. Under existing precedent, simply being an expressive association does not grant one a blank check to discriminate. The corporation would need to demonstrate that its discriminatory hiring practices were necessary to the maintenance of its expressive character. Even religiously expressive corporations need not necessarily be granted a waiver from antidiscrimination law, as most of their principles and values could be such that individuals of various religious backgrounds—and even no religious background at all—could readily toe the company line without problem. This was made abundantly clear in the case *Roberts v. Jaycees*, discussed in chapter 8.

In addition to these concerns over employment discrimination, there is also the specter of discrimination against customers as well. Many rightfully champion the goal of a marketplace that is open and tolerant. The ongoing battle against intolerance and discrimination in the marketplace has been a hard-fought one, and many view with great trepidation anything that risks undermining the progress that has been achieved. Given our multicultural, diverse, and pluralistic society, such openness and tolerance is not simply right and just, but essential as a practical matter. In light of this, it is easy to see why some view the notion of an expressive, "associational" business corporation as threatening. It conjures up images of the bad old days, including industrial ghettoization and shops that were off limits to certain populations. Although these concerns are also meritorious, I suggest that they overstate the risks entailed and, moreover, adopt an incorrect view of pluralism.

As a general proposition, and drawing upon the insights of John Garvey and Robert Vischer, twenty-first-century America should be considered capable of handling companies so committed to a set of values that they garner associational status.[15] In a society as incredibly diverse as our own, authentic pluralism can and should include an institutional component: we should welcome into our midst those institutions (including business corporations) that add to our diversity via their adherence to a particularized set of values and beliefs—even if idiosyncratic or unpopular. In other words, pluralism need not entail a "least common denominator" view of the world, in which every association's practices are deemed acceptable by all (or by the majority). Rather, in a diverse society, pluralism could and ought to encompass entities that add to our diversity via their very own lack of diversity. By analogy, instead of a rule requiring all restaurants to serve the same cuisine, we should tolerate (perhaps even welcome) restaurants that are strictly Italian, French, Cuban, Portuguese, or the like.

As Andrew Beerworth explains, "the structure of the Constitution—and the quintessence of American rights theory—embraces pluralisms and militates against artificially constructed uniformities."[16] It is precisely by allowing normatively divergent corporations to flourish that such groups can truly add to the mix of America's pluristic society and "counter government-induced homogeneity and cultural assimilation."[17] To quote Paul Horwitz once again: "The state should not be too imperial: it should not seek to make every sector of public and private life a reflection of its own values and procedures."[18]

This thinking harkens back to that of Tocqueville and the founders, recounted earlier in this book.[19] The natural right to association that they envisioned entailed a natural right to associate not simply for popular purposes, supported by the government, but also for purposes that might not comport with the desires of the majority, or of the state. As Roberta Romano explains:

> [A] pluralist democracy is conditioned upon the existence of numerous autonomous organizations. Such organizations curb state domination and thereby safeguard liberty, by serving as a counterweight to an expansive public bureaucracy and providing a clearly specified realm of private activity.[20]

Other prominent scholars, notably Frederic Maitland and Otto von Gierke, have pressed further. As they explained things, associations and "group entities" are not only of "vital importance," but rather are sovereigns of their own.[21] For any authentically free and pluralist society, it would be wrong to treat associations "as if they existed at the sufferance of the state."[22] Some have interpreted the First Amendment to endorse this perspective, at least with regard to religious entities.[23]

This admittedly presents a view of pluralism alien to most in the twenty-first century. Many simply do not question the role of the state as the superstructure of society, and have difficulty imagining a society in which the state itself is simply one of several spheres of authority. Consequently, most in Western society generally endorse a milder form of pluralism—one in which diverse groups and individuals are generally free to pursue their self-defined ends, absent harm to others. One need not go as far as Maitland and Gierke to endorse the view that generally, the state ought to prescind from interfering with private initiative, and ought to allow associations to serve as a means by which such initiative is fulfilled.

As alluded to earlier, the expansion of the state is such that few matters are wholly private nowadays.[24] Thus, the zone of private activity, free from the potentiality of state interference, has become smaller. This puts at risk precisely those groups in most need of protection: unpopular, heterodox groups that fail to fall in line with the spirit of the age. Ironically, in the name of liberal values such as freedom, tolerance, and equality, governments have been quite illiberal in their treatment of certain groups, denying to some the very liberty, tolerance, and equality demanded for others.

A vivid example of this was provided by the Supreme Court of the State of New Mexico, in the case *Elane Photography v. Vanessa Willock*.[25] The case concerned a commercial photography business (Elane Photography) that refused to photograph a "same-sex commitment ceremony" on religious grounds.[26] The court concluded that in so refusing, Elane Photography violated the New Mexico Human Rights Act (NMHRA). With regard to the business's First Amendment and religious liberty arguments, the court held that "[a]ssuming that Elane Photography has such rights, they are not offended by enforcement of the NMHRA."[27] The court found that the NMHRA was a law of general applicability and as such readily passed muster under First Amendment jurisprudence in the wake of *Employment Division* v. *Smith*.[28]

The merits of the decision, and how the court applied the rational basis test, are not what I find most interesting about *Elane Photography*. Rather, what I found most striking was the closing paragraph of Justice Bosson's concurring opinion. In this paragraph Justice Bosson attempts to explain why the deeply held principles of Elane Photography's proprietors must yield to the law as set forth in the NMHRA:

> In the smaller, more focused world of the marketplace, of commerce, of public accommodation, the Huguenins [the proprietors of Elane Photography] have to channel their conduct, not their beliefs, so as to leave space for other

> Americans who believe something different. That compromise is part of the glue that holds us together as a nation, the tolerance that lubricates the varied moving parts of us as a people. That sense of respect we owe others, whether or not we believe as they do, illuminates this country, setting it apart from the discord that afflicts much of the rest of the world. In short, I would say to the Huguenins, with the utmost respect: it is the price of citizenship. I therefore concur.[29]

In the paragraph that immediately preceded, Justice Bosson observed that "this case teaches that at some point in our lives all of us must compromise, if only a little, to accommodate the contrasting values of others. A multicultural, pluralistic society, one of our nation's strengths, demands no less."[30]

Justice Bosson's remarks ring right—perhaps some will even find them eloquent. What remains unexplained is why the "compromising," "tolerance," and "respect" must fall solely upon the shoulders of the proprietors of Elane Photography. The plaintiff in the case (Ms. Willock) certainly entered the "world of the marketplace" and "of commerce" when she decided to seek out a professional photographer for her commitment ceremony. Why must the photographers' values yield to hers, instead of the other way around?

Indeed, *Elane Photography* stands not for tolerance of diverse values, but rather the imposition of majoritarian values (as embodied in the NMHRA) upon those who would embrace different ones. If tolerance was the guiding principle, the court would have observed that Ms. Willock could have selected a different photographer for her ceremony, one who did not have any objection to the event, and need not have insisted upon the services of those who balked on account of their religious beliefs. Such is what a genuine commitment to pluralism demands consistent with the framers' efforts to "counter government-induced homogeneity and cultural assimilation" via the religion clauses of the First Amendment.[31]

Of course, even this approach has its limits and may be indefensible depending on the circumstances. This too Vischer has addressed thoughtfully.[32] Consider, for example, a state law that insists that pharmacies stock their shelves with the potentially abortifacient "morning-after pill." Some pharmacies have objected to dispensing this pill on moral and religious grounds. Were these pharmacies permitted to raise a free exercise claim against the law's implementation as applied to them, part of the court's evaluation of the claim (more specifically, the court's assessment of the government's interest in the law) ought to take into account whether other pharmacies in the area would be able and willing to supply the pill.[33] In other words, if litigated, the question need not be decided on a theoretical level, but rather on a case-by-case basis.[34] The weight of the government's interest in the law or regulation should be permitted to vary depending upon the context and circumstances of each particular case.[35] As with antitrust law, what is permissible for a given corporation to do may turn upon its relative power and importance within a particular market.[36] Although this certainly entails a bit more work for our courts, given the rights and principles at stake, and the need to thoughtfully balance them, this appears to be a thoroughly fair and appropriate approach.

An actual example of this scenario was provided by a high-profile case in Washington State, *Stormans v. Selecky*.[37] In *Stormans*, "Ralph's Thriftway," a pharmacy, together with certain pharmacists, asserted that state law requiring the dispensing of abortifacients conflicted with religious beliefs to which they adhered. After a long legal battle, in which the issue of corporate free exercise rights was raised but not resolved, the parties settled. Tellingly, in settling, the state conceded that permitting the conscientious objection that plaintiffs sought was "a time-honored pharmacy practice... often in the best interest of patients, pharmacies, and pharmacists." Moreover, the state declared that allowing the objection "do[es] not pose a threat to timely access to lawfully prescribed medications."[38] Although a similar conclusion might not be reachable in every situation, it should certainly be reachable in many.

Nevertheless, many persist in denying such freedoms to groups and individuals who dissent from the orthodoxy of the day. To them, such concessions are obstacles to progress and equality. Mark Hager articulates well my own thoughts on the subject:

> It cannot be considered progressive to restrict the free expression rights of organizations such as unions, churches, and associations. The activity of such organizations should be valued as expressions of associational freedom. Associational freedom, the power of citizens to find or pursue the good life through various voluntary groups, is crucial to the texture of democratic life. The democratic tenor of society can, in large degree, be measured by the intensity of associational activity among the citizens and the success of such activity in regulating and altering the terms of collective existence. It is important for democracy, then, that free expression rights for such organizations and groups be strongly defended. This can be called the "associational freedom" approach to understanding the free expression rights of organizational groups.[39]

It is critical to mention that Hager proceeds to specifically and vigorously deny business corporations access to these same freedoms, due to what he identifies as "crucial differences between the business corporation and other organizational entities."[40] As I have done repeatedly throughout this book, I acknowledge Hager's point as a general proposition. But when one digs into the "crucial differences" that Hager identifies, they vanish when the entity in question is the postmodern corporation.[41]

NOTES

1. I previously addressed these concerns, albeit much more briefly, in Ronald J. Colombo, *The Naked Private Square*, 51 HOUS. L. REV. 1 (2013).
2. *See* Eve Tahmincioglu, *Reconciling Religious Beliefs with Work*, MSNBC.COM (Sept. 30, 2007, 6:13 PM), http://www.msnbc,msn.com/id/20973408/ns/business-careers/t/reconciling-religious-beliefs-work/#.uprt4B3AF-4.
3. Maya Dollarhide, *When God Goes to the Office*, CNN.COM (Mar. 10, 2008 10:35 AM), http://www.cnn.com/2008/LIVING/worklife/03/10/religion.at.the.office/.
4. PAUL HORWITZ, FIRST AMENDMENT INSTITUTIONS 212 (2013).
5. A growth industry which has "grown fastest since 2001" and is expanding from its roots in the Bible Belt to regions across America. *See* Sue Shellenbarger, *Praying with the Office Chaplain*, WALL. ST. J., July 23, 2010, at D1; *see also* Karen C. Cash & George R. Gray, *A Framework for Accommodating Religion and Spirituality in the Workplace*, 14 ACADEMY OF MANAGEMENT EXECUTIVE 124, 124 (2000).
6. *See* Cash & Gray, *supra* note 5, at 125.
7. As David Miller put it: "The '60s was about race in the workplace; the '70s addressed women's needs; the '80s was about family-friendly policies and the Americans with Disabilities Act; the '90s was about sexual orientation, and now the big question is religion." *See* Eve Tahmincioglu, *Reconciling Religious Beliefs with Work*, NBCNEWS.COM (Sept. 30, 2007 6:13 PM), http://www.nbcnews.com/id/20973408/#.UtYoJ5GmBuY.
8. *See* Cash & Gray, *supra* note 5, at 132.
9. 42 U.S.C. § 2000e-2(a) (2000).
10. *See* Andrew C. Nichols, *Exemptions for "Religious Corporations" from Employment Discrimination States: Should Non-Profit Status Be Required?*, 3 GEO. J. L. & PUB. POL'Y 133, 134 (2005).
11. *See id.*at 137.
12. 42 U.S.C. § 2000e-2(e)(1) (2000).
13. *See* Nichols, *supra* note 10, at 137.
14. News of Chick-fil-A's financial support of groups that advocated a biblically based view of marriage made the company the target of a nationwide boycott. *See* Kim Severson, *Chick-fil-A Thrust Back into Spotlight on Gay Rights*, N.Y. TIMES (July 25, 2012), http://www.nytimes.com/2012/07/26/us/gay-rights-uproar-over-chick-fil-a-widens.html.
15. *See* ROBERT VISCHER, CONSCIENCE AND THE COMMON GOOD 4–6 (2010); John Garvey, *Introduction to AALS Symposium on Institutional Pluralism: The Role of Religiously Affiliated Law Schools*, 59 J. LEGAL EDUC. 125 (2009).
16. Andrew A. Beerworth, *Religion in the Marketplace: Establishments, Pluralisms, and the Doctrinal Eclipse of Free Exercise*, 26 T. JEFFERSON L. REV. 333, 387 (2004).
17. *Id.*
18. PAUL HORWITZ, FIRST AMENDMENT INSTITUTIONS 222 (2013).
19. *See* chapter 1.
20. *See* Roberta Romano, *Metapolitics and Corporate Law Reform*, 36 STAN. L. REV. 923, 949 (1984).
21. HORWITZ, *supra* note 18, at 214.
22. *Id.*
23. *See* Beerworth, *supra* note 16, at 387–88.
24. *See* REX AHDAR & IAN LEIGH, RELIGIOUS FREEDOM IN THE LIBERAL STATE 15 (2013).

25. 309 P.3d 53 (2013).
26. *Id.* at 59.
27. *Id.* at 63.
28. *See id.* The court also held that New Mexico's Religious Freedom Restoration Act was inapplicable because enforcement of the NMHRA did not implicate government action. *See id.* at 75. This is a questionable holding, but need not detain us.
29. *See id.* at 80.
30. *Id.*
31. Beerworth, *supra* note 16, at 387–88.
32. *See* VISCHER, *supra* note 15.
33. *See id.* at 174–75.
34. *See id.* That said, certain forms of discrimination might simply be off limits in virtually every situation. For example, the government might always have a "compelling government interest" in support of antidiscrimination laws that prohibit discrimination on the basis of race. This is because it could fairly be maintained that given our nation's particular history, coupled with the explicit text of the Fourteenth Amendment, "race is different." Sherrilyn A. Ifill, 13 GREEN BAG 2D 45, 54 (2009). Instructive here would be the Supreme Court case *Bob Jones University v. U.S.*, 461 U.S. 574 (1983). In *Bob Jones University*, the Court conceded the applicability of the free exercise clause to a religious school—but held nevertheless that "the Government has a fundamental, overriding interest in eradicating racial discrimination in education." *Id.* at 604. That said, "[i]t may be that as race relations in American improve, there will be greater scope for a robust form of freedom of association even where race is involved." *See* HORWITZ, *supra* note 18, at 234.
35. *See* VISCHER, *supra* note 15.
36. *See* William M. Landes & Richard A. Posner, *Market Power in Antitrust Cases*, 94 HARV. L. REV. 937, 937–38 (1981).
37. 586 F.3d 1109 (9th Cir. 2009).
38. Cristina Alarcon, *Religious Freedom's New Plan B*, NAT'L POST (July 10, 2010 4:14 PM), http://Life.nationalpost.com/2010/07/10/religious-freedoms-new-plan-b/.
39. Mark H. Hager, *Bodies Politic: The Progressive History of Organizational "Real Entity" Theory*, 50 U. PITT. L. REV. 575, 647–48 (1989).
40. *Id.* at 650.
41. Hager declares that a business corporation "is not essentially a collection of people, but rather, essentially a collection of capital" because they "find their purpose and unity in the organization of capital." *Id.* at 650. He contrasts this to nonbusiness organizations, which "find their purpose and unity in the organization of people." *Id.* He propounds this distinction by observing that "[t]he common bond among stockholders lies almost exclusively in their mutual hope of profits," whereas in nonbusiness organizations "[m]emberships . . . are typically held together by a broader and more complex range of social interests and purposes: political, educational, charitable, and fraternal, as well as economic." *Id.* at 651. As stated, and has been explained repeatedly, these differences largely evaporate once one substitutes the postmodern corporation for the modern corporation which Hager obviously has in mind.

Conclusion

Those who wield power are not typically prone to sharing it. Thus, to a large extent, the question of corporate constitutional rights reflects the perennial tug-of-war between government and those who would challenge its power.

For the First Amendment serves, primarily, to circumscribe government power, limiting the ability of the state to demand conformity with its vision for society. Any extension of the First Amendment serves, therefore, to curtail the government's reach. Expanding the amendment's applicability to include certain for-profit enterprises narrows the avenues by which the state can exert its influence and control; it carves out space for competing norms and competing visions of society to persist.

Admittedly, it is not only the state that opposes the extension of First Amendment protections to the business corporation: a large number of private individuals do as well. Their reasons for doing so vary significantly, and as such these opponents of corporate rights can be divided into at least two camps.

This first is the camp of those who support the prevalent (or ascendant) majoritarian norms and values of modern society. They are not interested in seeing these norms and values undermined by anyone or anything—including the business corporation. Further, even if not personally threatened by corporate forays into culture and politics, these individuals may simply not care to tolerate the heterodox. They disagree with the countercultural vision that certain groups embrace and wish to grant them no quarter, beyond that which is minimally necessary in a society that calls itself free. They do not hesitate, therefore, to seize upon an opportunity to scrub clean contrarian thought and opinion from the field of commerce and repel any toehold it may acquire upon corporate America and workplaces across the country.

I certainly hope that most people would reject this particular way of thinking. It is representative of the very intolerance and forced uniformity that the First Amendment's framers were resolute to protect society against. It matters not whether its purveyors may happen to carry a banner of purported tolerance, diversity, or open-mindedness (as is sometimes the case); efforts to stifle, marginalize, and exclude unpopular beliefs from society (and, consequently, those individuals who adhere to such beliefs) is decidedly illiberal and runs counter to the ideals of the First Amendment.

A second camp of opponents to corporate rights sets forth a far more persuasive argument. This camp is concerned primarily with what can be referred to as the unfairness or distortive effect of corporate influence upon culture and politics, and not as much with the particular ideological leanings or content of that influence. In chords analogous to President Eisenhower's admonitions against America's rising "military-industrial complex," this camp warns against the influence of corporate money in politics and the prospect that the regulated (big business) may come to control the regulators (government). Such concerns are difficult to readily dismiss, given the enormous amounts of money that must be spent in order to capture and retain political office and the concentration of enormous amounts of money in corporate coffers.

These concerns, coupled with the aforementioned importance of associational undertakings as both a bulwark against governmental hegemony and a refuge against majoritarian tyranny, require a carefully crafted solution. The key to the solution, as I have propounded throughout this book, lies in recognizing the fact that not all corporations are created equal. For once this is grasped, we can forge ahead in a manner that preserves the critical associational role that certain corporations play, while at the same time safeguarding society and politics from the pernicious influences that other corporations may exert.

In reverse order, the influences of certain corporations are pernicious for the very reasons that opponents of corporate First Amendment rights have identified over the last several decades. In what I have referred to as the modern corporation, a confluence of forces gives rise to conduct and communications that are largely dehumanized. First and foremost among these forces, the corporation is established as an entity contractually bound to maximize profits in whatever way is lawfully permissible, and its actions are directed to that singular end. Thus, the "values," "speech," and "expression" of the corporation are purely instrumental. Moreover, the values, speech, and expression of such entities are qualitatively different from the values, speech, and expression of human beings, be they the product of individual or group origin; they are simply not subject to the broad range of concerns, desires, emotions, and principles that mark their genuinely human manifestations. For this reason, we can confidently conclude that however we decide to ultimately characterize them, corporate speech and expression do not constitute speech and expression as contemplated and protected by the First Amendment. Put differently, the modern corporation is incapable of engaging in authentic, genuine speech and expression.

Not every corporation, however, is constituted as a modern corporation. Some reject the strictures of profit maximization, and instead embrace decision-making processes that are subject to the full range of human concerns. This includes adherence to values and principles that go well beyond profit making for its own sake. Such corporations, which I have labeled postmodern, are associations in the Tocquevillian sense of the word. As such, they are vital components of a free, diverse, and privately ordered society. They rightfully demand the full panoply of First Amendment rights that all associations rightfully demand.

Richard John Neuhaus's observation that religious institutions "threaten the totalitarian proposition that everything is to be within the state, nothing is to be outside the state" is relevant to such corporations within democratic societies as well.[1] For even democratically elected governments have a jealous streak and can subscribe to a vision of the state as the overarching source of sovereignty and authority in society, rather than as simple one of many sources of sovereignty and authority.

Of the First Amendment rights discussed in this book, the right to religious free exercise is perhaps the most consequential with regard to the postmodern corporation. For, to quote Neuhaus again, religion is the paradigmatic "loose cannon" on the deck of those who would construct "a neatly unitary social order."[2] As Neuhaus explains:

> [O]f all the institutions in society, only religion can invoke against the state a transcendent authority and have its invocation seconded by "the people" to whom a democratic state is presumably accountable. For the state to be secured from such challenges, religion must be redefined as a private, emphatically not public, phenomenon. In addition, because truly value-less existence is impossible for persons or societies, the state must displace religion as the generator and bearer of values.[3]

Recognizing the First Amendment rights of postmodern corporations, and especially the right to free exercise of religion, effectuates precisely what the framers of the First Amendment had hoped to accomplish. It provides an important space for deliberation, communication, and the transmission of values outside the reach and control of the government. Absent such recognition, Americans would be deprived of valuable freedoms in those contexts that occupy much of their time and energy. One of the most effective forms of organization and collaboration in the modern world, the corporation, would simply be off limits to those who wish to bring their values and voices to bear through such an entity within the marketplace. The freedom to manufacture products, provide services, and create workplaces all in accord with one's most cherished beliefs and practices would, to a large extent, be subject to the mercy of a government beholden to the whims of the majority. This cannot be what the framers of the First Amendment envisioned, nor the approach of country that deems itself free.

NOTES

1. RICHARD JOHN NEUHAUS, THE NAKED PUBLIC SQUARE 82 (1984).
2. *Id.* at 155.
3. *Id.*

INDEX